C000264973

THE STORY OF ROCK AND POP ON BRITISH TELEVISION

JEFF EVANS

THE STORY OF ROCK AND POP ON BRITISH TELEVISION

JEFF EVANS

OMNIBUS PRESS

London / New York / Paris / Sydney / Copenhagen / Berlin / Madrid / Tokyo

Cover designed by Michael Bell Design
Picture research Sarah Datblygu

ISBN: 9.781.78305.795.5
Order No: OP56254

Exclusive Distributors
Music Sales Limited,
14/15 Berners Street,
London, W1T 3LJ.

Music Sales Corporation
180 Madison Avenue, 24th Floor,
New York,
NY 10016,
USA.

Music Sales Pty Ltd
Level 4, 30–32
Carrington Street,
Sydney, NSW 2000,
Australia.

Printed in Malta

A catalogue record for this book is available from the British Library.

Visit Omnibus Press on the web at www.omnibuspress.com

Contents

To Alun and Julie,
for introducing me to pop music before I could even walk.

Introduction

Being the baby of the family does have its benefits. At a very tender age, I was introduced to pop music by my elder brother and sister. My brother, 10 years older, was into the Shadows and bought almost all of their singles before moving on to the Beatles; my sister, halfway in age between us boys, later helped me discover the Kinks, Traffic and the Moody Blues. From my earliest days, we also had other records in the house, an eclectic mix that included 'Hit The Road Jack' by Ray Charles, 'Like I Do' by Maureen Evans and 'Bobby's Girl' by Susan Maughan. I fell in love with these little plastic discs with their colourful centres, watching in awe as they were stacked six deep on the spindle of our Dansette record player that then proceeded to generate enough heat to warm the whole house as it belted out the music through its tiny speaker.

I was only two or three at this time but I already had a party trick I could perform to order. Sat on the sideboard alongside the player, I could pick up any disc and recite what it was called, who it was by and what was on the B-side. Quite obviously, I couldn't read, so I guess I worked this out by the feel or the smell of each piece of vinyl or, more likely, the shape of the words on the label. I have since encountered others who were also gifted this rare talent. Like me, their love of pop music has never faltered.

As I look back, music seemed to be everywhere in our lives. If we visited a café, it would be roaring out of the jukebox; when we went on holiday, it would be squeaking from the tinny transistor on the beach. And, of course, whenever there was music on television – that little box in the corner with its grainy, black and white picture, temperamental horizontal hold and constant threat of tube failure – then we had some of that, too.

My earliest television memories are not of *Andy Pandy*, *The Woodentops* or *Picture Book* – although they do come close – but of *Discs A Gogo*, *Thank Your Lucky Stars* and *Juke Box Jury*. I can't say I remember much about them but they are still there twinkling away in the back of my mind and that's one of the reasons I so wanted to write this book.

The era I've been talking about, of course, was the early sixties. I wasn't born in time to witness shows such as *Six-Five Special* and *Oh Boy!*, but I can imagine the excitement they brought to those who were teenagers at the time when all that had gone before was so stuffy and grey. I do recall, vaguely, the early days of *Top Of The Pops*, but I remember much better its glam-rock heyday, which coincided with the time that I began collecting singles of my own, a passion that then mellowed into albums when *The Old Grey Whistle Test* took a hold. For later generations, the same sort of buzz, I'm sure, will have come from *The Tube*, *Snub TV*, *The Word*, *TFI Friday* or *CD:UK*, perhaps.

Television – far from being just a visual add-on to the tunes we've listened to on the radio, on records, on CDs or via downloads – has also been fundamental to the very development of popular music. For a start, it has carried the message much faster and more effectively than any medium that came before it, actually showing young people around the country what might otherwise have been witnessed only in London and taking rock'n'roll and all its descendent genres to every part of the UK. It has also provided instant success for musicians whose careers might not have progressed so quickly if their material had only been experienced through radio – the moodiness of the young Cliff, the swagger of Jagger and the raunchiness of Madonna could not have been conveyed by sound alone. Then there is that pivotal television moment, a jaw-dropping epiphany capable of changing the mood of a nation, turning viewers' lives upside down or creating new stars on the spot. In the USA in the fifties it was Elvis on *The Ed Sullivan Show*; in the UK in the sixties it was the Beatles on *Sunday Night At The London Palladium*, and so it has continued: Bowie with 'Starman' on *Top Of The Pops*, the Sex Pistols on *Today* with Bill Grundy, Frankie Goes to Hollywood on *The Tube*, Adele on *The Brit Awards*.

This book aims to tell the whole story of pop music on British television, starting more than 60 years ago, before the arrival of rock'n'roll, when music on the UK's single channel was still dominated by dance bands, and running through to our present digital universe in which television is just one means of visually broadcasting music. It begins as the foundations of pop music on TV are laid through such shows as *Cool For Cats*, *Six-Five Special* and *Oh Boy!*, celebrating in particular the inspirational work of producer Jack Good. In the sixties, the excitement of the beat boom is mirrored in programmes such as *Ready, Steady, Go!* and *Top Of The Pops* and then an intellectual tone begins to emerge with documentaries such as *All My Loving* and the album-based music show *Colour Me Pop*. Glam rock and punk characterise the programmes of the seventies, captured in shows as diverse as *Supersonic* and *So It Goes*, while *The Old Grey Whistle Test* continues the album focus. In the eighties, Channel 4 arrives and with it *The Tube*, a *Ready, Steady, Go!* for a new generation. It is also the decade of MTV, Live Aid and "yoof" TV. The Britpop nineties are reflected in the controversy of *The Word*, the blank canvas of *The White Room*, the spontaneity of *TFI Friday* and the first coverage of Glastonbury, while Jools Holland embarks on a marathon stint as host of *Later*. Satellite channels appear and then turn digital during the new millennium, which is marked by the cheeky irreverence of *Popworld*, the unexpected triumph of the TV talent show and the eventual demise of *Top Of The Pops*. All kinds of popular music programmes are included in the following pages, from studio performances to documentaries, via live concerts, magazines, quizzes, award ceremonies, children's series and dramas.

There are a couple of points to make clear at the outset. Firstly, throughout this book, for simplicity I have used the term pop music as a generic name for what may cover anything from rock'n'roll to rap, heavy metal to house, soul to ska, although, where necessary, these precise terms are also employed. Secondly, the history of pop music on television has been overshadowed in recent years by disturbing revelations about certain individuals who were involved in important music programmes. While not wishing to ignore such matters, this book does not attempt to look into any of the detail surrounding those cases because, as serious as they are, they are peripheral to the story it is trying to tell. At the same time, this is an attempt to write a history and not re-write a history. Certain names need to be mentioned because they figure prominently in the story of televised pop music, but in such instances no glorification is intended.

We Hope You Have Enjoyed The Show has been a joy to research and to write and it allows me to say thank you to everyone in the worlds of pop music and television who has brought me so much pleasure over the years. I hope you find it as informative and entertaining an experience as it has been for me.

Jeff Evans, May 2016

Acknowledgements

I am immensely grateful to everyone who has so generously helped with this project, giving up hours of their busy schedules to talk to me about their personal experiences and providing insights into programmes that I would not have been able to discuss with any certainty otherwise. The list of those who set aside time to be interviewed reads like a *Who's Who* of pop music on television: Mike Appleton, Ayshea, Mark Cooper, Chris Cowey, Trevor Dann, Vince Eager, David Gell, Malcolm Gerrie, Jack Good, Johnnie Hamp, Bob Harris, David Jensen, Pete Murray, Janice Nicholls, Tony Palmer, Trevor Peacock, Tony Prince, Dougie Squires, Susan Stranks, Vicki Wickham and Marty Wilde.

I would also like to thank Samantha Blake and Kate O'Brien at the BBC Written Archives Centre for their assistance in digging out old pieces of correspondence, scripts and memos. In the absence of surviving film or video, these delicate papers have provided the only way of making sense of what was once shown on screen. Dr. John Williamson of the University of Glasgow and Don Smith were invaluably helpful in explaining the intricacies of the work of the Musicians' Union. John's book, co-written with Martin Cloonan, *Players' Work Time: A History Of The British Musicians' Union*, is published by Manchester University Press. Bernie Price and Terry Woolcock kindly shared their warm memories of *Discs A Gogo*.

I am also grateful to Sue Clark, Rosemary Gell, Elizabeth Melvin, Phil Swern, Tilly Tremayne, Joyce Wilde and Simon Winters for their help in setting up interviews and to my agent, Martin Toseland, for his encouragement and enthusiasm for the project. Finally, not many authors writing about pop music have editors with the knowledge and experience of David Barraclough and Chris Charlesworth at Omnibus Press to look over their work so, once again, I've been extremely fortunate in that respect.

THE FIFTIES

It's Time To Jive On The Old Six-Five

"The teenager was a modern invention, and an American invention at that," declares historian Dominic Sandbrook in his book *Never Had It So Good*, an account of life in the UK during the fifties. His assertion is based on the way the lives of young people changed dramatically during this period, with the prosperity of the post-war years, better education and more free time loosening the shackles of family life.

This sense of liberty expressed itself in numerous ways, in fashion, food and leisure, and when the influence of the USA – now the predominant world force – took a hold, through an invasion of cinema, magazines and music, Britain was never the same again. "No longer little adults waiting to become big adults, we luxuriated in a world of our own," explains Pete Frame in his history of pre-Beatles British rock'n'roll, *The Restless Generation*. "New youth and musical movements fused together in celebration as a generation gap opened."[1]

Reflecting such change proved problematic for the nation's sole broadcasting provider, especially when it came to music, a major part of its output. The BBC had been set up to run a radio service in 1922 and, under the guidance of its first director-general, the Scottish Presbytarian John Reith, adopted the role of a "moral guardian". Educate, inform and entertain were the three principles that Reith laid down and, although there was a commitment to offering both high-brow and low-brow programming, there was always an emphasis on what was worthy or sophisticated in those early days. This carried over to television when it arrived in 1936. A look at evening programming for the month of the BBC's 25th anniversary, November 1947, reveals a handful of plays, the opera 'Tosca', a Haydn cello concerto, some classical recitals and a couple of ballets, as well as documentaries on becoming a doctor and how the paintings at the National Gallery are cleaned. Music at this point was confined to variety shows – where it was squeezed in among comics and jugglers – the odd item on magazine programmes such as *Picture Page* (1936–9; 1946–52) and *Kaleidoscope* (1946–53), or a dance band showcase starring Geraldo & his Concert Orchestra.

Such starchiness became increasingly incompatible with the loose fun of what was coming from across the Atlantic and the generational differences that were beginning to shape British society. Something had to give. These were changing times that British broadcasting navigated with not a little difficulty.

★ ★ ★

At the dawn of the fifties the BBC's musical output remained much as it had been before the war. High-brow material – classical music – continued to dominate the schedules and the popular music of the time was still largely confined to big-band shows with guest singers, unless you count *Television Dancing Club* (1948–64), featuring the music of Victor Sylvester & his Ballroom Orchestra, and *Come Dancing* (1950–96; 1998). Then, in the summer of 1951, the BBC began making plans for a new and slightly more frivolous music show.

Aware of the viewing audience's increasing ambivalence towards dance-band programmes that amounted to little more than radio performances on television, the Light Entertainment department decided to go for something livelier and shamelessly rip off a show that had been running on the American NBC network for about a year. *Your Hit Parade* – borrowing a term that had been around since the thirties – was an extension of an American radio show that simply presented what were claimed to be the most popular songs of the moment. The basis for the popularity "chart" used in the show was rather vague but was said to cover both sheet music and record sales, juke box selections and radio plays. Each song, performed by the resident orchestra and band of singers, was given a dramatic treatment or dance routine, adding a visual dimension to what might otherwise offer little advance on the sound-only version.

The programme the BBC produced was strikingly similar, even though the title had been clipped back to *Hit Parade* and there was no commercial sponsor to call the shots as the Lucky Strike cigarette brand did in the USA. Having run into copyright issues with the panel game *What's My Line?*, BBC executives were wary of similar problems arising again but, after taking legal advice, it was felt that the format was sufficiently different for no rights to be infringed and the show went ahead, airing first on January 14, 1952 and then running once a fortnight. The *Radio Times* described it as "the most ambitious attempt yet made to present popular music on the screen in a directly visual way".[2]

Each edition of *Hit Parade* (1952; 1955–6) featured a collection of songs performed by Cyril Stapleton & his Augmented Orchestra with resident vocal groups Rita Williams & the Music Makers and the Stargazers. There were individual vocalists, too, Eve Boswell, Dick James and Lee Lawrence joining Carole Carr in the earliest shows, with Diana Coupland (later star of the sitcom *Bless This House*), Monty Norman (who went on to both marry Coupland and compose the James Bond theme), Bruce Trent and Jean Campbell later. In these days the song mattered more than the performer as far as the listeners or viewers were concerned, so the show wasn't obliged to book any particular artist to perform their latest hit. The Hit Parade Dancers supported the vocalists, visually bringing the lyrics of the songs to life. Featured songs were chosen on a similar basis to those for the American show – on sheet music and record sales, and the most popular requests on radio programmes – although there was also a band spot that allowed the airing of older tunes. Around eight songs were squeezed into each half-hour show and much was made of each song's position in the chart, with the relevant numeral somehow built into the performance or set design. The number one in the chart was the final offering.[3]

Audience reaction to the first programme was good with the effort made to provide a visual dimension to the music generally appreciated. That first show included tunes such as 'Some Enchanted Evening' from the musical *South Pacific*, 'Allentown Jail', 'Loveliest Night Of The Year' and even John Philip Sousa's 'Liberty Bell', later to become the theme tune to *Monty Python's Flying Circus*, although not all were so well received: one number, 'Rosaline', was considered by viewers to be "tasteless and embarrassing" because the setting used for illustration was a hospital ward. Cecil McGivern, Controller of Television Programmes, who had seen the original show on a trip to the States, also thought it was "a good effort", particularly liking the sound that had been achieved, but he felt things could have been done much better, criticising the lack of imagination in the staging of some numbers and urging a faster pace. One aspect of the show that got the thumbs down was the American voice that linked each item – clearly the US blueprint had been followed a little too precisely. McGivern was demanding and the show's producer, Bill Ward, concurred with some of his views but was also keen to point out that he didn't have the finances to present as slick a package as the American original. With its wealthy sponsor, that show had a budget of around £3,000 per programme; the BBC could find only £700.[4]

Hit Parade remained on air for less than a year, although it was strangely exhumed some time later. Petula Clark was the big name when the show came back in 1955, supported by the likes of Dennis Lotis, Shani Wallis, Jimmy Thompson, The Ken-Tones, Gillian Lynne, April Olrich and Terence Theobald. Cyril Stapleton's band had gone – replaced by the BBC's Concert Orchestra – and vocal support now came from the George Mitchell Singers. But Francis Essex, the new producer, really didn't care for it. He tried three different formats in the first three shows in an attempt to make it successful but ultimately concluded it was "not a very good programme idea". To take its place, he came up with a proposal for a wider-ranging programme that might include interviews and older material alongside the current musical favourites. Introduced by Billy Cotton, with remnants of the *Hit Parade* team, it was called the *Tin Pan Alley Show* (1956).[5]

It is easy to conclude that *Hit Parade* was just a cheap and not particularly successful copy of a programme that had proved popular on the other side of the Atlantic, but this would overlook its importance in the story of music on British television. Not only did the show pioneer the visual presentation of music but it also, for the first time, made a music chart the centrepiece of the show – indeed, pre-dating the first UK record chart published by the *New Musical Express* by exactly 10 months. Primitive it may have been – and certainly not rock'n'roll – but *Hit Parade* was a very clear forerunner of *Top Of The Pops*, *The Chart Show* and other such programmes.

★ ★ ★

In 1952, when *Hit Parade* was first broadcast, sheet music dominated the music industry with record sales slowly encroaching as a means of gauging the success of a song. Families with the means to afford one still gathered around an upright piano in the front room while mum – almost always mum – played the popular tunes of the day from sheet music that was stowed in a compartment beneath the cushion of her piano stool. By the time *Hit Parade*'s second run had ended four years later however, the world had changed and records had taken over.

The BBC decided to recognise this transformation with a new show that combined elements of behind-the-scenes documentary and studio performance. *Off The Record* (1955–8) took to the air from Hammersmith's Riverside Studios, with bandleader and radio presenter Jack Payne as host. In a two-minute filmed trailer for the series, Payne explained what it would entail. The programme would not only "bring to your screens some of the stars and personalities from this fascinating branch of the entertainment world" but also present the "latest news from the industry" and introduce "the people who make the records

– in both senses of the word". Payne featured in the *Radio Times*, too, encouraging viewers to tune in to what he described as "something different" and acknowledging how attitudes to recorded music had changed, with records now selling millions and many stars making their name via the recording studio. "British television," he said, "does not wish to overlook a form of entertainment that appeals to such a vast and increasing public."[6]

Payne presented the programme from a mocked-up office, introducing and interviewing performers, who were supported by the Concert Orchestra, conducted by Stanley Black, and the George Mitchell Singers. He also cued in outside broadcast items from venues such as theatre dressing rooms, where stars were preparing to perform, or pre-filmed sequences set in record pressing plants and the like.[7]

Over its three series, the 30-minute programme – produced initially by Francis Essex and later by Bill Cotton Jnr and James Gilbert – offered filmed visits to Abbey Road studios and the EMI factory, clips from feature films and various documentary-style items covering issues like record sales in Scotland and the German recording industry. It also provided an on-screen run-down of the current Top 10 records. The show relied heavily on co-operation from the recording industry and while it was still in the planning stages Ronnie Waldman, Head of TV Light Entertainment, invited bigwigs from EMI, Decca, Philips, Oriole and Polygon to the Lime Grove studios for drinks and a chat about the project, hoping to enlist their assistance. Not surprisingly, that assistance was readily forthcoming, the recording executives quickly grasping the value of the prime-time television exposure.[8]

Far from being begged to lend a hand, the record companies actually fell over themselves to grab a slice of the action. Letters flooded in from labels recommending their latest releases and pushing their artists – Petula Clark, Matt Monro, Mandy Miller and others. There was still a big-band, middle-of-the-road feel to the earliest studio guests, among them Max Bygraves, Alma Cogan, Winifred Atwell, Hoagy Carmichael and Edmundo Ross, but later in the show's run, skiffle and rock'n'roll had gained a foothold in the UK and artists such as Tommy Steele, Lonnie Donegan, Marty Wilde and Wee Willie Harris were featured.

In 1958, Buddy Holly & the Crickets were pre-recorded at Riverside for the very last show.

But the BBC's broadcasting monopoly had, by now, come to an end, and its rival – brasher and less bound by tradition – helped force the Corporation to find more effective ways of presenting new music on television. Competition, then as now, would encourage progress.[9]

* * *

The launch of commercial television in September 1955 tied in rather nicely with the arrival of rock'n'roll in the UK. 'Shake Rattle And Roll', the first hit by Bill Haley & his Comets, had entered the chart at the end of the previous year, and after a brief chart entry in January the follow up, 'Rock Around The Clock', roared back in the autumn, climbing to number one just a couple of months after ITV went on air. The following year, which saw ITV expand out of London and into the Midlands and the north of England, proved highly significant for pop music in Britain. Cultural shifts were taking place across the UK.

The new style of programming offered by ITV, with a greater emphasis on popularity rather than the worthy Reithian ideals still embraced by the BBC, paralleled the raw excitement of rock'n'roll in some respects, although broadcasters on both channels were still slow to recognise the importance of the new music. When ITV was launched, it was just as clueless about what young people wanted to watch and hear as the BBC and faced many of the same challenges as its older rival in moving with the times.

As the BBC discovered when it created *Hit Parade*, televising music was a much more complex business than playing it on radio. The same dilemma now faced ATV, one of ITV's first two contract holders, which was given the franchise to broadcast to London at weekends and – starting a few months later – to the Midlands on weekdays. The company noted the popularity of BBC radio disc jockey Jack Jackson and thought he would make a great addition to their opening line-up of artists. The question was, how to translate Jackson's success onto the screen.

Jackson, a trumpeter, studied at the Royal Academy of Music and worked with several high-profile bands before forming his own outfit. After the war, astutely spotting that dance-band music was on the wane, he reinvented himself as a disc jockey with Radio Luxembourg – a multi-lingual commercial station beamed into the UK from the tiny country in Western Europe – as well as the BBC. On his Light Programme show, *Record Roundabout*, Jackson developed a distinctive approach to music presentation, breaking free of the formal style typical of BBC announcers and developing instead a delivery that was both lively and witty. He was rather anarchic for the time, layering his music shows with bits of comedy borrowed from novelty and sound-effect records. Many who remember his programmes – which continued on BBC radio until shortly before his death in 1978 – point to his influence on the likes of later DJs, in particular Kenny Everett and Adrian Juste.[10]

Achieving the same effect on television, however, proved elusive. *The Jack Jackson Show* (1955–9) was first seen on a Saturday evening, just two days after ITV came on air. The programme came from the Embassy Club in London's Bond Street and was a mixture of interviews with stars, music and news from the world of showbusiness. Realising that the show wasn't working, after just a month ATV renamed the show *On The Town*, installing Australian actor Ron Randell as host. Jackson was nevertheless retained and a new *Jack Jackson Show* began on Sunday afternoons. Later subtitled 'In Record Time', this was a much better option, allowing Jackson to focus more on recording stars. It wasn't long before the programme transferred back to a late evening slot where it became a firm fixture in the ITV schedules.

From behind a desk, Jackson presented a fast-moving combination of music and comedy, chatting to guests and welcoming his own supporting company of comedians, headed by Glen Mason and Libby Morris but also including at various times Pamela Barrie, Paddie O'Neil (wife of Alfred Marks), Joan Savage, Barbara Windsor, Bernard Landy, Paddy Edwards and Pamela Manson. His cat Tiddles featured, too. As on his radio show, Jackson kept the audience on its toes with a constant barrage of sounds – snippets of music, snatches of conversations – using, on average, around 60 records in some form or other during each

30-minute programme. Preparation for each show involved a week's work in the specially-constructed recording studio at the bottom of Jackson's garden in Rickmansworth, with help from his son Malcolm – who also appeared on the programme – and the show's editor Mark White.[11]

Most of the music came from the usual combination of big band singers, vocal groups and stage performers but as rock'n'roll and skiffle began to take a hold so those at the forefront of the new music were also featured, initially Tommy Steele but also Lonnie Donegan, Cliff Richard and Marty Wilde, all of whom would feature heavily on – and benefit immensely from – rock'n'roll TV shows as the decade progressed.

⋆ ⋆ ⋆

On the same day that the original *Jack Jackson Show* took to the air, ATV also launched *The Music Shop* (1955–60). This went out under various titles, starting as *ABC Music Shop* and then becoming *ATV Music Shop*.* Initially hosted by Canadian broadcaster Gerry Wilmot who was cast in the role of 'Shop Keeper', its guests included the usual suspects seen on TV up to that point – Lita Roza, Anne Shelton, Joe Loss – with a sprinkling of new talent discovered by producer Dicky Leeman, such as close harmony singers the Tanner Sisters and a nine-fingered pianist called Bill McGuffie. There were also competitions, including a mystery voice challenge. The programme ran for a year and then was revived in 1958 with Teddy Johnson as host.

Another early ITV offering was *Penny For A Song* (1955), "a light musical adventure" starring zither-playing Shirley Abicair as Penny Lester who turns an old mews garage into a coffee bar called The Rattletrap, with the aid of her assistant Peter Crispin, played by Denis Quilley. The 15-minute episodes ran fortnightly. ITV presented a

* ATV broadcast as ABC for a few weeks before changing its name to avoid confusion with the other ABC that was going to be broadcasting to the Midlands and the North at weekends.

number of such contrived music programmes during its formative years. *Friday's Girl* (1955–6) was a 10-minute filler in which Sheila Mathews performed songs from the hit parade, with the gimmick of ringing a random telephone number live on air to invite a member of the public into the studio for the next show. Then there was *Housewives Call The Tune* (1956–7), shown at 9 a.m. on Saturday mornings and featuring Joan Edwards – a doctor's wife from Oldham – who played records requested by viewers while she cleaned the house and talked to a weekly visitor about such topics as hats or soufflés. More than 1,000 request postcards were received per week.

Big-band shows continued to be popular on ITV. *Top Numbers* (1957–9) featured "a non-stop selection from the hit tunes of the day", interpreted by singers like Steve Martin and Maureen Kershaw, accompanied by orchestras led by Dennis Ringrowe, Malcolm Lockyer, Geoff Love or Joe Loss and dancers choreographed by, among others, Lionel Blair. One memorable edition featured both Marty Wilde and the Big Bopper. *Top Numbers* alternated weekly for a while with *Top Tune Time* (1958), a show in much the same vein, featuring Jack Parnell & his Orchestra, Ken Morris and Joan Savage, which defiantly ignored the record charts and took as its guiding light sheet music sales.

Jerry Allen and his trio provided the focus for *Musical Cheers* (1956–7), hosted by a pre-*Crossroads* Noele Gordon, and the same musicians carried on into its replacement series, *Face The Mike* (1957), fronted by Don Peters, which aimed to bring through lesser-known performers – not all of them professionals. A later series, *The Song Parade* (1959–60), featured the Granadiers singers, under the direction of Cliff Adams, presenting "in their own inimitable style" a mixture of contemporary hits and standards (seven of the current Top 12 records plus three oldies in each show). When Ronnie Carroll took over as host, he was supported by singers Toni Eden and Gerry Dorsey (later to find fame as Engelbert Humperdinck).

ITV also enjoyed great success with the Granada presentation *Spot The Tune* (1956–62), in which contestants had to do what it said in the title, given just the odd note from a popular song. The show was fronted at various times by Ken Platt, "Desmond" O'Connor, Alfred

Marks, Jackie Rae, Ted Ray, Billy Raymond and Pete Murray but the stalwart of the series was singer Marion Ryan, mother of sixties duo Paul and Barry Ryan, who was originally booked for only six editions but stayed throughout its run. The format was exhumed as *Name That Tune* (1983–7; 1997–8), initially part of the variety show *Wednesday At Eight* from 1976 but then evolving into a series in its own right hosted by Tom O'Connor and then Lionel Blair. It was revived by Channel 5 in 1997 with Jools Holland as host.

★ ★ ★

All these programmes reveal that ITV was dabbling with rock'n'roll and skiffle, but was still mostly in thrall to easy-listening music. No doubt the shows were popular in their own way but teenage viewers, who finally had a genre of music to call their own, were not particularly catered for by any of the above. One show that did make them sit up and pay at least some attention was *Cool For Cats* (1956–61).

Launched on December 31, 1956 – the last day of a year that had seen the arrival of Elvis Presley, chart entries for 'Rock Island Line', 'Be Bop A Lula' and 'Rip It Up', and the release of the film *Rock Around The Clock* – *Cool For Cats* has been widely described as Britain's first pop music programme. It wasn't by any means full-on rock'n'roll – smoochy ballads and novelty records still dominated – but it was at least a showcase for the latest record releases, giving many of them their first television airing.

Originally broadcast only in London, *Cool For Cats* was a 15-minute, twice-weekly filler show in the early evening, but it later gained a longer, late-night edition on Fridays and was soon picked up by the other early ITV regions. The programme was put together by 50-year-old actress and theatre producer Joan Kemp-Welch, who had entered the world of television when Associated-Rediffusion came along and secured ITV's London weekday franchise. Directing *Cool For Cats*, she worked closely with *Daily Sketch* journalist Ker Robertson, a balding, bespectacled, middle-aged Scotsman who admitted his own personal taste was for "serious music" – an unlikely pairing for a project aimed at teenage viewers. The *TV Times* billed the show as "an intimate record programme in which Ker Robertson brings viewers the hits and near hits, the songs, music and stories of the people who make discs a £25,000,000 a year business", but the format didn't click and it was quickly decided that Robertson was better off behind the scenes, choosing the records, with someone younger taking his place in front of the camera.

Kenneth Walton Beckett was born to English parents in 1917 in Cairo and was educated at Charterhouse, the public school near Godalming, which seemed unlikely when you heard him speak. Influenced by Canadian air force colleagues during the war, the now-renamed Kent Walton had adopted a broad transatlantic twang by the time he began acting and broadcasting. His first TV role was as a sports commentator specialising in wrestling which was to dominate his career, drawing millions of fans to Saturday afternoon grappling contests on *World Of Sport* right up to 1988. Up to this point, music had been just a hobby for him – he once played drums in a semi-pro jazz band – but installed behind a desk on *Cool For Cats*, pulling on a cigarette, he built the show into a hit, helped by his laid-back presentation and the glamour of his accent.[12]

As other directors had discovered before, presenting music visually brought challenges for Kemp-Welch and her team, especially considering the programme's tiny budget and limited facilities. The show was broadcast live from Associated-Rediffusion's studios in Kingsway, London, and although some guest artists were booked to mime their latest releases, most of the music had to be interpreted by other means. This might involve the use of library film that was vaguely connected to the theme of the song, or simply showing a series of drawings as illustration, but most of the time it relied on the show's resident dance group, put together by a young hoofer from Nottinghamshire named Dougie Squires, who had been called in by Kemp-Welch after the show's early problems.

As the budget was so tight, Dougie would have to choreograph all the routines – little vignettes as well as full-on dances – and then take part himself. "It was my first choreographic job so I was nervous as hell," he recalls. "I went round to her house and we sat down with a pile of records and worked out a programme. I got together some dancers that I'd worked with before and we did the programme the next week. It was a success straight away."

The studios at Kingsway were located in the basement and this restricted Dougie's options. "There were very low ceilings so we couldn't do any high lifts or anything, so it was choreographed to suit the location," he says. This led to other parts of the building also being used as sets, with dancers on the stairs and in the hallways. "We used corridors and the offices and I think on the roof we did one routine as well. It was all live so we had to rush around doing quick changes." To help detract from the confinement of the surroundings, Kemp-Welch made good use of perspective, painting floors to fool the cameras, and she also superimposed images from more than one camera to create effects. Things became a little easier when the programme transferred to the company's larger new studios at Wembley.[13]

Working with Squires initially were assorted West End dancers: Pauline Innes, the Rambert-trained Mavis Traill, the comedian Tony Bateman, South African Angela von Breda and Jamaican dancer Roy Allen, whose inclusion was an important step in establishing mixed-race dance groups on television. Joining later, as they worked their way up the showbiz ladder, were names such as Una Stubbs, Amanda Barrie, Patsy Rowlands and Barbara Ferris. The routines Dougie put together were what he describes as "an integration of street rock'n'roll and theatre dancing", a professional take on what kids were doing in their local dance halls, but there was a lot of slow, balletic movement, too. Other choreographers took over when Squires headed off to bigger things. He eventually became one of television's most prolific dance directors, notably working with his Young Generation and Second Generation groups on showcases for the likes of Rolf Harris and Lulu in the sixties and seventies.[14]

During its time on air, *Cool For Cats* acquired a couple of strange subtitles in the *TV Times*, billed either as "A 'Square' Disc Programme" or "A Disc Programme for 'Squares'". This prompted an exchange on the letters page, with one reader who – as well as complaining about the "appalling lack of programmes for teenagers on television" – suggested that the term "square" had been inappropriately used, arguing that it applied to "people who do not like popular music". Other readers responded that the use was quite correct, one snootily explaining that a square was "a person who always follows the current trend in 'pop' music, be it rock'n'roll, skiffle or any other trash that deviates from good music".[15]

Cool For Cats, like *Top Of The Pops* in later years, very soon became an influential programme in determining which records became hits. On the occasion of the 100th edition, in May 1958, the show played its 1,000th record, prompting Kemp-Welch – who left the show at this point – to declare that she had been told by a big music publisher that "we have a 43 per cent influence on putting tunes into the Hit Parade".* That's an unfeasibly precise statistic but it nevertheless illustrates how important the show had become to the record industry. The assertion was backed up by *TV Times* columnist John Gough who, in October 1957, lauded Ker Robertson's ability to pick potential hit records, noting that 27 of that week's Top 30 discs had already featured on the show.[16]

Such influence did not go unnoticed in other areas. In April 1960, not for the first or last time, Labour MP Roy Mason questioned the relationship between broadcasters and the record industry in an adjournment debate in the House of Commons. He felt it unhealthy that people involved in such shows should also be associated with a record label. Ker Robertson, he claimed, was "attached to the Pye record firm", while Kent Walton "is employed by the Top Rank record firm". He didn't wish to single out *Cool For Cats* over other music programmes but pointed out the position such people were in to influence record sales, and asked the Postmaster-General to request that the BBC and the Independent Television Authority (ITA), which regulated ITV companies, look into the matter. His calls fell on deaf ears. The Government was happy to trust in the ability of the broadcasters to monitor the situation.[17]

Not long after being named in Parliament, *Cool For Cats* was seen for the last time. Its day was done. The presentation of music on television

---

* Joan Kemp-Welch (born Glory Vincent Green) continued to work in television, primarily on drama series, until the 1980s. She died, aged 92, in 1999.[18]

had moved on during its time on air and, although *Cool For Cats* hung around gamely until February 1961, by this time television had enjoyed greater success with livelier attempts at capturing the ever-changing pop music scene.

★ ★ ★

The first real injection of life into music programmes came, perhaps surprisingly, not on ITV but at the BBC. More precisely, it can be pinned down to just one man, a highly intelligent but rebellious young Oxford graduate who stubbornly refused to toe the Corporation's line.

Jack Good was a bright, confident lad from Palmers Green in north London. His early ambitions were theatrical and he furthered these enthusiastically at Balliol College by becoming President of the Oxford University Drama Society and directing an open-air production of *The Taming Of The Shrew*. On graduation, a bit-part in a West End play was followed by further attempts to make a name on the stage.

At Oxford a mutual friend introduced Good to another stage-struck north London boy named Trevor Peacock. They became close mates, shared accommodation later at a student hall in the East End and forged a comedy double act they hoped would entertain punters at the famous Windmill Theatre in Soho. By Good's own admission, they struggled. "The audience there wasn't in to see comedy sketches: they were in to see the girls with nothing on and so, as soon as we appeared on the stage, all the audience lifted up their *Sporting Reviews* and there was a sea of blank pages. They weren't interested in us at all." Undaunted, they took their performances to a room above the Royal Court Theatre in Sloane Square where, spotted by a man from the BBC named Royston Morley, they were beckoned to a table. "He wondered whether I was interested in becoming a TV producer," recalls Good, by this time newly married. "I lied outrageously and said how that was the peak of my ambition. Actually, the fact was that we had no money and I would have taken any job that offered prospects at all."

Morley secured a place for Good on a BBC training course at Alexandra Palace and, suitably qualified, he waited to be called into action. In the meantime, the BBC took advantage of his availability, tasking him with looking after a distinguished actor "who had trouble with his lines in rehearsal after lunch". "It was my job to make sure that he had enough to drink, but not too much, and then get him to the studios to rehearse," he says. On one of these occasions, having safely returned his charge to Lime Grove, Good decided to stroll around the corner to Shepherd's Bush and catch an afternoon showing of a film that was making newspaper headlines. As he settled back into his seat, the lights dimmed, the screen flickered into life and the way in which music was presented on television changed for ever.

The posters outside the cinema revealed that the afternoon's feature was a new American release called *Rock Around The Clock*, contrived as a vehicle for Bill Haley & his Comets and other early rock'n'roll stars. The film was already gaining a reputation, not for the quality of the movie itself but for the reaction it provoked. Young people, frenzied by the music, were breaking all the rules of cinema etiquette, turning the stalls and balconies into makeshift dance halls, and this is what really fascinated Jack Good.

"I scarcely looked at the film," he says. "I looked at the audience who were jumping up and down and climbing over the seats and I thought this was wonderful. If I ever get to do a show on the BBC, I'll get something like this going on." It was the sheer excitement of it that bowled him over, echoing the buzz that he had experienced himself in the heyday of the National Theatre, when he'd queue all night to buy a 1/6d ticket for the upper gallery to see Olivier and Guinness at their peak. Although in his mid-twenties – pretty 'old' in the currency of the era – he empathised with the new generation of young people. Their artistic interests may have been somewhat different but he understood why they responded as they did and, when the opportunity arose to reflect this on television, he grasped it eagerly with both hands.[19]

The arrival of ITV in 1955 had brought with it a challenge to the BBC's matronly approach to broadcasting. The new channel's more populist programmes contrasted sharply with the Corporation's rather precious output and forced it to confront changing times. Commercial pressures also began to build, with the independent broadcasters keen to maximise lucrative programming slots and claim more advertising revenue.

One area to come under scrutiny was the so-called Toddler's Truce. Designed as an hour's respite from television between 6 p.m. and 7 p.m. each evening, it supposedly allowed parents to put young children to bed and ensure older children were not distracted from their homework. Unlikely as it may seem today when an infinite number of channels broadcast 24/7, the Truce was rather quaintly observed by both channels until early 1957, when its abolition allowed ITV to march in with action series such as *The Adventures Of Sir Lancelot* and *The Buccaneers*. The BBC was more ponderous, filling the weekday slots with a new light-hearted, nightly news magazine called *Tonight*, presented by avuncular host Cliff Michelmore, with Sunday nights given over to a more respectful tone through a religious travelogue called *Sunday Special*. Saturday evening's slot, it was eventually decided, would go to a new programme for young people that had originally been earmarked for Mondays.[20]

In a piece explaining the demise of the Truce, the *Radio Times* trumpeted the new show, describing it as "designed for the young in spirit who like to keep abreast of topical trends in the world about them, with special emphasis on the world of entertainment". Music would play a major role, with rock'n'roll, skiffle and traditional jazz part of the mix. But, barely a month before the launch, the content and indeed the title of the show remained a matter for debate.[21]

Among the considered names for the new programme were *Hi There*, *Live It Up*, *Take It Easy*, *Don't Look Now* and *Start The Night Right*, but the favoured option was the railway-suggestive *Six-Five Special* (1957–8). This worked well because the programme was scheduled to begin at 6.05 p.m., after a five-minute news summary, and, explained producer Josephine Douglas, "trains and allusions thereto are frequently used in jazz parlance and this could be carried through to the billing – 'Those aboard the 6-5 Special tonight were …'."[22]

Jo Douglas, born in Huddersfield, had joined the armed forces as a WAAF recruit, and while there staged a number of entertainment shows. This led to a scholarship at RADA and acting work before training as a TV producer with the BBC in 1954. Aged around 30, she was one of the youngest producers on the BBC's books and this was clearly on her side in the decision to allocate her the new programme. But the BBC also needed to find suitable employment for an even younger, newly qualified producer so Jack Good, some five years Douglas' junior, was drafted in to share the duties. This was his chance to bring the excitement he had witnessed in that Shepherd's Bush cinema to the TV screen.[23]

From the outset, Douglas and Good saw the programme in rather different ways. The former played things close to the traditional BBC pattern, the Reithian commitment to "educate, inform, entertain" remaining firmly in place, which meant that music, while important, was not the be-all and end-all of the show. This was to be a magazine programme with a variety of features that might interest the youth of the day. Good, on the other hand, had a more simplistic view of what the programme should be. He just wanted to create a buzz, and the image of those teenagers, responding to new, noisy, lively music in the cinema stalls, remained at the front of his mind.

Although Good was initially co-opted only as associate producer, he was soon given parity with Douglas – a consequence of her doubling up as the programme's presenter – and they took weekly turns to produce and direct, their differing approaches inevitably reflected in the output. Pete Murray, hired as co-host, thought that "Jo Douglas's idea of the programme was very, very worthy. The first programme we did she had film clips in it of mountain climbing… whereas Jack was 100 per cent music and didn't bother with anything like that." He recognised Jack as an innovator, "a very wild, wonderful man with great ideas".[24]

Good was also crafty. He knew that with Douglas tied up in front of the camera he could get away with more than if she was constantly sitting next to him in Caravan 25, the makeshift production office outside the BBC Television Centre, which was still under construction. He began to take liberties, an early one of which proved fundamental to the instant success of the show.

At the BBC, audiences knew their place. Their role was merely reactive. Generally kept out of sight, they simply responded to music, comedy, panel games or whatever unfolded before them, their polite applause adding a little warmth to the often sterile studio atmosphere.

The *Rock Around The Clock* experience still reverberating through his brain, Jack Good decided to change all that. He wanted the audience not only in shot but as an intrinsic part of the programme, milling around the guest stars and dancing to the music. He knew the BBC would not be keen and he claims he kept the hierarchy in the dark about his plans by arranging with the designer to put wheels on the seating blocks so they could be surreptitiously moved to give the audience freedom just before the first show went on the air. This being a live production, there was nothing Good's bosses could do about it and, seeing the success of what he had attempted, they were subsequently reluctant to revert to the old way of handling the audience. There is, however, no written evidence of the BBC's disapproval of Good's action. Indeed, within two days of the first broadcast Cecil McGivern, Deputy Director of Television Broadcasting, was writing to Good and Douglas to comment that "overall this was a very good start indeed". Furthermore, by the time the programme was a year old, Kenneth Adam, Controller of TV Programmes, was demanding even more shots of the audience. "This was in my view part of the charm which put the programme on the map in the first place," he said.[25]

As the show progressed, the on-screen presence of members of the public inevitably caused a few problems. They sometimes stood in the way or strayed in front of cameras. Technicians struggled to manoeuvre around them, so microphone booms ended up in shot and it all became quite messy at times. But there's no doubt that having youngsters clapping and jiving in and around all the guest stars did imbue *Six-Five Special* with a liveliness and mild air of anarchy seldom seen on television before.

It's not clear how Jo Douglas viewed this unconventional approach to audience management but the power that Good had assumed while she was distracted by her dual role certainly seemed to trouble her. "She wasn't pleased by all that had happened and she went to Ronnie Waldman, who was the head of Light Entertainment, and complained, but really they couldn't do anything about it," Good says. "They had a major hit on their hands at a time when they desperately wanted one."

The selection of Pete Murray as Jo's co-presenter was another decision made by Jack Good. He was impressed with the urbane former Radio Luxembourg DJ – another actor with RADA training – and favoured him over an alternative candidate, a 26-year-old male model and body-builder from Edinburgh. "I think I was right," he says. "Sean Connery turned out to be great as James Bond but I didn't think he was cut out for introducing pop music."[26]

The third member of the presentation team was Freddie Mills, the former World Light Heavyweight boxing champion. Initially, Mills presented a sports slot that saw features on the likes of the Cooper twins (boxing), Reg Harris (cycling) and Judy Grinham (swimming). This needed to be handled delicately because of internal BBC politics, with the sports department having to be informed of plans in advance. A similar issue arose with the 'Star Spotlight' feature in each edition. Described by Jo Douglas as "an excuse to introduce a bit of 'glamour' into the programme", this was effectively a bit of cheap publicity for a film star, who took part in a pre-scripted discussion with Murray. Within the BBC, there were initial concerns that this would tread on the toes of the movie programme *Picture Parade*. Among those featured were Adrienne Corri, Tyrone Power, Julie Harris and Tony Britton. There were also musical clips from movies – Little Richard in *Don't Knock The Rock*, Elvis in *Loving You* – which helped cover up the lack of American talent on the show.[27]

The first ever *Six-Five Special* powered onto the air on February 16, 1957, driven by the urgent rhythm of the theme song – "over the points, over the points" – composed by former Keynotes vocal group member Johnny Johnston under his real name of Johnny Reine with lyricist Julian More. This was performed by the Bob Court Skiffle Group who had recorded it just three hours earlier, although their version was soon replaced by one from portly trombonist Don Lang & his Frantic Five, who became regulars on the show. Library footage of locomotives steaming down the tracks filled the title sequence, suggestive of drive, dynamism and relentless action. Douglas and Murray were suitably geed up for the premiere, causing the *Manchester Guardian*'s television critic to comment on their "synthetically bright look and fixed wide smile".[28]

Murray's opening lines seemed calculated to cause maximum bemusement: "Hi there. Welcome aboard the *Six-Five Special.* We've got almost a hundred cats jumping here, some real cool characters to give us the gas, so just get with it and have yourself a ball." But then, thankfully for older viewers, Douglas communicated that same sentiment in BBC speak: "Well, I'm just a square it seems, but for all the other squares with us, roughly translated what Pete Murray just said was, 'We've got some lively musicians and personalities mingling with us here, so just relax and catch the mood from us, will you?'".[29]

The same *Guardian* critic was suitably awed by the rest of the package – an "eyeopener" – describing a turbulent scene of "open mouths, staring eyes, unkempt girls, loutish youths, drummers, singers, and pianists white and coloured, bawling and shouting, jumping on the piano". Could this have been the same show in which the featured guests were Kenny Baker & his Dozen, Michael Holliday, the King Brothers, a youth choir and the Ukrainian classical pianist Leff Pouishnoff? Apparently so. The line-up doesn't scream rock'n'roll but it seems like the attitude was there at least.[30]

Reaction from the viewing public was mixed. A BBC Audience Research Report found that many older viewers were not keen, declaring it "quite intolerably noisy", although others were more accepting, believing that young people needed to be catered for. Younger viewers were also split, one claiming "this is what many of us have wanted for a long time", but another, despite the rather neutral guest line-up, questioning the amount of rock'n'roll now being directed at kids.[31]

Rock'n'roll authenticity hardened as the shows progressed – Tommy Steele, Britain's first, albeit short-lived, rock star, making the first of numerous appearances on the third programme and other British artists such as Tony Crombie & his Rockets, Terry Dene & his Dene-Agers, Marty Wilde & the Wildcats, the energetic Wee Willie Harris and unfeasibly cool Vince Eager following on, although American rock artists remained absent, thanks in part to those famously restrictive BBC budgets – just £1,000 a show.[32]

All the while, however, rock'n'roll was just part of the music mix. An early classical component proved short-lived but jazz always featured prominently, with names such as Humphrey Lyttelton, French violinist Stéphane Grappelli and Chris Barber all appearing. Skiffle lingered long, with appearances from Chas McDevitt's Skiffle Group, who in 1957 reached number five in the UK charts with 'Freight Train', Johnny Duncan & the Blue Grass Boys, who had a number two the same year with 'Last Train To San Fernando', and The Vipers, a skiffle finishing school that would go on to include among its members future Shadows Hank B. Marvin, Jet Harris and Tony Meehan and whose number 10 hit 'Don't You Rock Me Daddy-O' was produced by George Martin. Crooners like Dennis Lotis and band singers like Rosemary Squires were also made welcome. All these artists, with the odd rare exception, performed live with the minimum of rehearsal, slotting in their best efforts between the sport and cinema spots, wholesome features on hobbies or hairstyling, and a hefty dose of what aimed to pass as comedy but which the largely Oxbridge-educated BBC bigwigs thought rather lame and lacking intelligence.

As well as Mike & Bernie Winters, who became the resident comics, Good's old mate Trevor Peacock had been drafted in to write the continuity links, leaving the presenters to clown their way through fields of corn in the pursuit of a cheap laugh. There were also short sketches, some featuring Spike Milligan, who became a frequent visitor. Peacock, in particular, remembers involving the Goon in one surreal sketch about the invention of a machine that could detect jelly. Another sketch, involving actor Ian Carmichael and a chamber pot, was slated by Cecil McGivern, Deputy Director of Television, who found it off-colour, even if it had been shown on Boat Race Day. McGivern's intervention allows us a glimpse of the tension that existed between the show's two producers. In response to the criticism, Jo Douglas agreed with McGivern's comments and passed the buck to Jack Good as it was one of his programmes. Good's riposte was that the sketch was "satirical", poking fun at people who think chamber pots are funny. He apologised "sincerely – if not very profoundly".[33]

They may have criticised some of the comic elements but the show was generally well received by the BBC executives, although it is clear that in these circles rock'n'roll was tolerated only as far as it was part of the general provision for young people. Just a month after the programme came to air Tom Sloan, Assistant Head of Light Entertainment, was urging the producers to introduce more items of general interest "as Rock and Roll diminishes". His wishful thinking was repeated a year later when he told viewers: "There is a swing back to ballads. This will be reflected in future programmes." Rock'n'roll, or at least the fervour of rock'n'roll, would not go away, however, and the magazine items were gradually phased out as *Six-Five Special* became predominantly a music show.[34]

Six-Five Special was broadcast initially from Lime Grove and later from the Riverside Studios alongside the Thames in Hammersmith, but – often when dislodged by drama productions that needed the studio space – the programmes also took to the road for special outside broadcast editions. In May 1957 it was staged at the Scottish Radio and Television Exhibition and in December that year from the NAAFI Club in Plymouth. The relatively new Eurovision network was employed to present one edition from Paris. The most notable excursion, however, was just down the road to the 2Is Coffee Bar on Old Compton Street in Soho, a trawling ground for talent for the show and the place where Tommy Steele and other early British rockers were discovered.

In accordance with Jack Good's design, the studio audience continued to be the driving force behind the programme. Some 70 kids – recruited from youth clubs, art schools, coffee bars and jazz clubs – were able to get tickets for each show, although demand was considerably greater. Those who couldn't squeeze onto the floor to strut their stuff instead demonstrated the hand-jive – a seated piece of choreography involving crossing arms, twiddling fingers and tapping elbows – that they had borrowed from the cramped coffee bars of the West End where dancing was all but impossible. The result was a hand-jive craze that swept the country, with Jack Good even writing a book to explain all about it. This was just one of the merchandising spin-offs from the series, illustrating just how the programme took a hold on the youth of the nation. A couple of "various artists" albums were also released, one specially recorded for EMI with enthusiastic sleeve notes by Good, the other a cash-in from Decca, featuring re-heated old tracks, which Good described as "a museum piece" that left him cold. The *Daily Mirror* published a dedicated book, revealing how the show was put together, focusing on the stars, discussing dance moves and introducing readers to "Julie the Juke Box girl" – 21-year-old blonde model Julie Tucker who was often spotted next to the studio juke box.[35]

A feature film – *6.5 Special* – was also made and released in spring 1958. This starred Diane Todd as Ann, an aspiring singer, and Avril Leslie as Judy, her pushy flatmate, who board the 6.5 Special steam train from Glasgow to London in the hope of getting Ann an audition. Their luck is in as the train is full of star names, including Jo Douglas and Pete Murray who have been talent-spotting up north. Every possible device is employed by director Alfred Shaughnessy (later script editor for the TV series *Upstairs, Downstairs*) to allow guest stars to do their thing – there are musical interludes in compartments, in corridors, on a platform, in a galley kitchen and in a freight car – enabling the girls to meet the likes of Jim Dale, the Ken-Tones, Johnny Dankworth, Cleo Laine, Petula Clark and Joan Regan as they weave their way through the train. They finally track down Douglas and Murray who are suitably wowed by Ann's musical prowess and offer her a chorus role on the next programme. The film wraps up with studio performances from Don Lang, Russ Hamilton, the John Barry Seven, the King Brothers, Jackie Dennis, Dickie Valentine and Lonnie Donegan as the show is seen to go out live.

In essence, there is very little rock'n'roll in the movie and the songs that Ann herself sings are the stuff of light opera, but it does offer a rare glimpse of what the *Six-Five Special* studio looked like when very little of the series itself survives. A cut-down version of the film was later issued under the name *Calling All Cats*.[36]

It was another spin-off opportunity that finally led to the tenuous relationship between Jack Good and the BBC breaking down. Approaches were made by more than one impresario to turn the series into a touring stage show. Good claims that the BBC gave him verbal permission to get involved in one but then reneged. Some touring productions did result but Good's days at the BBC were numbered.

He was also bored. Jo Douglas was, at this point, still co-host with Pete Murray, but she relinquished her production role in September 1957. Her replacement was Dennis Main Wilson, an experienced radio variety and comedy producer who Good believes was brought in to keep him in check – something Good did not appreciate. Most importantly, the excitement on which he depended to make the programme a success had dissipated. The studio audience was no longer as naturally effervescent as it was at the outset. Good hated the way in which the kids had become conscious of their role and played up to the cameras. The electricity had gone. He also saw his bosses manoeuvring the show back towards the mainstream. "The BBC decided that rock'n'roll was a fad that was over," he says. "They were going back to big-band music." Good and the BBC parted ways at the end of 1957.[37]

His departure gave the BBC a chance to seize back control of the programme. Kenneth Adam, in a memo marked "urgent", declared: "The disappearance of Good is an appropriate moment to look again at this programme", going on to criticise the "Pressley-type" (sic) "bellyswingers" who featured in the show and looking to iron out the music policy: "The balance has gone further than ever in the direction of 'Rock and Roll' just at the time when straight jazz for jiving is on its way back".[38]

Dennis Main Wilson and Good's replacement producer, Duncan Wood, were immediately asked for a written report on the way forward. This was to include analysis of the way the programme had been produced, "with particular reference to any malpractices that existed or appeared to exist". Their response concluded that "the planning, booking, and administration of the programme in the past has certainly not been all that could have been desired". The booking of artists in particular was a cause for concern, with criticism of the over-use of some artists and a deterioration of important relationships with agents. The report also recommended retaining Pete Murray as host, while suggesting that Jo Douglas – who had "given over the last 10 months a fairly comprehensive exhibition of how technique can nearly overcome basic miscasting" – would be better employed in a different type of programme. With the sports features now long gone, it was felt that

Freddie Mills was no longer contributing much, apart from fooling around, and had thus also served his time.[39]

Six-Five Special kept on rolling for another year, with significant changes made in front of the cameras. Freddie Mills was indeed let go in March 1958 but Murray left at the same time, his agent – so the BBC explained – having asked for too much money. Jo Douglas followed them a few weeks later, looking forward, as the Corporation spun it, to "some weekends at home". She went on to produce the long-running soap *Emergency – Ward 10* for ATV and died in 1988. Mills – whose pugilistic looks contrasted with an amiable personality – died sooner, and in more tragic circumstances. He was found shot in a car in 1965.[40]

Installed as new host was the genial Jim Dale, who had impressed on the numerous occasions on which he had been a guest. Dale's arrival was convenient as his agent, Stanley Dale – from whom the Northamptonshire-born Jim Smith had acquired his stage name – had already negotiated a deal with Jack Good for the show to incorporate heats of his National Skiffle Contest – much to the annoyance of Dennis Main Wilson. Assisting Dale with links for a while was a group of girls called the Six-Five Dates. Other changes then ensued. Trevor Peacock had already followed Good out of the door, leaving Jeremy Lloyd as the continuity and gag writer and, later in the year, after a period of production from Bill Cotton Jnr, a new young producer called Russell Turner took the reins as the Tito Burns '6.5-ers' and Tony Osborne & his Brasshats became resident, or semi-resident, performers. Under this new regime, the BBC was steeling itself for competition. Word had filtered through that Jack Good was devising a rival music show for ITV.[41]

The BBC was right to be concerned about Good's plans for the other channel. When his new programme hit the air and immediately poached its audience, *Six-Five Special* finally ran out of steam and, to continue the metaphor, trundled into the buffers. Beaten into submission, the programme bowed out with *The Six-Five Special Party* on December 27, 1958. It had been on air for less than two years. In the annals of television music history, its legacy appears mixed. It is easy to point out that so much of the programme had little to do with rock'n'roll, but this is to ignore the fact that the show really did break new ground by providing young people with their own musical entertainment. Youth was now finding its voice and the BBC, to its credit, had moved to recognise the fact, albeit at a rather faster pace than it liked, thanks to the drive and rebellious spirit of Jack Good. The groundwork for presenting music for young people on television had been prepared. Somewhat inevitably, it now fell to that same young Oxford graduate to build on it.

★ ★ ★

On leaving the BBC, Jack Good did not immediately rush to the other side. No offers were on the table but he felt confident it would only be a matter of time before another chance arose. "I kept waiting because I thought that somebody would get the idea that they could do something that would knock *Six-Five Special* off the screen," he says. Finally, ABC – the ITV franchise holder for the Midlands on weekdays and the North at weekends – picked up the phone, offering Good the opportunity to pilot a rival to the BBC's Saturday evening show.

In fact, two sample programmes were produced, both staged at London's Wood Green Empire, a matter of yards from where Good was a grammar school boy during the war; a perfect setting for him to capture the thrill of young people's music in an even more exhilarating fashion than before. The BBC shackles were off: he was now his own man.[42]

In preparing his new show, Good recognised a simple fact. By televising popular music, programme makers ran the risk of neutering it. The challenge was to preserve the buzz that young people derived from listening to pop music and then, if possible, to enhance it. "How can vision be added to these sounds in such a way that, at worst, the excitement is not lost and, at best, it is boosted to an even higher level?" he asked. *Oh Boy!* (1958–9) was his attempt to solve the problem.[43]

The possibilities offered by the old theatre certainly helped. The stage was big enough to accommodate two bands so he brought in the John Barry Seven and assembled another outfit that he called Lord Rockingham's XI. Supporting the headline acts were two vocal groups and a lively singing/dancing troupe called the Vernons Girls.

The audience, as at *Six-Five Special*, would be crucial to the atmosphere. Good needed the "reaction and stimulus" they provided but he didn't want kids to become the stars of the show. He had seen how they had taken over *Six-Five Special* and so confined them to the circle and the balcony. Although they would occasionally be brought into shot there would definitely be no jiving among the musicians this time around. Nevertheless, he wanted the audience to be loud and vocal – "Nothing," he said, "is more depressing than bashing out a bouncy number and getting dead silence as a reaction" – and, to encourage this, he would present the programme as an all-action theatre show, ensuring everyone watching had a clear view of dynamic, brightly attired performers on top of their game. To heighten the experience, the whole package would be broadcast live, generating, as Good called it, "the thrill of actuality".[44]

The first of the two pilot shows was transmitted on June 15, 1958, a Sunday night, going out at the inconvenient time of 10.50 p.m., with the second aired two weeks later. Although described by the *TV Times* as an "Explosion of Beat Music", the shows featured a somewhat mixed bill, featuring the likes of young rock'n'roller Marty Wilde, crooner Ronnie Carroll and jazz and blues singer Bertice Reading. Despite its unhelpful transmission slot, the programme was a hit, and a full run was scheduled for Saturday evenings the following autumn.

When word of this reached the BBC, executives there immediately recognised the threat to *Six-Five Special*. In preparation for the competition, efforts were made to "strengthen the show" and a new set was commissioned, but it was a fruitless exercise. *Oh Boy!*, as a series, blasted onto the screens on Saturday, September 13, and blew the BBC away. By the end of October, the white flag had been waved and it was agreed that *Six-Five Special* would finish at the end of the year. Having canvassed opinion among younger viewers, Kenneth Adam, by now the BBC's Controller of TV Programmes, conceded that *Oh Boy!*'s "formula is better, more punchy, its camera work simpler and faster than ours".[45]

Correspondents to the *TV Times* echoed the BBC's findings. "*Oh Boy!* is the greatest and most entertaining programme ever," wrote

Birmingham viewers Margaret Keen and Sheila Brooks, although W.J. Eeles of Henley-on-Thames thought it "a cacophony of sound" that made his household reach for the volume button. They only turned the sound back up for Ronnie Carroll. "At least he can sing without including ditties about 'mah bayub' and other transatlantic monstrosities."[46]

Kenneth Adam's summary of the appeal of *Oh Boy!* is accurate but simplistic. It seriously underplays the attention to detail that Jack Good devoted to his new project and reveals just how off the pace the BBC had become in his absence. Now that it had been commissioned as a series, *Oh Boy!* was broadcast from a new venue, the Hackney Empire taking over from the now unavailable Wood Green Empire. This being smaller, it wasn't always possible to have two bands on stage, as in the pilots, so the John Barry Seven ceded the space to Lord Rockingham's XI, the band that Jack had put together with the programme's music director, Harry Robinson. "I wanted four saxes and an organ and drums and two guitars. I can't remember what else," says Good. "I think it added up to 13." To the fore was 23-year-old South African organist Cherry Wainer, who claimed to have the largest collection of shoes on television, not that you ever saw them as she was always concealed behind a strangely upholstered electric organ.[47]

The band's name, inevitably, sparked a lot of interest. A reader's letter to the *TV Times* questioned the identity of "Lord Rockingham" and elicited a concession that there was no such person but, a month later, the magazine ran with the idea and published a two-page spoof feature in which a reporter visited a country manor to meet up with the mysterious aristocrat. As well as supporting the guest stars, the band enjoyed its own particular popularity that sent two spin-off records into the UK charts. First came the effervescent if slightly cheesy sax-laden 'Hoots Mon', with its cod-Scottish interjections ("there's a moose loose aboot this hoose") – a number one in 1958 – followed by 'Wee Tom' a year later. Sadly, the Lord Rockingham concept soon became divisive, with Good and Robinson engaged in a legal battle for the rights to the name. "It was a shame," Good recalls. "Harry and I got on well together. He was a very, very nice bloke." Good was quoted elsewhere as suggesting the argument was between lawyers and agents and he and Robinson were unconcerned about the issue.* [48]

The two vocal groups that appeared in the pilots remained regulars on the show. Good knew the Dallas Boys from his days on *Six-Five Special*. Despite their Texan name, the lads came from Leicester and could be described as Britain's earliest boy band. The other group comprised four black rock'n'roll and doo-wop singers collectively known as Neville Taylor & his Cutters. The female interest, the Vernons Girls, was a singing group put together by the Vernons Pools company in Liverpool. Not all were actually employees of the company but they became vocal ambassadors for the business, the line-up constantly changing as members left to get married or have children. Like the Dallas Boys, Jack had booked the girls on to *Six-Five Special* and brought them over to ITV with him. Originally a 70-member choir, the group had been whittled down to a more manageable 16 by this point and, under the musical direction of Peter Knight and dance direction of Leslie Cooper, they became fixtures on *Oh Boy!*, often divided up into smaller groups. Visually, the most striking member was blonde-haired Maggie Stredder, who stood out because the ever-shrewd Jack had persuaded her – much against her wishes – to wear stylish horn-rimmed glasses on screen as a gimmick. Stredder later used her prominence to form a breakaway trio that, under the name of the Ladybirds, became backing singers on *Top Of The Pops* and many other shows. Two of Stredder's colleagues in the Vernons Girls went on to marry stars that Jack Good worked with and promoted: Joyce Baker to Marty Wilde and Vicki Haseman to singer/guitarist Joe Brown.[50]

Marty Wilde was important to *Oh Boy!* right from the start. He'd been auditioned and accepted by Jack for *Six-Five Special* and now Good wanted him on ITV. Wilde recalls just how focused the producer was when putting the programme together. "Our show was disciplined," he says. "You'd go to *Six-Five Special* on the day of the show and do your run through and do the show. But the *Oh Boy!* show you had to

---

* Robinson, whose real name was Henry MacLeod Robertson, later became a prolific composer of film scores. He died, aged 63, in 1996.[49]

rehearse through the week and then on Saturday you did the show. By the time you came to do that show, you were as professional as you ever were going to be. That was part of the secret of the success."

Jack, he says, worked like a film director, storyboarding each element of the production, drawing little squares to show artists how they were going to be shot. "He'd say: 'This is how you're going to look. I'm going to shoot under your jaw and we're going to come across here. You've got to keep dead still as you say that word and I'm going to move the camera round'. The whole thing was like a film. I'm still very aware of the things I was taught by Jack Good."[51]

Years ahead of his time, Good believed that you didn't need to be too physical in order to make your presence known on television. "Just a shift of an eye suddenly towards the camera and then away had a terrific impact on the screen," he says.[52]

Marty was just one of the artists who benefited from Jack's prescience. Cliff Richard owes his career to the advice he provided. The erstwhile Harry Webb came to Good's attention when an EMI plugger tried to persuade him to feature Cliff's first single on the show. The designated A-side was a song called 'Schoolboy Crush', which Good didn't care for at all but, out of courtesy, he asked to hear the B-side, a more dynamic track called 'Move It'. He thought it remarkable. At last here was a proper rock'n'roll record made by a British artist, not just a lame copy of what was coming from across the Atlantic. He played it to Marty Wilde and asked his opinion. Wilde was equally stunned. Good would indeed feature the record on *Oh Boy!* but it would be the B-side and not the A-side. EMI had little option but to flip the record over and, helped considerably by exposure on the programme, it reached number two in the autumn of 1958. More importantly, it established Cliff Richard as the UK's pre-eminent rock'n'roll performer and is still widely regarded as the best record he ever made.

But it wasn't just Cliff's music that Good influenced. His whole styling, he felt, needed an overhaul. "All he was interested in was being an imitation Elvis," he recalls. After signing him for the show, he persuaded him to find a new image. "I had a long session with him. I remember most of it took place in Leicester Square tube station, underneath, walking round and round and round." The upshot was that Cliff shaved off his sideburns and ditched his guitar. He learned how to play to the camera, curl his lip and hurtfully grip his arm as if stabbed by a syringe, and he has always credited Jack Good for turning a shy boy into a front man with presence.[53]

The moodiness of artists like Cliff and Marty was undoubtedly enhanced by the show's remarkable lighting. Singers performed in crisp spotlights, backing vocalists lingered in semi-obscurity and the rest of the stage lay wreathed in darkness. The inspiration was a European TV show that had imprinted itself on Good's mind for its innovative use of spotlights. "It wasn't a pop music show, I don't think. It may have been a drama, but it pinpointed the attention and when you changed the lighting everything got a jolt." The effect was emulated and put into practice by lighting technician Jim Boyers, working with programme director Rita Gillespie, a hugely talented former BBC colleague who became one of Good's close associates.[54]

This dramatic lighting, coupled with the sheer pace of the show, was an irresistible combination. From the start, Good declared that it would be "one of the fastest shows on television". "Cackle is cut to the minimum," he said. "No jokes, no long 'plugs' for the latest recordings." There was a host but his role was stripped back to brief introductions in each half of the show (there being a commercial break in the middle) and the odd voice-over. The job was shared by two presenters, working in alternate weeks, mouthing scripts penned by Good's old mucker Trevor Peacock. Jimmy Henney, a 25-year-old former Tin Pan Alley music promoter, whose daughter later married radio broadcaster Ed Stewart, was one; the other was Tony Hall, a jazz producer, who had unwittingly predicted his *Oh Boy!* role a year earlier by appearing as a concert compere in the film *Rock You Sinners*. But they knew their place: music was the boss on this show.[55]

Once the artists began hitting the notes, the tempo was relentless. Songs – original hits and covers of new American rock'n'roll tracks – were clipped and punchy, never allowed to outstay their welcome as cameras moved in and out to pick out the next performer who took over the spotlight without missing a beat. The pace was frenetic. Bang,

bang, bang. Non-stop medleys, mean looks and moody shadows. It was a breathless half-hour of television.

Even when the programme was over the excitement refused to die. Getting out of the theatre became a trial for the stars. Marty Wilde recalls "two-and-a-half thousand kids blocking the pavement and watching every escape route. Sometimes it could be a bit hairy. I used to get out eventually and get home and sit with my mum and dad, eating fish and chips. It was a strange old world."[56]

For Marty, already a star when the programme began, the arrival of Cliff Richard proved rather difficult. Wilde's manager, Larry Parnes, took issue with the amount of attention Good was apparently paying to Cliff and attempted to take matters into his own hands. "He turned up at the studios once, armed with a suit that he wanted Marty to wear," recalls Good. "It was useless, because in those days the camera couldn't deal with sparkly suits or anything like that: they just sent the cameras crazy." A row ensued when Good refused to play ball. "I got one of the guards to escort him out of the theatre, because he wasn't going to go." In response, Parnes withdrew Wilde from the show and other Parnes artists such as Billy Fury, Dickie Pride and Vince Eager were also prevented from taking part. "He thought he would teach me a lesson by not having Marty on the show when actually it was the worst thing that ever happened to Marty. Cliff got complete attention."[57]

Behind these headline names, *Oh Boy!* also gave exposure to a number of regular support acts and rising stars. These included Jamaican singer Dudley Heslop – nicknamed "Cuddly Dudley" by the Vernons Girls – sax player Red Price, future Beatles collaborator Tony Sheridan and balladeer Peter Elliott, who had competed for Great Britain in the 1948 Olympics as a diver. Stars of the future included Billy Fury, who had enjoyed only one minor hit by the time of his first appearance. American guests were still limited but viewers did get the chance to see 'Little Miss Dynamite' Brenda Lee and Conway Twitty whose recording of 'It's Only Make Believe' – one of many – went to number one in 1958.[58]

Oh Boy! only ran for one series, ending on May 30, 1959, but it had already generated a live stage show, and there was more to come. In June that year, Marty, Cliff and Lord Rockingham's XI were among the acts summoned to appear at a Royal Variety Performance, staged at the Palace Theatre, Manchester, in front of the Queen Mother. On a bill that featured such household names as Dickie Henderson, Arthur Askey and Liberace, their presence underscored the impact the series had made during its very short time on air.

The disappearance of *Oh Boy!* was partly the result of the decision by ABC to move production from the London theatre to its studios in a former cinema in Didsbury, Manchester. Jack Good hated it. "It was at the end of a season and I just said: 'I can't do *Oh Boy!* there.'" Instead, he came up with the idea for another music show, this time with the rehabilitated Marty Wilde as star. Screened nationally on Saturdays at 6.30 p.m. from the following autumn, *Boy Meets Girls* (1959–60) made Wilde the centre of attraction. As well as performing, he hosted proceedings, supported by the usual team of the Vernons Girls (the "Girls" of the title), Red Price and Cherry Wainer (now billed alongside her cousin, drummer Don Storer). There was a new band called Jack Good's Firing Squad, Harry Robinson giving way to musical director Bill Shepherd, and the pace was different, with steadier camera work and softer lighting.

"It was geared down to what they could give us in Manchester," Good recalls, but he also claimed at the time that the slower pace was deliberate, a reflection of the less frantic and more melodic tone popular music was developing at the time. There were more international names on the guest list than before, including Johnny Cash, Freddy Cannon, Little Tony from San Marino and, most notably, Gene Vincent, who, disappointingly for Good, was rather too polite and not quite the rebel he had seemed from across the Atlantic. To roughen him up, Good dressed Vincent in black and made him exaggerate a disability. "He'd had a crash on a motorbike and was trying to hide his limp. I was recorded shouting at him at rehearsals: 'Limp, you bugger, limp!'"[59]

The opposite approach was taken with Marty Wilde. Good now decided to groom Marty as less of a rocker and more as an artist acceptable to viewers of all ages, but it didn't go down well. "Jack wanted me in a suit, short haircut and all that," Wilde remembers. "He wanted me to style up a bit and be a much smoother entertainer. I understand what he was trying to do but I would really, really have liked to stay the way I was."

Good was disappointed with the series but Wilde insists the standards remained high. "The production was superb and Jack's direction was magnificent," he says. Discipline was still at the heart of the show and when Joe Brown missed the start of one rehearsal, Good didn't waste the opportunity to drum this home. "I stopped everybody and pointed him out," he says, telling everyone: "This man has arrived late for rehearsal. If he turns up late again, he will be out!"

"I shamed him in front of everybody," recalls Good. "He still remembers that and is a great disciplinarian now himself."[60]

Boy Meets Girls ran for six months, ending in March 1960 and leaving Jack Good with a month to come up with another Saturday evening music show for the ITV network. The answer was *Wham!!* (1960), described in the *TV Times* as "A Fistful of Songs". Tried-and-tested Good collaborators were once again brought together – Trevor Peacock, as for *Boy Meets Girls*, in charge of scripts; the Vernons providing the glamour; and Joe Brown, Jess Conrad, Billy Fury and Little Tony as regulars, although Good guaranteed he would feature at least one new name in each show. Among those given some important airtime were Tommy Bruce and Johnny Kidd & the Pirates, whose influence would be felt for decades to come. DJ Keith Fordyce was installed as the programme's host and the house band – a 20-piece brass ensemble – was now known as Jack Good's Fat Noise.

As rather clumsily revealed by the double exclamation mark in the name, *Wham!!* was a conscious attempt to pick up the pace again after the violin-stringed hiatus of *Boy Meets Girls*. A bold, brassy title, Good called it, for a bold, brassy sound, but just eight programmes were made and *Wham!!* had disappeared by June. By Good's own admission, it wasn't a success. "I tried to get some energy back but I don't think it was very good." In his defence, maybe the show was just too good a reflection of the blandness that had descended on the British music scene at the turn of the sixties, when the freshness of rock'n'roll had turned stale and the Beatles had yet to arrive.[61]

The demise of *Wham!!* signalled the end of the first great chapter in the history of rock and pop music on British television. For Good, it was time to move on. He decided to chance his arm in America, still harbouring ambitions in front of the camera and Hollywood seemingly the best place to further these. He met with some success, appearing with Cary Grant and in a few sitcoms and, some years later, featuring alongside Elvis in the film *Clambake*. But in the interim, with three children and a wife to support, he needed to earn a living. Hugely unimpressed by Dick Clark's *American Bandstand* on US TV, he decided he could do better. "*American Bandstand*s were rubbish, absolute rubbish, because they were just lip-synching and having one person on after the other and then loads of commercials and Dick Clark mouthing off," he says. "I thought I need to make some money so I went round all the networks and told them that I could do better than that. They were very kind as they showed me to the door."

As for so many, his luck turned with the arrival of the Beatles. Good was asked to produce a TV special featuring the band (*Around The Beatles*), which then led to his own music series called *Shindig*, a programme that, like *Oh Boy!* in the UK, changed the rules for music on US television. *Oh Boy!* was the template, with Good choreographing the artists, the action fast and relentless and only minimal input allowed from host Jimmy O'Neill. It ran for two seasons, fading into mediocrity during the second without its guiding light, who, typically, had decided to leave rather than compromise his principles. "It was very difficult to keep the quality up with the American idea that the sponsors came first and we came a very poor second," he explains.

Good later worked with the likes of Andy Williams and the Monkees, and away from television conceived and directed a stage musical based on Shakespeare's *Othello* called *Catch My Soul*, which premiered in 1968 in Los Angeles with Jerry Lee Lewis as Iago. He then returned home to bring the same show to London's West End, also producing a film version that was directed by actor Patrick McGoohan, star of the cult series *The Prisoner*.[62]

Still committed to the stage, Good went on to co-write and direct the show *Elvis The Musical* but he was tempted back to television when ATV decided to revive *Oh Boy!* in 1979. The move was inspired by an *Oh Boy!* stage show that Good had directed on Sunday nights at London's Astoria Theatre. It featured the cast of *Elvis The Musical*, with some added star names, who decamped to the ATV studios in Birmingham for the recording. It was a purely retro show, featuring among others Les Gray of Mud, Alvin Stardust, Shakin' Stevens, one-eyed piano-player Freddie "Fingers" Lee, new teenage discovery Johnny Storm, compere GBH (Grievous Billy Hartman, later to play Terry Woods in *Emmerdale*) and Joe Brown, who generally avoided rock'n'roll revivals but would have done anything for Jack Good. These were supported by the Oh Boy! Cats & Kittens, the Oh Boy! Boogie Band and Fumble, a group Good had worked with on the Elvis musical. For Good, this wasn't a nostalgia fest, whatever message its juke box set, fifties fashions and Teddy boy studio audience sent out. "It's no more nostalgic than Verdi's *Requiem*," he said. "It's classic material – not so much 'Do you remember' as 'How can you forget?'" Sadly, the revival wasn't a huge success, despite lasting two series – three if you count a follow-up, which went out under the title of *Let's Rock* (1981), with Lulu and Den Hegarty of Darts added to the regular cast. "I just thought that television had lost something with the *Oh Boy!* attitude gone and I could sort of bring it back, but I couldn't," Good concedes. "It was a failure. I had a good cast – Lulu was great – but it wasn't the right time to do it. I didn't do another series."[63]

The Jack Good story wasn't quite over, however. In 1992, a biographical musical reached the London stage. *Good Rockin' Tonite*, written by the man himself and co-produced with Bill Kenwright, related the whole *Six-Five Special*/*Oh Boy!* scenario as it unfolded in those exciting years in the late fifties, continuing Good's story through to America and *Shindig*. Philip Bird picked up an Olivier Award nomination for his portrayal of Good, taking over from Greg Wise who had played him in the original run in Liverpool. Wise was so enthused by Good's story that he produced a documentary about him for BBC2 in 2005 (*A Good Man … Is Hard To Find*), tracking down the now reclusive producer/director to a chapel in New Mexico, where, after toying with the idea of becoming a monk, he had taken up a hermit's existence, painting religious scenes.

At the time of writing, Good lives in retirement in rural Oxfordshire, somewhat dismissive of the influence his work has had on the televising of popular music and on popular music itself. This is the man who made stars out of Marty Wilde and Cliff Richard and gave breaks to scores of future big names, from Adam Faith to Tina Turner, the man who showed future generations of television producers and directors how things could and should be done. And yet, when asked about his legacy, he says rather quietly: "I don't think of it at all."[64]

Others who experienced those heady days recognise Good's achievements and the excitement he created for both viewers and performers. For Marty Wilde, there has never been anything to better *Oh Boy!* in terms of music television. "The atmosphere on these shows was absolutely electric because we knew we absolutely had to get it dead right, on the button – sing in tune, remember the bars, remember our moves – and we did it, week after week. Every weekend, when the ABC chimes went out on the little screen in front of me, I knew that I was going to be in front of millions of people."[65]

★ ★ ★

Jack Good may have given BBC executives a nagging headache during his time at the Corporation but this turned into a nasty migraine once he settled in at ABC. *Oh Boy!* was deliberately conceived to sink *Six-Five Special* and was ruthlessly scheduled against it on a Saturday with a five-minute head start – it went on the air at 6 p.m – to twist the knife. This early-evening slot was strategically significant for programmers. Whichever channel came out on top stood to retain much of the audience through the big family Saturday evening viewing period and, for ITV, that translated into enhanced advertising revenue.

After Good's departure, the Corporation struggled to revive *Six-Five Special* for some time. The show had clearly lost some of its style and energy but when *Oh Boy!* exploded onto the airwaves BBC executives knew their programme's time was up. Within a month, Head of Light Entertainment Eric Maschwitz had instructed producer Russell Turner to come up with a replacement. He wanted this new programme to run for 30 minutes, instead of 55, and to appeal to the same age-group and interests, but it should also have "quite a different setting and formula so as to give the impression of a brand-new show". That said, Maschwitz still felt there was mileage in the old name, requesting that Turner keep what he called "the '6-5' designation", perhaps calling the new programme "'Six-Five Record Club', or something similar".[66]

Plans seemed to be coming together by early November 1958 when Kenneth Adam remarked to a colleague that the programme's fortunes would dictate "the success of our new Saturday night plan". His memo was marked "Private and Confidential" and ended with a further indication of the secrecy attached to the new project: "Do you want a pilot, or will that set the tongues wagging?".[67]

The resulting programme, *Dig This!* (1959), went on air in January 1959. Nominally, the *Six-Five Special* connection may have been jettisoned but the *Radio Times* still added the strapline "The new Six-Five Show" to the billing. This time, the audience was back in its accustomed place, leaving the performers to generate all the enthusiasm, not least the resident band, Bob Miller & the Millermen*. Host of the show was actor/singer Gary Marshal but his input was purposefully minimal, the cheesy linking patter of *Six-Five Special* now – thankfully, thought many viewers – abandoned. The first show was not without its fans but, overall, it was a poor start in the opinion of those questioned for the BBC's audience research. Even though around a third of the respondents were aged under 30, many were unable to "find a good

* Miller, a conservatoire-trained saxophonist and clarinettist, played with various bands before forming his own ballroom ensemble. They successfully auditioned for the BBC and featured on *Come Dancing* and radio's *Friday Dance Date*, before getting their own Light Programme show. After *Drumbeat*, they continued to broadcast on TV and radio – handily filling airtime with cover versions of current tunes when there were strict limits on the amount of recorded music that could be played ('needle-time'). They were heard in shows such as *Parade Of The Pops* and *Saturday Club*, as well as supporting acts like Cliff Richard on tour.[68]

word to say about the programme". "I disliked *6.5 Special* more as time went on," declared one panellist. "This programme I'm sure I shall dislike intensely throughout."[69]

Clearly, this was not good but *Dig This!* soldiered on in its prime Saturday evening slot until the end of March, with the Millermen joined as regulars by the likes of Barry Barnett, Barbara Young, the Polka Dots, Susan Jons and Al Saxon, most of whom were largely unknown even at that time. It stood no chance against *Oh Boy!*

Still cornered, the BBC needed to make more changes and, on March 28, *Dig This!* disappeared to be replaced a week later by a new show called *Drumbeat* (1959). In one respect, this signified the waving of a white flag, as the programme was now rescheduled to avoid direct competition with *Oh Boy!* The American western series *Wells Fargo* would now start at 6 p.m. and *Drumbeat* would follow at 6.30, once *Oh Boy!* had finished. It would last for half an hour. In other respects, though, this was very much a fightback by the BBC, *Drumbeat* being a far better attempt at wooing the *Oh Boy!* audience than its predecessors. Bob Miller & the Millermen were still in residence but they were now joined by the John Barry Seven, giving the show a little of that *Oh Boy!* magic. Pre-broadcast publicity also turned up the heat, the *Radio Times* describing the show as "thirty fast-moving minutes of music in the ultra-modern manner, that will make the old-fashioned 'rug cutters' feel like members of a knitting circle".[70]

The initial host of *Drumbeat* was Gus Goodwin, a young DJ who had made a mark with his *Rockabilly Show* on Radio Luxembourg, but he was soon replaced by Trevor Peacock, brought back from ITV and thrust before the cameras.* The powerful theme tune was called 'Bees Knees'. The musical line-up, as the series progressed, was certainly more relevant than seen in *Dig This!*, with Adam Faith, Cliff Richard

* Trevor Peacock later became a prolific character actor, best known for his role as Jim Trott in the sitcom *The Vicar Of Dibley*. ("No, no, no, no, no … yes"). He also has notable songwriting credits to his name, including the hits 'That's What Love Will Do' for Joe Brown and 'Mrs Brown You've Got a Lovely Daughter' for Herman's Hermits.

and Marty Wilde all featuring at various points, supported by regulars such as Vince Eager, Roy Young (widely described as "England's Little Richard"), 17-year-old South African crooner Danny Williams and young, dark-haired singer Sylvia Sands. Also seen were the vocal groups the Barry Sisters, the Kingpins, American girl trio the Poni-Tails and the Raindrops*. But, this being the BBC, there still had to be room for the likes of Dennis Lotis, Russ Conway, Petula Clark, Lita Roza and Malcolm Vaughan, which watered things down somewhat. The fact that no episodes appear to have survived – the show being broadcast live – makes it hard to judge its quality but there are plenty of people who did rate it, not least Vince Eager.

"*Drumbeat* was a great show," he says. "It was obviously along the lines of *Oh Boy!* but that's what people wanted in those days." Its popularity is also suggested by the spin-off records that were released and young people, crucially, were on the whole positive about it. BBC audience research revealed that viewers were largely split by age in their opinions, those over 30 really disliking it – some claiming that the featured music "had an unwholesome, sexual derivation which was harmful to young people", which suggests that the BBC was actually doing something right for a change. Those under 30 were far more favourable, although they felt more "top-line artists or hit-parade numbers" should be included.[71]

Drumbeat was broadcast from Riverside Studios in Hammersmith but occasionally came from Lime Grove. Production-wise, it was handed to a new recruit, a big, stocky former cinema manager (his dad owned a chain of them) named Stewart Morris, who went on to become one of the BBC's long-serving light entertainment producers, as well as marrying Sylvia Sands.[72]

Sadly, after a reasonable start, the rhythm of *Drumbeat* seems to have slackened as the weeks passed and BBC executives finally gave up on the idea, calling time on the series in August, just a couple of weeks before Jack Good launched *Boy Meets Girls*. They just couldn't compete with

* The Raindrops was a quartet put together by musician Len Beadle. Other members were Johnny Worth – better known as the songwriter Les Vandyke – Jackie Lee, later to have hits with 'White Horses' and 'Rupert', and Vince Hill.

the man who had turned things on their head. By that time, however, as Good recognised on that second ITV series, the early excitement of rock'n'roll had waned. The tempo was slowing, allowing the BBC to guide its youth music output back into safer waters. A replacement programme for *Drumbeat* was already on air, a programme in a rather different vein that was to become one of the best-remembered music shows of the sixties, albeit ensconced once again in the safe, comfortable bosom of "family viewing" rather than a prickly stand-alone for kids. After two consecutive misses, the BBC was now cultivating a hit.

THE SIXTIES

The Weekend Starts Here

For six months, over the autumn and winter of 1953, national fame came fleetingly to a largely unknown DJ and talk show host when his panel game was given a slot on the ABC network in the US. In the show, Peter Potter lined up four celebrity guests and asked them to review the latest record releases. They could comment on the song, the performance, the arrangement and every other aspect of the production but the only thing that mattered ultimately was whether they thought the disc would be a "hit" or a "miss". Potter himself took on the role of presiding judge, introducing the music and banging down his gavel with every verdict. The show, *Juke Box Jury*, despite being popular in Los Angeles, where it had started during the forties, lasted barely six months. Peter Potter* faded quickly from view, but the programme he devised and presented went on to become an influential and durable player in television's coverage of popular music – although that happened a decade later and on the other side of the Atlantic.

Any disappointment Potter may have felt when his show was cancelled by ABC was surely assuaged when *Juke Box Jury* (1959–67; 1979; 1989–90) was picked up in the UK. The BBC showed an interest

---

* Peter Potter was born William Mann Moore in 1905 and died in 1983.[1]

in early 1959 and started making plans for a dry run, adapting the format for British audiences. Copyright was a key issue and it was eventually agreed that Potter would receive £50 for each of the 13 editions the BBC planned to produce. This figure was to rise steadily over the years as the agreement was extended and, by the time the series ended in 1967, Potter had done rather well out of his creation.[2]

Such longevity was not predicted by the programme's host, the velvet-toned disc jockey David Jacobs. After the unaired pilot programme, he thought that "this might be a show with limited appeal for record fans" but did not "count on it being anything like a big hit". His enthusiasm had diminished even further by the time the show went live on air on Monday, June 1, 1959. He found the whole thing "so very dreadful that by the middle of it I was wishing I could just get up and go". Luckily, BBC executives were considerably more upbeat and the show was given a chance to make its mark.[3]

That first programme featured a panel made up of fellow DJ Pete Murray, singers Alma Cogan and Gary Miller, and a young aspiring actress named Susan Stranks, whose role was to speak for the youth of the nation. "I was cast as being a typical teenager of the time, with the ponytail," she recalls. "I think somebody who knew me and knew my parents suggested I might be right for it. I was about 18. They probably thought that they couldn't go too young." The same panel presided for the next two programmes before producer Russell Turner began to mix things up, bringing in different guests for each show. While Pete Murray remained a semi-regular contributor over the next seven years, in an apparent effort to consolidate the "family viewing" experience, other seats on the panel were generally given to stage and screen personalities, some of whose knowledge of the music scene and youth culture was limited to say the least. Actress Peggy Mount was gracious enough to admit as much on air, but you do wonder to what extent Sid James, Gilbert Harding and Kenneth Wolstenholme were in tune with British teenagers. Some of them had never even heard of the featured artists. "Everybody wanted to appear on it because it had a terrific following," says Pete Murray. "And 90 per cent of them knew nothing about music."[4]

Although the panellists changed weekly, and the programme itself soon switched from Mondays to replace *Drumbeat* on Saturdays, the format remained constant. After a burst of the theme tune, 'Hit and Miss'*, the unflappable Jacobs presented a selection of new record releases, pushing a button on a dummy juke box to set each disc spinning. Up to 10 records per show were featured, not played in full but long enough for the judges to decide if they were going to be successful. Again, with the aim of appealing across the family, tracks covered all aspects of popular music. One running order from 1965 reveals releases from Ted Heath and Vince Hill alongside discs from the Kinks and the Supremes.

Unlike in Peter Potter's version, there were no performers to watch while the music played. Instead, the cameras panned over the deliberating guests and also explored, via close-ups, the reactions of the studio audience. A positive verdict from the jury saw Jacobs ding a bell to indicate a hit; if the feeling was negative, he sounded a derisory klaxon.† If the panel was evenly split, a secondary jury, made up of members of the audience, was asked to cast its deciding vote. But panellists needed to be tactful. Lurking behind the scenes could be one of the artists whose records were under review and, having slated a disc, jurors were often taken aback to see the performer brought before the cameras. "You had to face them afterwards, when you'd made your decision," recalls Susan Stranks. "It was pretty mean, that, I thought. I know that once or twice I was embarrassed because I said something rude about something and then out came the poor person that you were judging."[5]

Two programmes from *Juke Box Jury*'s long run stand out. On December 7, 1963, the Beatles filled all four of the panel chairs in an edition presented from the Empire Theatre, Liverpool. Among the songs they reviewed were 'Kiss Me Quick' by Elvis, 'Hippy Hippy Shake' by the Swinging Blue Jeans and 'I Think Of You' by the Merseybeats.

---

* A 1960 hit for the John Barry Seven. This had replaced an earlier signature track called 'Juke Box Fury' by Ozzie Warlock & the Wizards – a pseudonym for bandleader Tony Osborne.

† In 1964, the *Radio Times* reported that a survey had shown that, in terms of predicting hits, panellists were right two-thirds of the time.[6]

The show was recorded earlier that afternoon, just before the band gave a concert that was partly screened on the BBC later that evening under the title *It's The Beatles*. Then, on July 4, 1964, an extra chair was added to the set to allow the Rolling Stones to become the jury. Sadly, unlike the Beatles, they didn't endear themselves to the viewing public, showing little sign of wit and reinforcing their bad-boy image by trashing every record that was played.[7]

This wasn't the last time that the make up of the panel caused consternation at the BBC. At the end of 1966, it was decided to make the jury more professional and four of the nation's best-known music broadcasters were signed up for an eight-week run. Pete Murray was brought back and sat alongside Simon Dee, Alan Freeman and Jimmy Savile. It was not a popular decision. Audience feedback found that teenagers disliked having the panel confined to "middle-aged disc jockeys" and the lack of juror variety from week to week deterred others. Worse still, the DJs' "silly" behaviour and "disgusting" manners incensed viewers. "They are supposed to be there to criticise the records," railed one caller to the BBC's Duty Office. "They are just having private jokes."[8]

Clearly, after nearly eight years on air, *Juke Box Jury* was foundering. It was finally sunk when Paul Fox, Controller of BBC1, became concerned about the show's rising costs – the copyright fee for Peter Potter included – and called for a replacement. Like many viewers who enjoyed their weekly half-hour of new releases sandwiched between *Grandstand* and *Doctor Who*, David Jacobs – who had clearly got used to the idea – was sorry to see it go, claiming that the programme had provided "a patch of sanity in a rather odd world of pop". After being shunted to Wednesday evenings, to make way for the *Dee Time* chat show, the final edition was broadcast on December 27, 1967, with Lulu and Eric Sykes on the panel alongside original jurors Pete Murray and Susan Stranks, who was soon to become one of the original presenters of ITV's children's magazine, *Magpie*.[9]

For those who missed the programme in the sixties, a chance to see what *Juke Box Jury* was all about came in 1979, when the BBC revived it with Noel Edmonds in the chair for one series. It was a largely unmemorable affair, apart from the edition where Johnny Rotten walked off before the end. Ten years later, David Jacobs and Pete Murray were reunited for a one-off edition to mark the centenary of the juke box, prompting yet another revival, this time with Jools Holland as the host.

★ ★ ★

Just as *Juke Box Jury* was getting into its stride, providing the BBC with a lasting record show, the UK's other television channel found itself without a weekly music programme that could be seen by the whole country – or "networked" as the industry term put it. Jack Good's third ITV series, *Wham!!*, finished in 1960 and this left individual ITV companies to come up with lower-key equivalents, usually available only to their local, regional viewers.

Tyne Tees in the North-East was the first into the frame with an "exceedingly vivacious and noisy" show called *Young At Heart* (1960) that gave Jimmy Savile his first TV break. Savile's co-host was band singer Valerie Masters, who also had her own show on Radio Luxembourg. Westward Television in the South-West offered *Spin Along* (1961–3), hosted by Alan Freeman, and followed this up with *Move Over, Dad* (1963), for which the Beatles once recorded an interview while on tour in Plymouth. In the North, Border Television offered three series of *Beat In The Border* (1962–3) while, in Northern Ireland, Ulster put together a show called *Now Hear This* (1963), following up with *Pop Scene '64*, a year later. In the South, Southern Television thumbed through a dictionary of jive speak and came up with *Dad You're A Square* (1963–4), a programme in the *Juke Box Jury* mould in which records were voted hits or misses by contrasting panels of enthusiastic teenagers and dour curmudgeons. Rejected discs were symbolically smashed by a cannonball rolled down a slide.

A further variation on the *Juke Box Jury* format came from Associated-Rediffusion. *Needle Match* (1962) – a head-to-head battle between the latest releases from the USA and the UK – wasn't fully networked but was seen in large swathes of the country. The show featured a young actor by the name of Oliver Reed, billed as the "British Promoter", against Radio Luxembourg's Canadian DJ, David Gell, the "American Promoter". Gell explains the format. "We would each play a new record – one British, one American – and members of the audience would then vote by holding up either a small British flag or a small American flag to indicate which record they preferred. A young, relatively unknown chap by the name of David Frost would then run around and collect the flags. The flags were counted and the winning song announced."[10]

The audience that Gell refers to was a neutral international jury composed of young students. Members of the public could also vote for the best new disc of the week by sending in postcards. *Needle Match* was "refereed" by Keith Fordyce and also included guest artists and dance routines. Later "promoters" included Wally Whyton and Don Moss, with Jim Dale also sitting in for Fordyce on at least one occasion. David Gell then moved on to host a *Spot The Tune*-type game show, entitled *Music Match* (1963–71), for Anglia Television's local viewers. Under the musical direction of Peter Fenn, it proved considerably more durable that an earlier attempt by the same company called *Disc Quiz* (1960).

Needle Match was not David Frost's only involvement with pop music at the time. In 1962, just six months before he "rose without a trace" (as writer Kitty Muggeridge is said to have declared) as host of the BBC satire show *That Was The Week That Was*, he could be found presenting a trio of 15-minute programmes about the twist dance craze. Most of the ITV regions carried the shows, which were made by Associated-Rediffusion and took the form of a competition. *Let's Twist To Win* saw the best dancers in London battle it out, with the winners heading across the Channel to take on the French in *Let's Twist In Paris* and then *Let's Twist On The Riviera.* Other ITV regions also held competitions, as youth music became increasingly important to schedulers – the *Westward Beat Competition* (1964), for example, and Border Television's *Isle Of Man Beat Contest* (1965).

* * *

One of the most unlikely ITV companies to succeed with pop music programming was TWW. The company, which broadcast to Wales and the west of England, contributed very little to the ITV network in the 10 years it held its franchise. The semi-operatic *Land Of Song*, featuring Ivor Emmanuel and other Welsh singers, was probably the most prominent, but the fondly remembered *Discs A Gogo* (1961–5) ran it close.

This show was first broadcast from the company's studios in Cardiff, using a set designed to resemble a cellar coffee bar ("Gogo's"). Here teenagers danced to tracks, usually mimed, by stars of the day. Billed in the *TV Times* as a visit to "the gayest coffee bar in town", the programme was hosted by Kent Walton, who had been snapped up by TWW along with scriptwriter Ker Robertson after *Cool For Cats* had ended. Also signed was animator Harry Hargreaves, who created a mascot for the series called Gogo the fox, which featured in sketches illustrating some of the music and appeared on the little badges worn by audience members.

Discs A Gogo soon transferred to TWW's Bristol studio, which made things easier for artists heading across from London, and the show was also picked up by more ITV regions. When it started, it was accessible to only around two million viewers; within two years – when a Decca EP, featuring tracks by Billy Fury, the Vernons Girls, Karl Denver and Jet Harris, had been issued as a cash-in – it had gained an audience of nine million. At its height, all ITV regions offered the programme (if not at the same time) except the big three of London (Associated-Rediffusion/ATV), the Midlands (ATV/ABC) and the North (Granada/ABC).[11]

For local teenagers, a place in the audience was highly coveted but not easily obtained. Only those with dancing ability and fashion sense were invited. "If you went to the Top Rank and you were deemed to be a bit of a face or an okay dancer, they would come and ask you if you would like to be on *Discs A Gogo*," regular Bernie Price recalls. "When you got there, for your services, you got the choice of a hot dog or a hamburger and a Coke or a glass of milk." "We used to take girls sometimes," says his mate, Terry Woolcock. "You'd get two tickets. So we were quite popular people." But, he adds, they weren't so keen on the weekly 'Smooch Spot', when the pace slowed and the youngsters had to get embarrassingly close and intimate for the cameras.

Discs A Gogo also featured a married couple as regular dancers. They were exceptional performers, but it was a brave move by producer Chris Mercer to make them a fixture of the show, as the husband was black and mixed-race marriages were still some way from being accepted in Britain. In later editions, a female dance troupe called the Gojos, who were also the first resident dancers on *Top Of The Pops*, added their own interpretations of hits.

Getting bands down to the Bristol studio proved to be no great problem, such was the coverage the show offered – even the Beatles made it in December 1962 – although whether the sleepy West Country was quite ready for some of the livelier acts was another matter. "We saw people like the Kinks, the Who, the Animals, those sort of bands," says Bernie in a warm West Country burr undiminished 50 years on. "I remember dancing with Cher and Sandie Shaw. She said I sounded like a farmer. I also remember the Who. They had sparkly stuff in their hair." Terry was just as shocked. "They had make up on, which we weren't accustomed to, so they looked a bit freakish to us."[12]

Helping Kent Walton in the studio was Frank Harding, who manned the coffee counter with the help of a girl named Connie Greengrove, but he was later replaced by a 20-year-old DJ from Oldham, who had come to Bristol to work at the Top Rank ballroom. Singer Tony Prince had been thrown out of the Musicians' Union for daring to play records between his songs and so he turned to spinning discs as a full-time job. When a local beauty queen took him to a *Discs A Gogo* recording, he seized the opportunity to cheek Chris Mercer into considering him for a job. Prince successfully auditioned and was thrown in at the deep end as a temporary replacement for Kent Walton, who was required by ITV to work on the Olympic Games in Tokyo. When Walton returned, Prince kept his place on the show, poking a little fun at the host from behind the coffee counter.*

With his youthful ear close to the ground, Prince also became Mercer's record librarian and musical advisor, recommending acts to book on the show. He once used it to his advantage, suggesting

* Kent Walton died, aged 86, in 2003.[13]

that a pirate radio DJ named Tony Blackburn be invited to perform his latest record release. "The song was called 'Don't Get Off That Train'," Prince recalls. "Blackburn got off that train in Bristol and came to TWW and he filled my heart full of love for this exciting job he'd got as a pirate DJ on Radio Caroline." It was a life-changing moment. Using a contact name provided by Blackburn, Prince approached the station and secured himself a job on the pirate ships, joining shortly after *Discs A Gogo* was finally taken off air. "Caroline were really thrilled. They were getting themselves a TV personality," he says. "I was more thrilled that I was going to become a radio personality, quite honestly. It was wonderful." That was the start of a career that saw Tony become one of Radio Luxembourg's best-known voices during the seventies and eighties.

When *Discs A Gogo* ended just before Christmas 1965, it was swiftly replaced by another TWW youth programme entitled *Now!* (1965–6) that featured two or three bands per week. This was seen only in the TWW and Border areas and lasted only until the following July, but it is notable for giving Michael Palin his first television presenting job.

In 1967, during the scheduled franchise reviews, TWW lost its ITV contract to Harlech Television (HTV). It went off air in March 1968 but, on its penultimate evening, it brought back *Discs A Gogo* for one last outing with – ironically for Tony Prince – Tony Blackburn as host. Prince may not have had the show's last word but he remains a big fan of the series. Its contribution to the music scene of the early sixties, he feels, is very much underrated. "It's an unsung hero," he says. "It used to break a lot of records. Obviously, its impact was diluted because it wasn't on Rediffusion and Granada but all the groups came down. It was fantastic, no other word for it."[14]

* * *

Another ITV region trying to develop a national music show was ABC, whose pre-eminence in this area of programming had taken a knock with the departure of Jack Good for America. The company's next attempt began rather quietly. Recorded in studios at Teddington

Lock, *Thank Your Lucky Stars* (1961–6) was broadcast initially only in the Midlands, North, Scottish and Tyne Tees ITV regions. The first show featured Pete Murray as host and guests included Hughie Green, Anne Shelton and the Five Dallas Boys – perhaps not the most auspicious line-up, but other early headliners included Gene Vincent, Billy Fury, Johnny Kidd & the Pirates and the Shadows as the series began to find its feet. By the time the show became almost fully networked five months later (only Anglia remained temporarily out of the loop), the 25-minute production had been extended to 40 minutes and, going head to head in the same time slot, was giving *Juke Box Jury* a real run for its money on a Saturday teatime.

There was very little groundbreaking about *Thank Your Lucky Stars*. It was a simple pop showcase, featuring the biggest stars of the day who would mime to their latest releases or biggest hits. But there was a twist, at least initially, when it set out the idea that established artists would not simply perform but would also introduce up-and-coming bands and singers – "their tips for tomorrow's hit parade", as the *TV Times* phrased it. In October 1961, 14-year-old star Helen Shapiro introduced a likely lad four years her senior by the name of Shane Fenton. Fenton's first hit, 'I'm A Moody Guy', entered the charts just three weeks later and he went on to notch three further minor successes before becoming far more famous in the seventies as Alvin Stardust. Otherwise, *Thank Your Lucky Stars* was largely derivative, a pop music take on the established light entertainment format. It was also a magpie, stealing from *Juke Box Jury* to create a segment named 'Spin-A-Disc', in which a panel of teenagers reviewed three of the latest releases from the USA.

This part of the show was hosted by Brian Matthew, presenter of the hugely popular *Saturday Club* on the BBC's Light Programme, who then joined Keith Fordyce as a full co-host when the series went national and Pete Murray stepped down. Also participating in Spin-A-Disc was a roster of guest DJs, who had their say on the records after the teenagers had given their verdicts. Among those dispensing wisdom were Barry Alldis, Jimmy Young, Sam Costa, Steve Race, Don Moss, Shaw Taylor, Desmond Carrington, Keith Skues, Simon Dee, Robert Holness and Catherine Boyle (sic). One week the job fell to comedy partnership

Bob Monkhouse and Denis Goodwin. Rather than declaring whether a record would be a "hit" or a "miss", as on *Juke Box Jury*, Spin-A-Disc panellists gave each release marks out of five. This simple format wouldn't seem to offer much scope for personality development but it was enough to propel a teenager from Wednesbury to national stardom in February 1962.

Watching one week as part of the live audience, Janice Nicholls learned that ABC was on the hunt for more teenage jurors. She promptly wrote in, successfully auditioned and was invited to take part in the following week's show – a lightning-fast chain of events that was to change the 16-year-old's life. Asked for her score for one of the discs, Janice's broad Brummie accent declared "Oi'll give it foive", which tickled both the production team and viewers. She was immediately asked to return and remained with the show for three years.

Such fame led to Janice quitting her post as a junior factory clerk in favour of a job booking acts at The Adelphi ballroom in West Bromwich, which she did while writing a record column for the local *Sunday Mercury* newspaper. "Oi'll give it foive" soon became a nationally used expression of approval for anything and everything – heard in pubs, playgrounds and workplaces – and, at the end of 1962, Brian Matthew, asked by the *TV Times* to decide for whom, musically, it had been a good year, included Janice in his list for having done "the hardest thing in the world – coin a catch phrase".[15]

Janice's bold regional accent was just what ITV needed to help build the character and identity of the show and develop a useful contrast to the very BBC, London-centric *Juke Box Jury*, and it led to other panellists' chairs being filled by similar kids from other parts of the country. Meanwhile, Janice's popularity continued to grow. She made a couple of commercials for Cadbury's chocolate, answered questions about pop on the quiz show *Double Your Money* and, only a year after first appearing on *Thank Your Lucky Stars*, cut her own record for Decca, a rather contrived affair in the Mike Sarne comedy vein entitled 'I'll Give It Five', which failed to chart. Given such national prominence, friends at the time assumed Janice was earning a small fortune until she revealed that all she was paid by ABC was three guineas a week (later rising to seven), although, if Janice's money was poor, there were at least other benefits, especially the chance to mingle with the biggest stars of the day. Few turned down the chance to appear on a "plug" show like *Thank Your Lucky Stars* that was guaranteed to boost record sales. But Janice's time in the limelight was coming to an end. Like many young women of her era, she decided a settled future was worth more than a career and she left the show in 1965 to marry long-time sweetheart Brian Meacham, singer with the Birmingham band Brian Gulliver & the Travellers. She later trained as a chiropodist, trading pop for corns.[16]

Production-wise *Thank Your Lucky Stars* offered nothing adventurous. The set design was elementary, usually just consisting of a row of light bulbs and a few artistic props. Sometimes outsized graphics displayed the names of the performers and now and again there were a few fake trees. The host simply introduced acts from behind a desk or perched on a stool, occasionally snatching a few words as he handed a guest a gold disc. Special effects were few. In its rather traditional presentation, *Thank Your Lucky Stars* had clearly learned little from *Six-Five Special* and *Oh Boy!* Audiences – while often extremely vocal – remained comfortably out of shot and there was no attempt to hide the fact that everyone was miming. Guitars were not plugged in and there weren't even any microphones to hold. But some artists would tell you that an appearance on the show was not as easy as it seemed, considering the travel involved in those pre-motorway times and the long studio days.

After the first series, production had switched to the Alpha Television Studios in Birmingham – a former cinema that ABC shared with ATV. The show was recorded on a Sunday, for broadcast the following Saturday. Stars and presenters alike would be shipped in from London or Liverpool and needed to arrive early for rehearsal. Host Brian Matthew reflects on the demands of the production in his autobiography and concedes that he was often glad of a drink at the end of a tiring day under the studio lights. The problem was that pubs near the studio were not the most salubrious and there was insufficient time to reach more suitable establishments before closing time at 10.30 p.m. The solution – pointed out by guest DJ Kent Walton, who had stumbled on it while returning from one of his wrestling commentaries – lay in a pub located between Birmingham and Coventry where the landlord welcomed after-hours drinking in his restaurant area. This pub soon became the team's regular watering hole, with many of the guest stars joining them for an illicit tipple on their way home, occasionally entertaining the regulars with a few impromptu performances.

Matthew was, by this time, well ensconced as the sole presenter on the show but his promotion owed much to an industrial dispute called by the actors' union, Equity. Union member Keith Fordyce fell in line and withdrew his services but Matthew, although an actor himself before becoming a DJ, no longer considered himself part of the union, having not paid his annual dues for nine years, and continued to work. This angered the union's hierarchy, who considered he was only a lapsed member and therefore still subject to its rules and regulations. They called him in to face the consequences. Despite a plea for leniency from Richard Attenborough, he was suspended from the union for a year and ordered to pay nine years' back subscriptions. Matthew complied and fell back into the Equity fold but the real loser was Fordyce who, when the industrial action ended, was not asked to return.

Brian Matthew's tenure as host lasted four years – not including the summer months when the programme, retitled *Lucky Stars Summer Spin*, employed other presenters. Pete Murray ran the 1963 summer season, with an assortment of guest hosts brought in for 1964, among them Joe Brown, Dusty Springfield, Adam Faith and Dave Clark. For 1965, the series was handed to Jim Dale, who took time out from appearing as part of the *Carry On* team to front the show. When that run of *Summer Spin* concluded, and *Thank Your Lucky Stars* returned, Dale was retained as host. Brian Matthew had been moved aside, the production team picking up on his waning interest in the pop music industry. By his own admission, Matthew was sick of all the teenage screaming and hysteria that made it impossible to hear much of the music.[17]

It's quite possible that this change of presenter was also hastened by the fact that the BBC now had an established competitor in *Top Of The Pops*, and also that the show's position as ITV's leading music programme had been eroded. For the last two years, *Thank Your Lucky*

Stars had faced a much livelier rival in the form of *Ready, Steady, Go!*, which had begun to win awards. In response, the way *Thank Your Lucky Stars* was billed in the *TV Times* began to subtly change. Up until April 1965, it was described as "TV's top pop show". This was carefully amended to "TV's top-rated pop show" for a while but for its final year on air the strapline became "a musical spectacular for all the family with today's top recording stars" – recognising that the programme's appeal was to a wider audience than the teenagers who adored its competitors. A glance at the guest lists of the time reinforces this idea. While *Thank Your Lucky Stars* still offered plenty of artists who might and, indeed, did appear on *Ready, Steady, Go!*, it also accommodated acts such as the Bachelors, Matt Monro, Lance Percival, Libby Morris, Cleo Laine and the Seekers.

Perhaps Brian Matthew could see the writing on the wall. That 1965–6 season was to be *Thank Your Lucky Stars*' last. Interest began to fade around the country and ITV regions started to allocate their peak-hour Saturday evening slot to other programmes. In April 1966, London ITV switched the show to the middle of Sunday afternoon, to make way for a new soap opera called *Weaver's Green*. In June, the capital lost interest all together and the show ceased to air there, as it already had in other parts of the UK.

Thank Your Lucky Stars battled on for a couple more weeks in its Midlands home and then drew to a close, one other key factor precipitating its demise. A ruling by the Musicians' Union that year meant that artists appearing on such shows would no longer be able to mime to their records. *Ready, Steady, Go!* had anticipated this by turning itself – at great additional expense – into a live music show a year before. But for *Thank Your Lucky Stars*, a miming show at heart, it meant the end of the road.

The programme's five years on air, however, had witnessed the biggest shake-up in music since the arrival of rock'n'roll and, like its TWW counterpart *Discs A Gogo*, *Thank Your Lucky Stars* had more than played its part in facilitating this change. Countless major stars had gained vital early promotion on the programme – from Gene Pitney to Gerry & the Pacemakers. Most importantly, the series also gave the first national television exposure to another Liverpool group, their appearance on the show on January 19, 1963, a watershed moment in their career even though they were way down a bill that also included Acker Bilk, Petula Clark, Mark Wynter, the Brook Brothers, Chris Barber's Jazz Band and David Macbeth. That night the UK was virtually at a standstill thanks to a snowfall of Arctic magnitude, so after digesting their tea many more families than usual were snuggled up in front of TV sets to watch this hugely engaging young group perform their second single. Everything about them captivated the frozen nation that night: their cheeky smiles beneath fringes that concealed their foreheads, the way they shook their heads and wiggled their guitars, the perfect symmetry of how the guitar played by the one on the left pointed in the opposite outward direction to the one on the right. Their record, 'Please Please Me', entered the UK Top 40 the following week and reached the top three two weeks later. The Beatles were on their way.

The appearance had an even greater impact on former singer Dick James, who had secured the group a place on the show with a phone call to his friend, the programme's producer Philip Jones. It was a trade-off James had agreed with the Beatles' manager Brian Epstein for the rights to publish the band's music. It's fair to say that the man who was previously best known for singing the theme to the ITV series *The Adventures Of Robin Hood* will have had less productive days at the office.[18]

★ ★ ★

Although major music showcases such as *Juke Box Jury*, *Discs A Gogo* and *Thank Your Lucky Stars* were few and far between in the early sixties, pop music was creeping into the schedules in other ways. Children's series were seen by record labels as a good way to get exposure. *Crackerjack* (1955–84) was well into its stride by the time the sixties broke and starting to feature artists such as Cliff Richard and Marty Wilde. Adam Faith, Joe Brown, Mark Wynter and Frank Ifield followed until, with the arrival of Merseybeat, pop music became a central plank of the programme, slotted in among the slapstick sketches and games like 'Double or Drop'. The Searchers, the Swinging Blue Jeans and the Applejacks were among the first of the new bands to feature, with later names including Georgie Fame, the Hollies, Tom Jones, Manfred Mann, the Small Faces, Roy Orbison, Lulu, Eric Burdon, Cat Stevens, the Bee Gees and even the Who (miming to 'Magic Bus' during a temporary lull in their career in 1968). *Crackerjack* didn't get the Beatles or the Stones, but almost everyone else who mattered trod the stage of the BBC Television Theatre in Shepherd's Bush, in front of a raucous audience of excited school kids. *Crackerjack* also offered its own novel treatment of some of the latest hits, concluding each week with a medley of chart numbers with corny new lyrics added.

One show that did secure the Beatles was *Pops And Lenny* (1962–3), a reincarnation of *The Lenny The Lion Show*, which had begun in 1957 as a vehicle for ventriloquist Terry Hall and his bashful lion puppet. Three guest artists normally appeared in each half-hour show. ITV also began to build pop music into its own kids' TV programmes. One of the earliest was *Lucky Dip* (1958–61), an Associated-Rediffusion magazine show that included a guitar course from Bert Weedon, author of the famous *Play In A Day* tutorial. This was replaced by the similar *Tuesday Rendezvous* (1961–3), which snared the Beatles a couple of times and in turn gave way to the more successful *Five O'Clock Club* (1963–6), sometimes billed as *Ollie And Fred's Five O'Clock Club* and *Five O'Clock Funfair*. Although former continuity announcer Muriel Young, initially supported by Howard Williams and again Bert Weedon, was the human host – with Marjorie Sigley taking over for *Five O'Clock Funfair* – puppets were the real stars of these shows, most notably the owl Ollie Beak, voiced by former Vipers Skiffle Group singer Wally Whyton, and the dog Fred Barker, the creation of Ivan Owen. Owen was also the voice of Basil Brush and the idea of mixing contemporary chart music with children's comedy continued through him in the BBC's extremely popular *The Basil Brush Show* (1968–80).

The growing appeal of pop music was hard to resist for producers of other kinds of programmes, too. In 1961, ATV launched *Harpers West One*, a soap opera set in a London department store. While mostly following the daily lives of the store's employees, it also introduced guest characters with their own story to tell, one of which turned out to be a pop singer named Johnny St Cyr, played by actor John Leyton, fresh from the children's series *Biggles*. St Cyr was written into the storyline to open the shop's new record department and perform his latest release. This was a new creation put together by songwriter Geoff Goddard and maverick record producer Joe Meek, a song about a distressed guy who hears his deceased lover's voice calling to him "blowin' in the treetops" from beyond the grave. The atmospheric production of 'Johnny Remember Me' made a huge impact on the viewing public and, issued as a single in its own right, it broke into the charts within two weeks of airing on the show, going on to give Leyton a huge number one hit.

A similar stunt was pulled by the producers of *Coronation Street* two years later when Chris Sandford was cast as Liverpudlian window cleaner Walter Potts, the lodger of *Street* siren Elsie Tanner. When it was discovered that Potts could sing, Tanner's son Dennis renamed him Brett Falcon and attempted to make him a star. The result was a spin-off hit called 'Not Too Little, Not Too Much'. Sandford even had publicity shots taken with the Beatles at the Granada studios.*

Once the Beatles had conquered all before them, makers of programmes of all genres found the power of pop hard to resist. The Fab Four themselves featured briefly in an episode of *Doctor Who* (the first part of a dalek story called *The Chase*) when they were spotted on a monitor in the Tardis performing 'Ticket To Ride', although this was actually a recording shown first on *Top Of The Pops* in April 1965. A year earlier, an episode of Gerry Anderson's underwater puppet series *Stingray* – entitled *Titan Goes Pop* – centred around the kidnap of a pop star named Duke Dexter.

---

* Rival soap *Crossroads* also had its pop successes. Actress Sue Nicholls (who played singing waitress Marilyn Gates) scored a Top 20 hit with 'Where Will You Be' in 1968 and there were further spin-offs in the seventies and eighties for Stephanie De Sykes ('Born With A Smile On My Face'), Simon May ('Summer Of My Life'), Paul Henry ('Benny's Theme') and Kate Robbins ('More Than In Love').

* * *

Documentary makers began to take an interest in the new music enjoyed by young people at the end of the fifties. In March 1959, the BBC's news magazine *Panorama* had run a feature on manager Larry Parnes and his troupe of young performers, which included at the time Marty Wilde, Vince Eager and Billy Fury. Reporter Christopher Chataway investigated and asked how the boys felt about the way Parnes peddled their talent. But again it was the arrival of the Beatles that really ignited the interest of film-makers who were keen to explore why Liverpool had suddenly become the epicentre of the music industry.

Two particular documentaries stand out. In October 1963, the BBC aired *The Mersey Sound*, a film made by Don Haworth. The opening narration, over images of screaming girls as the Beatles performed 'Twist And Shout', explained: "This is the story about a special kind of noise, a noise worth a small fortune." The following 30 minutes featured various local musicians discussing the nature of the music and the reasons for its success, including the time locals had to practise through being on the dole. The film explored how kids got into music and the local club scene, and there was also an interview with Bill Harry, editor of the influential *Mersey Beat* newspaper. Grim shots of Mersey ferries and run-down, often derelict, terraced houses were intercut with contributions from local bands the Undertakers and Group One as well as more clips of the Beatles – in performance and in interview – some of which have been used, out of context, time and again over the years.

Despite Haworth's pleas for a network showing, only viewers in London and the North saw the first transmission of the film, other regions being allowed to opt out with their own programmes in the post-10 p.m. timeslot it had been allocated. But, in recognition of the pull of the Beatles, an early evening, nationwide repeat was scheduled for just over a month later. Another reason for the quick repeat was the knowledge that Associated-Rediffusion had its own documentary ready to roll. In *Beat City*, which was shown on Christmas Eve 1963, reporter Dan Farson delivered his own 45-minute take on the Liverpool music scene. Asking the question "Why Liverpool?", Farson's less serious film visited the Cavern and Blue Angel clubs, crossed the Mersey to Birkenhead and featured a wider selection of local performers, from Gerry & the Pacemakers and Rory Storm & the Hurricanes to the lesser known Faron's Flamingos and the Chants. The Beatles didn't appear, as the BBC had signed them for *The Mersey Sound* before Associated-Rediffusion could reach them.[19]

The commercial channel was to bite back, however, as the first transmission of *The Mersey Sound* was followed just four days later by the Beatles' live appearance on ITV's *Sunday Night At The London Palladium* (1955–67; 1973–4). This long-running variety show, with its big American stars, captured the attention of the nation from the moment it began. Although generally built around crooners, comics and dancing girls, with games interludes like 'Beat the Clock', the programme had enjoyed the odd rock'n'roll moment – most notably when Buddy Holly & the Crickets appeared in March 1958 – but it had seen nothing like the interest the Beatles would attract. ITV need not have worried about its thunder being stolen by *The Mersey Sound*; a whole new storm broke when John, Paul, George and Ringo topped the bill. They didn't just win over the audience inside the theatre, they also blocked the roads outside, as screaming fans surged around Oxford Circus hoping for a glimpse of their new idols. It was the moment when Beatlemania became a recognised phenomenon, a story that was splashed across the front pages of the Monday newspapers.

Less than a month later, the Beatles confirmed their superstar status with a barnstorming performance at the *Royal Variety Performance*. Staged on November 4, 1963 at the Prince of Wales Theatre, just off Leicester Square, and broadcast by ITV six days later, it saw the band on a bill that included such names as Buddy Greco, Marlene Dietrich and Tommy Steele, as well as *Steptoe And Son*'s Wilfrid Brambell and Harry H. Corbett, Charlie Drake, Eric Sykes, Hattie Jacques and puppets Pinky & Perky. John Lennon – now famously – encouraged the audience to join in with the band, asking people in the cheaper seats to clap their hands and the rest – with a nod to the Queen Mother in the royal box – to just rattle their jewellery.

By this time, the Beatles had become practised television performers, largely through regular appearances on Granada's weekday news magazine, *Scene At 6.30* (1963–6). This was not a networked show but, as Granada's transmission area covered all of the north of England and north Wales, it provided plenty of early exposure and broadcasting experience for the band. In charge of the programme's musical content was a young producer by the name of Johnnie Hamp, who had been brought in from the theatrical side of Granada's business where he worked as a booker of artists. His job was to put together music spots in each edition and he toured the North's pubs and clubs in search of new talent.

The Beatles were already on Granada's radar, having been filmed at the Cavern Club for a programme that had never been shown, reportedly because the technical quality was poor, although it was later revealed it was actually because a linked film, featuring the Brighouse & Rastrick Brass Band, would have been too expensive to broadcast, with members of that band needing payment at Musicians' Union rates. Manager Brian Epstein desperately wanted the Cavern film on air to give the group publicity but Granada wouldn't budge. Eventually, a compromise was reached whereby the Beatles went instead into the studio for *Scene At 6.30*'s predecessor, *People And Places*, in October 1962 to perform two songs, 'Some Other Guy' and their new single, 'Love Me Do'. It was their first television appearance.[20]

Johnnie Hamp – who had first seen the band in Hamburg in early 1962 – continued to foster their fledgling career on *Scene At 6.30*, offering them regular appearances throughout 1963. But it wasn't just the Beatles who benefited as the programme developed into a significant outlet for pop music during its three years on air and, with five editions to fill a week, Hamp was able to bring in lots of hopeful locals as well as big-name international stars. "We had everyone that made a record, from the Beatles onwards," he recalls. "The Stones, a lot of the Americans – people like the Righteous Brothers and Sonny & Cher, the Byrds – the Who." Most were captured in the Granada studio but some were recorded on location in what, in effect, were early music videos. Three trains were hired, for example, so that Little Eva could perform 'The Locomotion'.

While it didn't contribute a networked music series during the early sixties, Granada did make a number of significant one-off programmes alongside *Scene At 6.30*. *I Hear The Blues* (1963) saw Hamp giving airtime to a group of touring blues musicians, including Muddy Waters, Sonny Boy Williamson and Willie Dixon. He repeated the idea with *Blues And Gospel Train* (1964), which featured Waters again, plus Sister Rosetta Tharpe and Sonny Terry & Brownie McGhee, performing at a disused station in Chorlton that was dressed up as a railroad halt from the Deep South ("Chorltonville"). Rock'n'roll came under the Granada spotlight with *It's Little Richard* (1964), in which the star was supported by the Shirelles and Sounds Incorporated. This was a particularly popular show. Some 50,000 letters were received, asking for a repeat and encouraging Hamp to come up with another rock'n'roll revival called *A Whole Lotta Shakin' Goin' On* (1964) that brought Jerry Lee Lewis, Gene Vincent and the Animals to the Manchester studios. Distinctly more laid back was Hamp's 1965 offering, *The Bacharach Sound*, allowing Burt Bacharach to work through his catalogue of hits in the company of Dionne Warwick, the Searchers, Dusty Springfield, the Merseybeats and Chuck Jackson.

Hamp rounded off that year with the biggest showcase yet when he enticed the Beatles into making *The Music Of Lennon & McCartney* (1965), which Granada sold all around the world. The band members themselves only appeared in parts of this programme, leaving the interpretation of their songs largely to Cilla Black, Lulu, Peter & Gordon, Marianne Faithfull and Billy J. Kramer & the Dakotas, with Henry Mancini flying in to give a piano rendition of 'If I Fell'. The group did perform two numbers, 'Day Tripper' and 'We Can Work It Out', the latter featuring John Lennon at a harmonium that had been dragged out of the Granada storeroom and was usually played by Ena Sharples in *Coronation Street*.

The show is probably best remembered for actor Peter Sellers' version of 'A Hard Day's Night', performed in the character of Shakespeare's Richard III (as depicted in film by Laurence Olivier). Having heard the Sellers recording, Johnnie Hamp decided he wanted him on the show, but didn't think he would oblige. "He was a superstar at that time and I really didn't think that he would do it," he says. "I rang him at home.

We were weeks off production and he said: 'Yes, I'll do it next Tuesday. I can't do it later because I'm off to Hollywood.'" Hamp quickly booked three hours in a London studio and four days later Sellers turned up with his own make-up guy and Shakespearean costume. It proved to be a difficult, if hilarious, session. Being far too tricky to mime, the piece had to be re-recorded over a backing track and Sellers could not remember the words. "He took 10 takes to get it in," recalls Hamp. "If you look on YouTube, you'll find all the outtakes. They're very, very funny."[21]

The Music Of Lennon & McCartney was not the only Beatles special ITV screened around this time. In May 1964, Rediffusion (as Associated-Rediffusion had been rebranded by then) presented *Around The Beatles*, a one-hour showcase, with Jack Good as producer and Good's regular assistant, Rita Gillespie, as director. Unfortunately, preparations for the show were hindered by the fact that the group were working on their first feature film, which left Good, a stickler for rehearsal, somewhat frustrated. To compensate and to fill out the hour, he added a number of other acts, including Long John Baldry, the Vernons Girls and P.J. Proby, whom Good had discovered in America and introduced to the UK in this show. The Beatles mimed a few numbers but also clowned around in a version of *Pyramus And Thisbe*, the play-within-a-play from Shakespeare's *A Midsummer Night's Dream*. John Lennon was happy to lark about in this way, Good claims, but Paul McCartney was not so keen and needed encouragement from his *A Hard Day's Night* co-star Wilfrid Brambell to do it. Good at this time was resident in the USA and it was this programme that enabled him to finally break into American television and led to his creating *Shindig* for ABC.[22]

The BBC also dabbled in Beatles specials. *It's The Beatles* (1963), recorded and broadcast the same day as their *Juke Box Jury* appearance, was eagerly awaited by fans but not an unqualified success, with many quick to report their disappointment with the camerawork and sound. The Corporation, in the form of producer Barney Colehan, cited a lack of rehearsal time – just 20 minutes – for the problems.[23]

The BBC also presented a behind-the-scenes programme exploring the band at work on the film *A Hard Day's Night*. *Follow The Beatles* (1964), introduced by Robert Robinson, showed the group on set and featured interviews with other cast and crew members. Two years later, the BBC snapped up the chance to show *The Beatles At Shea Stadium* (1966), a 50-minute film shot the previous summer while the group were performing in front of nearly 60,000 New York fans, mostly hysterical girls screaming themselves silly. Again, there were complaints about excessive crowd noise and jumpy camerawork, although any fault this time lay with Bob Precht (son-in-law of US TV great Ed Sullivan) who produced the film for NEMS Enterprises, the Beatles' management company. But "fault" is a very harsh word to levy in this instance as all Precht did was to capture – exceptionally well – the sheer frenzy and deafening excitement of the occasion. In hindsight, films like this have become valuable historical artefacts that offer a priceless insight into the Beatles phenomenon.

* * *

Through the unparalleled success of the Beatles and the bands that followed in their wake, it became increasingly difficult to deny pop music a place on British television. Associated-Rediffusion responded by selling a programme called *Here Come The Girls* (1963) to a number of other ITV regions. This was an occasional, 15-minute offering hosted by Alan Freeman, who interviewed one of the leading female stars of the day around performances of some of their hits. Susan Maughan, Carol Deene, Billie Davis and Kathy Kirby were among those featured. This evolved into *They've Sold A Million* (1963–4), with Freeman usually again as host and artists such as Gerry & the Pacemakers, Joe Brown, the Ronettes, the Crystals and the Searchers in the frame. These programmes proved handy as last-minute fillers for schedulers.

A similar format was used by Southern Television for *Ladybirds* (1964–5), a 30-minute series directed by Mike Mansfield. "What are the top girl singers really like when they step into their own private lives?" asked the *TV Times*. Interviewers Terence Carroll and Shaw Taylor tried to find the answer from the likes of Petula Clark, Françoise Hardy, Dionne Warwick, Cilla Black and Sandie Shaw. The same team followed up with the similarly themed *The Chart Busters* (1965), which included Dave Clark as one of the guests.* ABC, meanwhile, delivered a collection of short programmes called *The Pop Spot* (1964–5) that, once again, conveniently filled a hole in the schedule for the ITV regions when needed. The format consisted of just one artist/group – the Migil 5, Cilla Black, Sounds Incorporated, Dusty Springfield, etc. – performing a few songs.

⋆ ⋆ ⋆

Looking back on the early sixties, for all the regional output and the best efforts of *Thank Your Lucky Stars* and *Discs A Gogo* in particular, there still wasn't a nationally televised programme that quite got to grips with what young people wanted to see and hear musically on television. The fifties had gifted *Six-Five Special* and *Oh Boy!* but, in this new decade, there was nothing that really demanded the attention of kids in quite the same way. But things were about to change.

The day before *Thank Your Lucky Stars* celebrated its 100th edition, ITV launched a pop programme that was to shake up not only its Saturday-night rival but also influence the way that music was presented on television for decades to follow. On August 9, 1963, *Ready, Steady, Go!* (1963–6) burst onto the screen, bringing a buzz to early Friday evenings and, for many teenagers, living up to its bold subtitle 'The Weekend Starts Here'.

The programme was the brainchild of Elkan Allan, head of entertainment at Associated-Rediffusion. Allan, a 40-year-old former *Picture Post* reporter, had broken into television in the fifties and was once editor of the current affairs show *This Week*. He saw *RSG!* as more of a magazine than a pure pop showcase in the style of *Thank Your Lucky Stars*, and, from the start, he aimed to include a variety of items of interest to young people in the capital, who were the initial target audience.

---

* Mansfield resurrected the idea 20 years later for Channel 4. *Ladybirds* (1983–4) this time featured such names as Lynsey de Paul, Barbara Dickson, Bonnie Tyler, Elaine Paige, Bertice Reading, Jane Birkin, Janis Ian, Dana and Kiki Dee.

A pilot show was put together but it didn't work. Changes were needed. Allan recognised that the pop element was the best part but, with the audience seated, even that fell flat. So, prompted by his 14-year-old son, he decided to remove all the seating to see if giving the audience room to dance would perk things up. It certainly did. This was the first evidence of Allan very sensibly deferring to those with a better understanding of what would appeal to teenagers. The future success of the show was built on such deferral and the person he grew to rely on most was Vicki Wickham.[24]

A farmer's daughter from Berkshire, Vicki had accepted a job in publishing when she first arrived in London and then took on a radio production role at the BBC. Now, in her early twenties, she decided to give that up in pursuit of a career in television. A friend introduced her to Elkan Allan and, hearing of his plans for a new music show, she decided to work as his secretary/PA on condition that, if the programme was given the green light, she could transfer onto the production team. The excitement generated by the project was too much, even though her knowledge of the popular music scene was somewhat limited.

"I honestly knew nothing about contemporary music," she concedes. "I'd been brought up on Gilbert & Sullivan; I didn't even know who the Beatles were. Anyway, the show got picked up. So I went on as what was called an 'editor'." Allan reluctantly gave up an excellent secretary and soon realised he'd been very wise to do so as Vicki quickly embraced the latest sounds and drove the programme forward.

With the format ironed out, *RSG!* was sold to most of the other ITV regions and scheduled for broadcast at 7 p.m. on a Friday evening, preceding the popular nursing soap *Emergency – Ward 10.* In keeping with Allan's original intentions, it was by no means just a pop programme. The *TV Times* listings information suggested that viewers could "Meet" (guest stars), "Listen" (to music), "See" (performers), "Dance" (to the music) and "Find Out" (what's going on) during the course of the 30 minutes the programme was on air. Among the performers on that first show were Brian Poole & the Tremeloes and Billy Fury, but Vicki and her young team were given plenty of rein to expand the repertoire of guests.

"We were young and they had faith in the fact that we kind of knew what we were doing and would have good instincts," she remembers. "In retrospect, it paid off because we were kids that were hanging out with the people that were the artists. We knew everyone. London was very small at the time. You all went to the same restaurants, the same clubs, so it was very easy to get to know people. We could literally say: 'Come on the show.'" The only artist that Allan himself asked them to book was Donovan, who became a star in very short order after a number of appearances.[25]

Although experience had ceded ground to youthful enthusiasm behind the scenes, the front-of-camera responsibilities were still only entrusted to a practised presenter, with ex-*Thank Your Lucky Stars* host Keith Fordyce, aged 34, installed as the anchor, aided for the first few months by 33-year-old former *Needle Match* panellist David Gell, whose job it was to mingle with the kids, chat to them about dancing and ask if they had any record requests. Gell recalls how the programme took time to take shape.* "In the early days, we were just finding our feet, so to speak. In some ways the show was similar to the BBC's *Six-Five Special*; in others, it was a ground-breaking concept. There was a very exciting, energetic atmosphere… we were constantly surrounded by new, ground-breaking music… and we were right in the heart of it. The Beatles had just released their debut album, *Please Please Me*, a few months before; 'She Loves You' had just hit the charts, the British Invasion was about to take the world by storm and London was the place to be. Everyone seemed to be enjoying themselves, both audience members and performers, despite the organised chaos!"[26]

RSG! was broadcast live from Associated-Rediffusion's home at Television House in London's Kingsway, a very handy location, not least because established artists, even those not performing, could easily

* David Gell – who also hosted the early-sixties game show *Concentration* – continued to broadcast in the UK until 1977, including taking on the TV commentator's role – later made famous by Terry Wogan – for the *Eurovision Song Contest* in 1969 and 1970. He then moved back to his native Canada.

drop by to add glamour to the audience, or to whip up a party in the green room, behind the scenes.

"The green room was run by a Joyce Grenfell-type woman called Isobel," Vicki Wickham recalls. "The idea was that everybody came in and had 'a drink'. It became like the social scene. Mick, Eric, everybody would be up there on a Friday, whether they were on the show or not. And they all worked out a way that they could get extra drinks and drink themselves silly by the end of the night."[27]

Meanwhile, viewers switching on were taken into what appeared to be a claustrophobically crowded cellar bar filled with trendy, dancing teenagers. Artists stood and swayed on plinths, bits of scaffolding or a battered spiral staircase – part of the original studio fabric called into service as an impromptu stage – as they mimed to their latest releases. Cameras barged through the throng, pushing to the front for the next close-up, as dancers skipped hurriedly out of the way. Presentation-wise, it was much closer to *Discs A Gogo* than *Thank Your Lucky Stars* – indeed, heavily borrowed from the TWW show – with a touch of the warts-and-all open studio look pioneered by the BBC's satire series, *That Was The Week That Was*. Just as Jack Good had found with *Six-Five Special*, this liberal embrace of the audience and the workings of television proved vital, delivering energy and spontaneity.

Regular features and competitions included an "amateur disc jockey" slot that saw a celebrity or audience member introducing a favourite record, and a miming competition for the studio crowd. Future knight of the realm Tim Rice took part one week, but his impersonation of Billy J. Kramer singing 'I'll Keep You Satisfied' failed to impress judge Chris Sandford. On another occasion, a distinctly unenthused Paul McCartney was called upon to judge four girls as they mimed to Brenda Lee's 'Let's Jump The Broomstick'. He chose 13-year-old Melanie Coe as the winner. Strangely, it wasn't the last time Paul and Melanie's lives were to cross. The same girl featured in a story in the *Daily Mirror* four years later. Discovering herself pregnant and worried about her parents' reaction, she had run away with a croupier. Around the same time, McCartney was inspired to write his plangent *Sgt Pepper* song 'She's Leaving Home', admitting it was triggered by reading a newspaper story – now widely believed today to be the one concerning Melanie Coe.[28]

RSG! gained such a reputation among the youth of Britain that the few ITV regions that hadn't originally taken the show soon demanded it, leading to full network status within six months of its launch. But not all regions screened the show early on Friday evening; for viewers in some parts of the country, the weekend didn't so much start here as end there.

By autumn 1963, the programme had been extended to 45 minutes and moved to a slightly earlier slot. The control young people had of the programme was also consolidated. Joining Vicki Wickham on the team were 18-year-old Michael Aldred, a boy-next-door type with an encyclopaedic knowledge of music, and a pelmet-fringed 19-year-old secretary from Streatham named Cathy McGowan, who were appointed "teenage advisers" after answering an advertisement in a national newspaper and fighting off competition from 3,000 other applicants. It was McGowan's commitment to fashion that led Elkan Allan to choose her over future DJ and *Old Grey Whistle Test* presenter Anne Nightingale. When asked later what special qualifications she had for the role, McGowan replied: "Perhaps it's just that I mix five nights a week with with-it teenagers in the right places." It sounds simplistic but it was such credibility within the production team that made the programme relevant to the youth of the day. Cathy, with Vicki Wickham, even chose the audience by touring London clubs such as The Speakeasy and Revolution and selecting youngsters she felt would add to the show through their dancing skills or clothes sense.[29]

In January 1964, with Manfred Mann's '5-4-3-2-1' replacing the Surfaris' 'Wipe Out' as the show's theme tune, Aldred and McGowan were pushed in front of the cameras to provide a youthful onscreen balance to the more mature Fordyce. Aldred remained with the programme only until May but McGowan was destined for stardom, even if her transition from backroom assistant to onstage presenter was not at all easy. The contrast between Fordyce's slick, Radio Luxembourg-honed communication skills and McGowan's nervous, hesitant fumbling was impossible to ignore. But she shrewdly turned this to her advantage.

The way she stumbled over her lines, blushing self-consciously, often star-struck during interviews, offered a natural appeal. She came to be seen as someone just plucked from the crowd, rather than part of the broadcasting Establishment. "Cathy was not a natural but, in retrospect, it was part of her charm because I think everybody watching felt they could do better," says Vicki Wickham. "She wasn't good at remembering names and there were lots of 'smashings' in there but she managed it and people loved her." Her prominence led to her becoming a style leader, one of the faces of the sixties, working closely with designer Barbara Hulanicki and her Biba clothing brand. George Melly, looking back on the show, went so far as to declare that McGowan had "destroyed the class basis of fashion, gesture and speech".[30]

The look of the programme slowly changed, too, as designer Nicholas Ferguson drew on the world of pop art to dress the studio walls with giant paintings, collages and Mod symbols like arrows and bullseyes. Indeed, the Mod influence became increasingly important, culminating in a major outside broadcast edition in April 1964. Entitled *Ready, Steady, Go! Mod Ball*, the event was presented at the Empire Pool, Wembley, with ticket sales benefiting the children's charities of the Variety Club of Great Britain. Demand was instant and overwhelming, with more than 25,000 applications for the 8,000 available tickets (2,000 for dancers and 6,000 seated). The show was partly screened live and featured, among other names, the Rolling Stones, Manfred Mann, Cilla Black, Freddie & the Dreamers, the Searchers, the Fourmost and the Merseybeats.[31]

Later the same month, the programme decamped to Switzerland for a one-off edition called *Ready, Steady, Goes To Montreux*, which was recorded at the town's casino, an ill-fated lakeside venue later celebrated in Deep Purple's 'Smoke On The Water'. This was an opportunistic move designed to show delegates at the International Contest for Television Light Entertainment Programmes "how a live mod pop show is produced". The programme itself was not part of the competition: ITV's official entry was a Merseybeat edition of *Thank Your Lucky Stars* from the previous December.[32]

In June 1964, the series generated a spin-off talent show called *Ready, Steady – Win!* Each week, six groups took part in a contest to find the best new beat combo, with £1,000 of musical equipment the top prize, followed by a second prize of a £750 van and £250 worth of clothes for third. Keith Fordyce, assisted by Michael Aldred and actress-singer Gay Shingleton – later known as Singleton when her acting career took off – hosted proceedings as each band played a couple of numbers, including an original song. They were then judged on their personalities as well as their musical ability. Names on the changing roster of judges included Mick Jagger, Lulu and Helen Shapiro. The victorious band emerged from a finale entitled *Ready, Steady – Winner* in September, with Beatles manager Brian Epstein and rock'n'roll pioneer Bill Haley part of the judging panel. Runners-up were a Stockport band, the Toggery Five, but first place was awarded to the Bo Street Runners from Harrow. Despite securing a Decca recording contract, and enjoying the exposure the programme provided, they failed to register a chart hit.

RSG! packed so much into its first year and generated such excitement that, when its first anniversary came around – marked with an edition subtitled 'Year Two Starts Here' – the *TV Times* asked: "Can you remember a time when there was no *Ready, Steady, Go!*?" Its popularity then continued, ensuring both Christmas Day and New Year's Eve editions (*The New Year Starts Here*) that year.[33]

The next year proved to be even more momentous, for various reasons. One of the highlights was a spin-off programme entitled *The Sound Of Motown*. This featured an array of Motown talent, fresh from their recent British tour. The idea for the show came from Dusty Springfield, who had accompanied Vicki Wickham to one of the concerts. "It was amazing but there was nobody there," Vicki recalls. "Nobody knew who the hell Motown was. It was really disappointing so Dusty said: 'We really should do this on television. Why don't you talk to Elkan? Explain to him why it's so important. Explain that this is the music of the future'." Elkan Allan was receptive to the idea and agreed to the proposal, on the condition that Dusty – who had assisted Keith Fordyce on some early *RSG!* programmes – would agree to be the host.

The programme has been credited with breaking Motown in the UK, although by this time the Supremes had already notched up three hits on this side of the Atlantic and Martha & the Vandellas had scored a minor success with 'Dancing In The Street', so it was not entirely responsible. But the exposure this programme gave to the Motown sound and the show's other stars – Stevie Wonder, the Temptations and Smokey Robinson & the Miracles, all hit-less at that point in the UK – was clearly important.

In March 1965, Keith Fordyce and *RSG!* parted company. At the same time, the programme turned an important corner and abandoned miming in favour of studio performances. Elkan Allan was trying to keep things fresh and reignite interest in the show that was just beginning to fade. Adding to the pressure for change was the Musicians' Union. Its long-standing grumble over the way records were replacing live music on television led eventually to a blanket miming ban in 1966, but the decision by Allan to go live a year earlier was a brave one and expensive, too. The show's weekly budget needed to rise by 50 per cent to cover the cost of backing singers, musicians and arrangers, and a five-figure sum was spent on acquiring the latest equipment to guarantee high-quality sound reproduction. But, according to Vicki Wickham, it was "obviously the thing to do", given how the music world had moved on and the sort of artists the show was now presenting – talented musicians eager to show live what they could do. "Now they were performers, writing their own material, putting it across, so it was inevitable that we had to do it." [34]

The move coincided with a change of studio. For all its convenience, Television House had always had a problem with numbers. Fans were known to queue around the block to try to get into the show or catch a glimpse of the stars. The new location, Associated-Rediffusion's Wembley Studios, offered not just more space but also better facilities. While efforts were made to recreate the intimacy of the original set, artists were now not so tightly hemmed in by fans and probing cameras, and dancers – up to 250 per programme – were given more room to show off their latest moves. To formalise the selection of audience members, a club was formed, welcoming around 2,000 "dancer-members" who were invited to take part on a rota basis. Their clothes sense was closely monitored, with the threat of ejection from the studio and loss of club membership if they didn't show up "looking smart and up-to-the-minute". As for the music, "We don't claim to produce an authentic 'record' sound," explained producer Francis Hitching.* "What viewers will see and hear is comparable to a live stage performance … with all its accompanying excitement".[35]

In order to kick-start the new format, the programme changed its name to *Ready Steady Goes Live!* and the first performers into the brave new world included Manfred Mann, Dionne Warwick, Cliff Bennett & the Rebel Rousers and Zoot Money's Big Roll Band. After nine weeks, the old title was brought back, with briefly-seen co-host David Goldsmith stepping aside and Cathy McGowan now fronting alone. To retain the emphasis on the live approach, a new subtitle – 'The All-Live Pop Show' – was coined.

Anyone watching *RSG!* in 1965 will also have noticed more adventure in the camera work, courtesy of a new director named Michael Lindsay-Hogg. The ambitious, Oxford-educated 24-year-old son of an English baronet and an Irish Hollywood actress found his way into the director's chair after working for Irish television and took full advantage when he got there by constantly looking for angles and approaches that would add to the show's excitement. His proactive direction was designed to enhance the thrill of the live performances, rather than simply capturing the images. This is well exemplified by his treatment of the Rolling Stones' 'Paint It Black', for which he dimmed a bank of lights after every verse so that, by the end, only singer Mick Jagger was left illuminated, camera effects making his face shudder in a dramatic finale.[36]

"Michael understood that people wanted to see the artist," says Vicki Wickham. "You wanted to see their face; you wanted to see their bodies; you wanted to see them reacting. You didn't want to see just hands on a guitar. We'd all seen that. He would cut in really close to girls dancing. He was innovative and creative. Michael was *Ready, Steady, Go!* He gave it its look, its mark."[37]

---

* Francis Hitching went on to become a noted authority on the paranormal and evolution, writing several books on such issues as dowsing, ley lines and the work of Charles Darwin.

For Lindsay-Hogg, *RSG!* was a career changer. His work was noticed by the Beatles, who asked him to direct some promotional videos as well as their last feature-length film, *Let It Be*. Later, in television drama, he directed episodes of the epic series *Brideshead Revisited*.

Technological advances continued to be grasped by the programme, such as when on New Year's Eve 1965 small cameras called vidicons – the size of a shoebox – were introduced, allowing closer, more intimate shots of the artists and audience. Special editions also continued. In March 1966, one was built around the American soul star James Brown, although the production team was somewhat shocked by the reaction of the viewing public, some of whom – in racially abusive language – phoned up to complain. "It was the first time that it ever struck me that there was a different attitude to black artists than white artists," says Vicki Wickham. "It absolutely never entered my mind. We were horrified. He was a physical, sexy man and I think a lot of people just couldn't deal with that." [38]

Another special edition was *Ready, Steady, Allez!*, broadcast via Eurovision from La Locomotive, described at the time as the "top teenage club in Paris". French music and fashions came under the spotlight but there were also performances from the Yardbirds and the Who, *RSG!* favourites whose second single 'Anyway, Anyhow, Anywhere' became the show's theme song not long after its release in May of 1965.

Despite all this innovation, 1966 was to be *RSG!*'s last year on air. Rediffusion decided to call time on the series in the face of rising costs and the fact that the BBC had launched a new pop show that was now ahead in the ratings. But *RSG!* remained relevant and innovative to the end. Otis Redding was introduced to the UK in a special in September and guests in the penultimate show included Jimi Hendrix and a young Marc Bolan. On December 23, the series drew to a close with a grand finale entitled *Ready, Steady, Goes!*

Over the course of nearly 180 programmes, the series had featured almost all the big names in pop music from the Beatles and the Stones to American stars such as Roy Orbison and Little Richard. Perhaps less widely remembered are acts such as Van Dyke & the Bambies,

Johnny Milton & the Condors, and Glenda Collins & the Orchids. Not every artist who enjoyed *RSG!* exposure followed it up with chart success. Another "failure" was Rod Stewart who began his appearance inauspiciously by tripping over his own feet and literally stumbling into view. But his evening was not a complete disaster. He then headed off to a Soho pub and struck up a friendship with a stranger named Ronnie Wood.[39]

After the series' demise, Elkan Allan's career took a few further turns. He wrote a number of episodes of the American drama series *Batman* and, leaving production, became a noted television critic and listings editor, working for the *Sunday Times* and the *Independent*. He died in 2006. Vicki Wickham went on to become manager of Dusty Springfield and other stars such as Labelle, Morrissey and Holly Johnson. She was awarded an OBE in 2013. Keith Fordyce, who died in 2011, remained in broadcasting, both nationally and, latterly, in the West Country. Cathy McGowan also continued working in the media for a while, most notably as an entertainment reporter for the BBC's regional magazine *Newsroom South-East* and as host of the 1990 Brit Awards ceremony. She married actor Hywel Bennett in 1970 but, for many years, her partner has been actor-singer Michael Ball. The one-time "Queen of the Mods" now prefers to be out of the spotlight and that's a shame as her programme's legacy has been immense.

RSG! – possibly the most colourful series ever to be made in black and white – is the first name on critics' lips when it comes to sixties music programmes. It was the show that took the buzz of Swinging London – the music, the dancing, the fashion, the attitude – and generously shared it with the rest of the UK. The time when Scotland, Northern Ireland, Wales and the English provinces took months to catch up with London's latest sounds, looks and trends was over. *RSG!* revealed everything on a weekly basis.

The programme's day was not quite done, however. Edited episodes also pleased a new audience when they were broadcast on Channel 4 in the eighties, courtesy of former pop star Dave Clark, who had acquired the rights to the series. They offered a fascinating counterpoint to the channel's own major music series of the time, *The Tube*, which, broadcasting live on a Friday teatime, more than doffed its hat to Elkan Allan, Vicki Wickham, Cathy McGowan and *RSG!*'s other inspirational figures.

⋆ ⋆ ⋆

The new BBC show that was partly responsible for the demise of *RSG!* was, of course, *Top Of The Pops* (1964–2006). Noting the success of ITV's music programmes, the BBC decided to launch a weekly competitor and settled on a shamelessly populist format built tightly around the best-selling singles of the week. Producer Johnnie Stewart was charged with bringing it to air.

Stewart, a former radio producer, had been working in television since the late fifties, including a stint on *Juke Box Jury*. For the new show, he set out two hard-and-fast rules. Firstly, only records going up the singles chart could be featured. Any disc on its way down was yesterday's news. Secondly, each programme would conclude with the current number one single, whether or not the artists were available for the show. This immediately added to the pressure of putting the show together. Not only did Stewart have to predict which records would be heading the right way but he also had to find a way of presenting the chart topper in the absence of the performer. This initially entailed piecing together bits of archive film, news footage or some still shots. There were no videos in those days.

With the format in place, the BBC commissioned *Top Of The Pops* for six programmes and the first edition went out live on New Year's Day 1964 from a converted church in Dickenson Road, Rusholme, Manchester, the BBC's hub in the North-West, where there happened to be some spare production capacity. The first, 25-minute show opened with a drum-laden theme called 'Percussion Piece', performed by Bobby Midgley, and featuring studio appearances from the Rolling Stones – who kicked things off with 'I Wanna Be Your Man' – Dusty Springfield, the Dave Clark Five, the Hollies and the Swinging Blue Jeans. The Beatles stood at number one with

'I Want To Hold Your Hand' but were not available, so Johnnie Stewart put together the first of many visual collages to cover. Radio Luxembourg's Jimmy Savile was the host; local youngsters were brought in to dance and mill around the stages. *Top Of The Pops* was up and running.[40]

No one at the time could have predicted that the show would run for 42 years but reaction to the first programme was extremely positive, with teenagers, according to a BBC Audience Research Report, "wildly enthusiastic", although they thought the dancers were apathetic, "in need of a pep pill" – a criticism that was to dog the show for much of its long life. The BBC must have been rather pleased to hear that "the selection of current hits, the appearances of some singers and groups ... and the presentation in general – smooth, slick and lively" were very well received.[41]

Such a warm response ensured that *Top Of The Pops* survived its trial run and was commissioned as a permanent weekly series. From then on, around 150 local youths were invited each week to the church-studio that featured a soft-drinks bar, a DJ station – complete with turntables and TV monitors – and a back projection screen displaying giant portraits of stars. Prominently displayed, the programme's *raison d'être* – the latest singles chart – offered the nation the first glimpse of the week's best-selling discs, the programme going out live at 6.35 on a Wednesday evening, a day before other charts were published in the music press.

The chart used for the show was the same as compiled by the BBC for the radio programme *Pick Of The Pops*. This was not a new piece of sales research but simply put together by amalgamating information produced for the different charts featured in the music weeklies: *New Musical Express*, *Melody Maker*, *Disc* and *Record Retailer* (whose chart was also published in *Record Mirror*). Although considered by many music fans in the sixties as the "official" arbiter of chart position, because of its use on television and radio, the BBC chart does not correspond to the charts referenced in most "hit singles" books, as these defer only to the *Record Retailer* chart. From 1969, the BBC collaborated with *Record Retailer* to commission a new chart that has been used as the official source by the BBC ever since, although the ownership, compiling agency and methodology have changed over time.

Top Of The Pops quickly settled into this Wednesday time slot, where it stayed until September 1964, when it switched to Thursdays, giving producer Johnnie Stewart a little more time in which to put the programme together. He'd normally receive the chart on a Tuesday and then spend the next day or so finding acts or arranging filming sessions. The predictable success of some records did allow Stewart to book or record some material in advance but his clairvoyance inevitably let him down at times, leading to stressful moments in the hours before the show went out.

From the start, there was no pretence that the music was actually being played live. *Top Of The Pops* was unashamedly a show in which artists mimed to records and this idea was reinforced by showing a female assistant pretending to start each record, physically lifting the stylus onto the vinyl.* This was a rare excursion into miming at the time for the BBC, which still stuck rigidly to live music wherever possible, but the Corporation declared that, as this was a record show, it was the "noise" created in a recording studio that mattered, and not the performance. That was what the teenage audience was buying and that was what should be reflected in the show.[42]

Alan Freeman introduced the second ever programme, David Jacobs the third and Pete(r) Murray the fourth. With Savile, these elder statesmen of pop broadcasting continued to alternate as hosts, providing the bedrock of the show, although they were very nearly toppled by Tom Sloan, the BBC's Head of TV Light Entertainment, in 1965. Sloan wanted a clear out, claiming "we really must begin to find M.C.s of this type of output who are nearer to the generation they are catering to", but change didn't come until David Jacobs retired from the show towards the end of 1966. He was temporarily replaced by former pirate

* The longest serving and most recognisable "disc girl" was former model Samantha Juste, who went on to marry Monkee Micky Dolenz, after they met on the show. They divorced in the seventies and she died in California, aged 69, in 2014.[43]

DJ Simon Dee, who then skipped off to host his own chat show, *Dee Time*, leaving the three remaining presenters to carry on alone, until they were joined as co-hosts by presenters from the newly launched Radio 1, among them Tony Blackburn, Kenny Everett, Emperor Rosko, Mike Raven, Chris Denning, Mike Lennox, Keith Skues, Dave Cash, John Peel, Ed Stewart, David Symonds and Stuart Henry, who finally became the fourth regular DJ in 1968. Henry was himself then replaced by Tony Blackburn the next year. Pete Murray and Alan Freeman bowed out at the end of 1969.[44]

Reflecting the changing music scene of the sixties, *Top Of The Pops* morphed in other ways, too. A new brassy theme tune was supplied by Harry Rabinowitz and the programme also moved home. For a 13-week period in summer 1965, while the Manchester studio was being refurbished, the show switched to BBC Television Centre in London. By the end of that year, executives had concluded that Dickenson Road was no longer the right venue for this programme, the cost of travel to Manchester being a key factor in the decision to relocate to London permanently in January 1966, first to Television Centre, then to Lime Grove.[45]

An increasingly regular feature of the programme was the specially recorded film insert, designed to cover the absence of a performer who was in the chart. These were often made on demand in the USA, as there was little chance of getting an American artist on the show at short notice. An element of risk-taking pervaded the process, with Johnnie Stewart having to commission a film more than a week in advance so that it could be made and flown over in time for broadcast. This led to urgent messages racing back and forth across the Atlantic, such as when Gladys Knight's release 'Take Me In Your Arms And Love Me', which had been steadily climbing the chart, unexpectedly dropped in August 1967. Stewart was forced to telex the film agency in Hollywood to ask them to edit the footage into a film for her next release instead, in the hope that it could be used if that record made the chart. Performances by the Beatles were also mostly pre-recorded, taped in advance at BBC studios. The only time the band appeared in the show as it went out live was in June 1966, when they mimed to both sides of their latest hit, 'Paperback Writer' and 'Rain'*.[46]

Shortly after that Beatles performance, a new challenge confronted *Top Of The Pops*, one that threatened to undermine the whole basis of the show. From August 1, 1966, the programme was forced to rethink its miming policy as a Musicians' Union rule came into force banning the practice – although the change was diplomatically explained to the world as a voluntary decision made by the BBC and ITV companies after representations by the Union. Miming – described in the *Times* newspaper at that point as "the practice of distorting the features as though singing, sobbing, etc., while the sound is supplied by a gramophone record" – was not outlawed completely. If songs were recorded only for use on a programme, using the same musicians featured in the programme, then miming was permissable, which is why variety shows such as *The Black & White Minstrel Show* were able to carry on regardless. But for *Top Of The Pops* it was a major issue. The solution was to get artists either to perform live – backed by the new house orchestra directed by Johnny Pearson and the Ladybirds vocal trio (ex-Vernons Girl Maggie Stredder, Gloria George and Marian Davies) – or to re-record their music specially for the show. They could then mime to this re-recording on the programme itself. *Top Of The Pops* wasn't the only pop music programme affected. *Ready, Steady, Go!* had already gone live by this point, and *Thank Your Lucky Stars* had just drawn to a close, but there were consequences for other ITV programmes, such as Granada's *Scene At 6.30*, the kids' series *Five O'Clock Club*, and *Now!*, TWW's replacement for *Discs A Gogo*.[47]

The logic behind the ban was based on the idea that miming to records deprived musicians of employment, especially those who, as session musicians, had appeared on original recordings, as Musicians' Union archivist John Williamson explains. "When, for example, Lulu went on TV and mimed to the performance of the session musicians, the Union believed that this was putting them/other musicians out of

* In an honour not normally bestowed on others, the Beatles' B-sides as well as A-sides regularly featured on the show.

work – i.e. they should have been playing live in the studio," he says. "The Union thought that if the musicians couldn't accompany the acts in the TV studio then they would at least get paid for a three-hour recording session reworking the track, which the artist could then mime to. In the Union's eyes, it was also acceptable if the artist was playing with one of the house orchestras, as this was still creating employment for musicians. Of course, this really misunderstood (a) how records were made – it became a bigger and bigger problem as production techniques became more sophisticated – and (b) was open to abuse."[48]

To negate such abuse, the Union employed a session organiser, who claimed the right to call into any recording studio without notice to see that the Union's rules were being observed. His job, for *Top Of The Pops* and other shows, was to ensure that artists recorded a new backing track, but he had his work cut out. Some groups belonged to a different union and were known to cheat by booking a studio for a re-recording, not showing up and then turning up at the BBC the next day with a tape they claimed to have produced the night before. To stamp out the practice, it was made clear that any re-recording sessions had to be declared in advance and a BBC official had to be present, with a Union official possibly in attendance, too.

Don Smith took on this job for the Union in the early seventies, and *Top Of The Pops* became part of his weekly schedule. "I'd be there pretty much every week on the Wednesday when they recorded the show," he says. "Tuesday night there would be backing tracks taking place and I'd try and get from one to another to see what was happening." For its own part, the BBC required artists to sign statements declaring: "We certify that we own the above tape and have the right to allow the BBC to use it in connection with [the] *Top Of The Pops* series and that this is a privately made tape and not recorded during the making of the commercial record."[49]

The Union's rules did have some unforeseen consequences, which took some lateral thinking by bands to resolve. "I remember a funny one with Mud," Smith says. "They were okay as musicians; they could do their stuff. But a number was going up the charts and they had a backing-track session to do. Their manager phoned me and said: 'Look, we have got a real problem. The drummer, Dave Mount, can't do it because he is involved in a film and he can't get out of it. Can we use a session drummer?' I said: 'Yes, of course you can.' 'But,' he said, 'Dave can be there on the Wednesday to mime to it.'" This was a breach of the rules, as no one was allowed to mime to another person's performance, so a clever solution was found. The band re-recorded the track with the session drummer and then, on the Wednesday at *Top Of The Pops*, placed the session drummer behind a curtain in front of which sat Dave Mount at the drum kit. The session drummer's hands then came through the curtain to play while Dave sat there smiling at the audience.

Another example of miming madness came when the Boomtown Rats performed 'Rat Trap' and didn't invite the musician who provided the sax riffs to join them on the show. Bob Geldof was going to mime it. Warned off by Don Smith, he put the sax mouthpiece on a candelabra and pretended to play that instead.[50]

Despite Don's best efforts, tales of tape swapping are rife, with bands either trying to cut corners or genuinely not wanting any re-recordings to go out. They had a point. It wasn't easy to recreate in a few hours, the day before a *Top Of The Pops* appearance, a sound that may have taken weeks to achieve in a studio. Those artists who braved it and decided to sing live with the *Top Of The Pops* house orchestra also took a chance. The BBC musicians were top notch but they didn't always have the right feel for the music and it showed.

Other significant changes took place on *Top Of The Pops*, too, as it cruised through the sixties. Towards the end of 1964, a female dance unit called the Gojos (Linda Hotchkin, Jane Bartlett and Pat Hughes), choreographed by Jo Cook, had been added to the show, providing cover for those all-too-regular instances when there was no artist available for a climbing record. The Gojos were then replaced in 1968 by a group of experienced dancers that had come together two years earlier under the direction of American choreographer Flick Colby. Joining Flick were Ruth Pearson, Andrea Rutherford, Barbara (Babs) Lord, Dee Dee Wilde and Louise Clarke. As Pan's People, they became a fixture of the show for eight years, scaling dizzying heights of popularity in the seventies.

Towards the end of the decade, the show also lost its father figure. Having established *Top Of The Pops* as the number one pop music series on television – a programme record labels were desperate for their artists to appear on because of its influence on the buying public; a show that commanded prime Christmas Day and Boxing Day timeslots for its annual highlights packages – Johnnie Stewart decided to take a break, leaving Colin Charman and then Mel Cornish – who oversaw the first colour transmission in November 1969 – in the producer's chair. But Stewart's time on the programme was not over. He was to return a couple of years later as "the swingiest, zingiest, most successful pop show of them all", as the *Radio Times* described it, headed into an exciting new decade for music. Arguably, the heyday of *Top Of The Pops* was still to come.

* * *

From the moment it hit the air, *Top Of The Pops* dominated the BBC's presentation of pop but it wasn't the only music show made by the Corporation in the mid-sixties. *Juke Box Jury* still had a few years of life in it and there were several other attempts to capture the excitement the beat boom was generating. The arrival of BBC2 in April 1964 also gave the broadcaster more flexibility and it was for the new channel that *The Beat Room* (1964–5) was commissioned.

The programme aired on Monday evenings at around 7.30 p.m., but it will not be remembered by many viewers as, in its early months, BBC2 was only available in London and the South-East. Coverage was extended to the Midlands by December 1964 but didn't reach other parts of the country until the following year, by which time the series had ended. Many viewers at the time also lacked a set that could receive the new channel, as it was broadcast on the new 625-line system, as opposed to the 405 lines of BBC1 and ITV.

In keeping with the more upmarket, more intellectual slant of the new second channel, *The Beat Room*, declared the *Radio Times*, had "quite an air of sophistication about it". To avoid screaming teenagers, no one under 18 was allowed to join the studio audience and the 25 minutes of non-stop music – performed live, not mimed – were only interrupted by an unseen compere (Irish DJ Pat Campbell) who introduced the acts or The Beat Girls dance group (featuring future Pan's People Babs Lord and Ruth Pearson, as well as Gojos founder Jo Cook). It was a show with pace and life. Guests on the first edition were the Animals, Lulu & the Luvvers and Millie, backed by the resident group, Wayne Gibson with the Dynamic Sounds, who, in later shows, supported the likes of Long John Baldry, Manfred Mann, the Pretty Things, Herman's Hermits, the Kinks and Chris Farlowe. From across the Atlantic, the Beach Boys, Jackie de Shannon and the Isley Brothers were among those who made appearances. *The Beat Room*, for all its virtues, proved short-lived, taken off air after only six months at the end of January 1965.

The word "beat" was big in 1964. The same year BBC2 (sharing coverage with BBC Radio's Light Programme) also screened segments of four concerts staged at the Royal Albert Hall under the name of *Top Beat*. These were hosted either by Alan Freeman or Jimmy Savile and featured such names as Gerry & the Pacemakers, the Rolling Stones, the Searchers, Big Dee Irwin and the Caravelles. The same channel also covered the final of a national beat group contest, in aid of Oxfam, in 1964. *It's Beat Time*, from the Prince of Wales Theatre, London, was hosted by Don Moss, with David Jacobs chairing a jury that included Ringo Starr, Brian Epstein, Cilla Black and Alan Freeman.

With few exceptions, pop music, at the BBC, was still generally seen as family entertainment, rather than just a young persons' thing. This was evident in the creation of a strange early-evening programme called *The Cool Spot* (1964). The show was actually derived from a series called *Hot Ice* (1961–3), which saw professional ice-skaters judged on their interpretation of contemporary records, instead of the usual classical pieces. *Hot Ice* came from Nottingham's Ice Stadium and was hosted by sports commentator Alan Weeks but it was taken over for the final series by David Jacobs, at which point the *Radio Times* appropriately began to describe it as "the Cool DJ Show". Jacobs remained in place for *The Cool Spot*, which – if you ignore the fact that the artists were all stranded on ice, performing in and around the skating – offered a fairly impressive line-up of guest stars, from the Yardbirds and Kiki Dee to

Lulu and the Spencer Davis Group, with of course a bit of Kenny Ball thrown in to keep the grown-ups happy. The programme's strapline, "Television's new Ice-Discery", was only marginally more clumsy than the concept itself.

Another hybrid music show was *Gadzooks! It's All Happening* (1965), the BBC's replacement for *The Beat Room*. Introduced by singer Alan David and future *Crackerjack* presenter Christine Holmes from the BBC Television Theatre, this offered a mixed bag of musical styles – some blues, a bit of country, a burst of gospel. Being on BBC2, it wouldn't have been seen by most of the nation but those who were able to tune in could have caught the Animals, Marianne Faithfull and Tom Jones in the first show. Mike Leander was resident (with his Combo), as was blind keyboard player Peter Cooke, the Three Bells – a vocal group featuring three sisters – and the Beat Girls dance group. Later guests included the Graham Bond Organisation, Screaming Jay Hawkins, Donovan, the Who, the Moody Blues and Alexis Korner's Blues Inc., and there was an early outing for David Bowie with his band Davy Jones & the Manish Boys. After three months, the show briefly changed its title to *Gadzooks! It's The In Crowd*, with Lulu joining Alan David as host and Marianne Faithfull installed as a fixture, before finally ending up simply as *Gadzooks!*, which added Rog (sic) Whittaker to the cast as a replacement for Cooke and Faithfull.

The BBC regions were also contributing music shows at this time. Elements of *Gadzooks!* could be found in BBC Scotland's *Stramash!* (1965–6) – "The Big Noise from Glasgow" – an energetic, fast-moving show with lots of screaming from the audience.* Lulu & the Luvvers were the headline act, but the Three Bells and Peter Cooke also followed her north from *Gadzooks!*, the latter changing his name for the series to Peter London. Other regulars were singer Chris McClure and a seven-man band known as the Senate with Sol Byron. The series, which was screened early in the evening on BBC1 across most of the UK, ran for barely three months – a month longer in Scotland – but it

* The show's name is a popular Scottish term for a riot.

did book some notable guests, including the then London-based Paul Simon and Tom Jones. Also featured were the Stramashers, a six-girl dance group, and the Lindella Movers, six local couples brought in as additional dancers.

Meanwhile, in Wales, a Welsh-language music show was soon in production. *Disc A Dawn* (1966–73) – the title translated as "disc and talent" – covered both pop and folk, with artists such as Meic Stevens and Dafydd Iwan often featured. Although primarily made for local consumption, editions were shown nationally in the afternoons on BBC1 between 1969 and 1973. A spin-off album was released by BBC Records in 1970.

* * *

Other important pop programmes in the early- to mid-sixties were once-a-year special events such as the *NME Poll Winners' Awards* (1961; 1964–6) and the *Glad Rag Ball* (1964–5). Highlights of the *NME* Poll Winners Concert were first broadcast by ABC in 1961 as part of a series called *Big Night Out*. The company later returned to the idea, covering the annual Empire Pool show over two programmes under various titles – *Big Beat '64*, *Poll Winners Concert* and then the more explanatory *The New Musical Express Poll Winners Concert*. The Beatles appeared on all three *NME* Poll Winners shows, but their May 1, 1966, appearance – their last ever live performance in the UK* – wasn't screened because Brian Epstein was unable to agree terms with the TV company.

Glad Rag Ball was a charity music event, also staged at the Empire Pool, that was televised by Associated-Rediffusion in association with its organiser, the London Students' Carnival. In the first year, Jimmy Savile and Anne Nightingale were the hosts, introducing highlights of such acts as the Rolling Stones, the Animals, Long John Baldry, Susan Maughan and Humphrey Lyttelton. Jimmy Tarbuck presented the second event, welcoming the Hollies, the Who, Georgie Fame, Donovan, Wilson Pickett and a young Marc Bolan to the stage, but it

* Aside from the unadvertised Apple rooftop show on January 30, 1969.

was Frankie Vaughan who, rather oddly, topped the bill. The BBC later covered *The Record Star Show* (1968–9), a similar charity event.

Anne Nightingale – having narrowly lost the *Ready, Steady, Go!* gig to Cathy McGowan – was nevertheless well thought of at Associated-Rediffusion. She was often seen in the *RSG!* studio and was soon offered her own show, partnering documentary-maker Dan Farson on *That's For Me* (1964–5). This was a request programme, seen only in London and the south of England, that allowed selected studio audience members to choose a piece of current music, something older or even a clip from a film or a cartoon. Nightingale also worked alongside presenter Ronan O'Casey on a musical quiz for Rediffusion called *Sing A Song Of Sixpence* (1965), which paired contestants with celebrities to try to identify song lyrics. Her job as "bimbo TV game-show hostess" (her words) was to add up the scores. Thankfully for Nightingale's credibility, the show didn't last long.[51]

* * *

By the mid-sixties, broadcaster attitudes to popular music were slowly changing. As the music became more sophisticated, and the talents of the performers more widely appreciated, there was a gradual shift in the treatment it received on television. This was particularly illustrated by a handful of individual showcases and documentaries.

In June 1965, BBC1 offered two half-hour shows dedicated to Bob Dylan. The *Radio Times* still described him as a folk singer at this point, even though he had just embraced electric on his most recent album, *Bringing It All Back Home*. The recordings at BBC Television Centre took place only a matter of weeks before Dylan was roundly heckled at the Newport Folk Festival for opening his set with electric songs before returning to perform two acoustic numbers as an encore.

Not long afterwards, ITV turned the spotlight on the performer once touted as the UK's own Bob Dylan. Rediffusion, which had helped Donovan become a star with those regular *Ready, Steady, Go!* appearances, now devoted an hour to the 19-year-old Scottish singer, describing *A Boy Called Donovan* (1966) as neither a variety show nor a documentary but "a lyrical evocation of a young man who has found success but treats it casually".

As well as featuring a number of songs, the film, directed by Charles Squires, reflected on the bohemian life the musician had previously led in St Ives, Cornwall, where he had camped out and busked for a living, and contrasted it with his new prosperous existence in London. Also seen was 'Gypsy' Dave Mills, one-time fellow wanderer, now employed as Donovan's road manager. For the film, Dave helped to organise a beatnik party, in which much wine was drunk and one guest was seen to be smoking hashish, and this was to have serious consequences. Six months later, both men were fined £250 for possessing cannabis resin after a raid on the singer's Edgware Road flat. It seems that the drug squad had been watching.

At this time, there was also evidence that the BBC was beginning to view pop music in a broader cultural context, most notably with the launch of *A Whole Scene Going* (1966). This 30-minute weekly programme was the brainchild of producer Elizabeth Cowley, who had worked out the format after extensive national research, using reporters from the BBC regions. The show had a wide "pop" remit: it wasn't just about music but about youth culture in general, covering, through live and filmed reports, items such as fashion, art, sport, travel, clubs and cinema as far as they were of interest to those aged under 21. Broadcast live from BBC Television Centre at 6.30 every Wednesday evening, it was given a 13-week commission, which, despite numerous teething troubles, was soon extended.[52]

The hosts – deliberately chosen for their relative youth, so they didn't talk down to the target audience – were 25-year-old Oxbridge-graduate Wendy Varnals, an actress, and Barry Fantoni, a year older, who was an artist/cartoonist for the *Observer* and *Private Eye*. On this programme, musicians didn't just perform: they were also put in a "hot seat" to be questioned by the probing studio audience. Lulu and the Who featured in the first programme, with Pete Townshend describing a Beatles' backing track as "flipping lousy" and attracting much publicity by discussing drug-taking in the band; later guests included Sandie Shaw, the Kinks, Mary Quant, Peter Hall and Charlton Heston. Some also took on the role of agony aunts, answering viewers' problems – Spike Milligan in the first show! – and viewers sent in poems to be read on air.

After a scheduled summer break, there were plans to bring back the programme in the autumn, but, out of the blue, and to the huge disappointment of Elizabeth Cowley, the decision was reversed and *A Whole Scene Going* was axed. During its six-month run, the programme had attracted generous quantities of both praise and criticism. Those that disliked it railed against everything from Fantoni's long hair to its irresponsible discussions on teenage morals, one of the sternest critics being a key figure in the BBC hierarchy. Tom Sloan, Head of Light Entertainment, didn't mince words, calling it not just "awful" but "harmful". "For God's sake, please take it off", he begged, just a month after it went on air. Those in favour of the show pointed out how brave the BBC was to attempt such a programme, a new take on the pop idea, which, it was felt, was long overdue.[53]

The show did make a shaky start, but it then seemed to find its feet and was beginning to realise its potential by the time it was cancelled. Audience figures had grown, although competition from *Crossroads* on ITV meant that it was always fighting a losing battle in its time slot. The show was eventually killed by Michael Peacock, Controller of BBC1, citing those low audience figures and his own feeling that the show was not quite good enough. He added that, had he known there would be so much pop music in the show, he might not have commissioned it in the first place.[54]

Although not mentioned by Peacock, one other significant factor contributed to the series' demise. The new Musicians' Union miming ban that was to cause *Top Of The Pops* so much hassle would also have applied to *A Whole Scene Going*. It appears it was easier to get rid of the show than to try to work around this, too.

* * *

From the example of *A Whole Scene Going*, it is possible to deduce that, although progress was being made, British television still wasn't quite ready at this point to fully embrace popular music as a topic of cultural value. While adventurous producers like Cowley were having some success in breaking the mould, it seems that the executives who ran the broadcasting companies – BBC and commercial – still saw pop as simply one element in their light entertainment provision. Their arguably cynical transformation of the more mainstream pop performers into prime-time television presenters supports this.

Turning chart stars into hosts of their own series was a handy way of keeping the family audience together during peak viewing hours. Cliff Richard had been given his own series as early as 1961, when ATV partnered him with the Shadows, the Vernons Girls and guests for a weekly half-hour simply called *Cliff!*, and the company continued to use him intermittently throughout the sixties. The BBC then signed Richard for shows such as *It's Cliff Richard* (1970–2; 1974) and *It's Cliff – and Friends* (1975–6). ATV next produced *Tom Jones!* (1966–7), a series based around themed songs, before splashing out on *This Is... Tom Jones* (1969–71), a collection of all-star spectaculars that was sold to the USA.

Dusty Springfield, having honed her presentation skills on *Ready, Steady, Go!*, was offered *Dusty* (1966–7) and *Decidedly Dusty* (1969) by the BBC, with *It Must Be Dusty* (1968) for ATV slotted in between. Lulu, after headlining in *Gadzooks!* and *Stramash!*, was signed up for a BBC series called *Three Of A Kind* (1967), which she shared with impressionist Mike Yarwood and comedian Ray Fell. She was then given sole billing in *Lulu's Back In Town* (1968), *Happening For Lulu/Lulu* (1968–9), *It's Lulu* (1970–4) and, once again, *Lulu* (1975). The BBC also attempted a series called *Scott*, later expanded to *Scott Walker* (1968–9), but this proved less successful, despite the attentions of *Top Of The Pops* producer Johnnie Stewart. Undoubtedly, the most successful of the pop stars-turned-TV hosts was Cilla Black, who embarked on a stellar on-screen career with the BBC series *Cilla* (1968–9; 1971–4; 1976).

The BBC's decision to create *The Sandie Shaw Supplement* (1968) must have been influenced by the singer's success in the 1967 *Eurovision Song Contest*. This annual display of mutual hostility was first staged in 1956, as a showcase for the new Eurovision network, which linked broadcasters across the Continent. The UK didn't enter that year, although some of the event – which was won by Lys Assia for Switzerland with the song

'Refrain' – was broadcast on the BBC. For the next event, the UK sent Patricia Bredin to wave the flag. Her song, 'All', came seventh, paving the way for years of British failure. In 1960, the BBC hosted the event for the first time from the Royal Festival Hall, London, and hosted it again, from BBC Television Centre, in 1963, but there was still no British winner. By 1967, despite the best efforts of Teddy Johnson & Pearl Carr, Bryan Johnson, the Allisons, Matt Monro and Kathy Kirby, who had all come in second, the BBC was still firing blanks, although perhaps this wasn't surprising as some of the performers and songs were hardly indicative of what was happening in the British music scene in the sixties. When Kenneth McKellar, in full Highland regalia, could finish no higher than ninth in 1966, it was clear that a change of direction was needed. Scottish tenors were out and Britpop, sixties style, was in.

Sandie Shaw was chosen to turn things around and she appeared weekly on *The Rolf Harris Show* to sing each of the songs in contention to be the UK's entry. The victorious number, Bill Martin and Phil Coulter's 'Puppet On A String', then went on to slay the opposition in Vienna and re-boot the UK's love-hate affair with the competition. With Cliff Richard running in second with 'Congratulations' in 1968 and Lulu one of four tied winners with 'Boom Bang-A-Bang' in 1969, the country was riding high in Europe as the sixties drew to a close.

⋆ ⋆ ⋆

A new concept on British television in the sixties was the chat show. Originating in the USA, it was a programme format that had obvious appeal to anyone with something to promote, as it provided cheap publicity. The film and fashion worlds were keen to supply guests and so was the record industry, especially as between all the chat there was generally time for a song or two. There was even greater interest when the BBC announced the launch of a new twice-weekly chat show, one that would be broadcast in the big-audience, early-evening time slot and hosted by one of the rising stars of the era.

Simon Dee was a 31-year-old privately educated broadcaster with dashing blond looks, a playboy image and a somewhat inflated ego, who had shot to fame on the high seas as a DJ with Radio Caroline. Like Cathy McGowan, he was undoubtedly one of the faces of the Swinging Sixties, indeed claimed by some to be the inspiration for the film character Austin Powers. His show, *Dee Time* (1967–9), was bold, lively and expressive of what was happening at the time, a fast-moving mix of chat, comedy and music. There were some serious moments but generally it was a fun show with celebrities, musicians and people in the news all welcomed as guests. Included in the first programme were Cat Stevens and the Jimi Hendrix Experience and respected artists just kept on coming – Manfred Mann, Donovan, the Move, the Turtles, the Small Faces, P.P. Arnold, Eric Burdon and more – interspersed, of course – this being "light entertainment" – with middle-of-the-road performers such as Marion Montgomery, Donald Peers and Vince Hill.

Recorded initially in *Top Of The Pops*' old stomping ground, the former church in Dickenson Road, Manchester, *Dee Time* hit the ground running and, five months into its run, was switched to early Saturday evening, displacing the long-running *Juke Box Jury*. The show – which is perhaps best remembered for its closing sequence in which the host roars away in a white open-top E-type Jaguar, "dolly bird" at his side – ended when Dee moved to ITV for more money. It wasn't a good decision. The ITV programme was soon dropped and Dee's career came to an end as rapidly as it had begun. Despite a few attempted comebacks, he was barely seen or heard from again.*

★ ★ ★

Pop music also began to invade comedy. One of the main outlets for music on ITV during the late sixties was *Doddy's Music Box* (1967–8), produced by ABC. Shown in most of the country in that popular early Saturday evening slot, this was "a very slick, punchy mixture of comedy and music, featuring people in the charts", in the words of its star, Liverpudlian comic Ken Dodd. Dodd's musical guests ranged from Wayne Fontana and Herman's Hermits to Paul Jones and the Love

* Simon Dee was born Cyril Nicholas Henty-Dodd. He died, aged 74, in 2009.

Affair, with the "family balance" provided by the likes of Russ Conway, Rosemary Squires and Joe Henderson. The series also saw future Radio 1 presenter David Hamilton – whom Dodd nicknamed "Diddy" – employed as a straight man.

There was also a role for pop in alternative comedy. In the BBC's short-lived *Twice A Fortnight* (1967) – a primeval broth of future Pythons and Goodies, produced and directed by Tony Palmer, whose importance to the contemporary music scene was yet to be realised – one artist or band was featured each week among the sketches. So, sharing the post-*Match Of The Day* slot on a Saturday night with Bill Oddie, Graeme Garden, Jonathan Lynn, Dilys Watling, Michael Palin and Terry Jones were performers such as the Who, Simon Dupree & the Big Sound, the Moody Blues and Cream.

The major fusion of comedy and pop music at this time, however, came in an imported series from the USA. Inspired by the success of the early Beatles films, American producers Bert Schneider and Bob Rafelson had dreamt up the idea of a TV series based around a manufactured pop group. They advertised for band members – "4 insane boys, age 17–21" – and came up with Micky Dolenz, one-time child star of the series *Circus Boy*, former *Coronation Street* actor Davy Jones and two folk musicians, Peter Tork and Michael Nesmith. In this way, the Monkees were created.

The Monkees (1966–8) was a half-hour madcap comedy, drawing heavily on Richard Lester's direction of the Beatles in *A Hard Day's Night*, slapstick routines and Keystone Kops chases as the band members lurched from scrape to scrape in and around their sunny beach house. Inventive camerawork, over-exposed film and speeded up sequences kept viewers on their toes, Davy usually fell for a pretty girl and a couple of songs were slotted into every show, encouraging fans to go out and buy the records.

The Monkees' music was originally provided by session players, but later in their career the band took charge of their own output. Throughout, the output was slick and well conceived. The repertoire of hits was impressive – 'Last Train To Clarksville', 'A Little Bit Me, A Little Bit You', 'Daydream Believer', 'Pleasant Valley Sunday' and more, penned by such names as Neil Diamond, Gerry Goffin & Carole King, and Tommy Boyce & Bobby Hart – but the show also generated lucrative sales of Monkee merchandise, anything from badges to collectors' cards. The first episode went out on BBC1 on New Year's Eve 1966, a few months after its US premiere, and the band's first UK hit, 'I'm A Believer', entered the singles chart the following week.

The humour in *The Monkees* was pretty juvenile stuff, although not quite as infantile as in most of the cartoons arriving from the US. Some of these were beginning to accommodate pop music in some way, recognising its pulling power. In 1967, BBC1 began screening *Frankenstein Jr And The Impossibles*, a Hanna-Barbera series that split into two sections. The Frankenstein Jr bit was all about the adventures of a rocket-powered robot and his child genius inventor, Buzz Conroy; the Impossibles, in the other part of the show, were a three-man pop group who morphed into superheroes – Coil Man, Fluid Man and Multi Man – to foil criminal masterminds as they toured the world. It wasn't a million miles away from *Josie And The Pussycats* (1972–3), another Hanna-Barbera offering that became *Josie And The Pussycats In Outer Space* (1973–4) when the crime-conquering, feline-themed band – lead singer Josie, tambourine shaker Valerie and drummer Melody – were accidentally blasted into space aboard a NASA rocket.

There were also two major US animations that didn't transfer to the UK. For four years from 1965, the Beatles lent their name to a kids' cartoon series made by King Features under producer Al Brodax, who later co-scripted and produced the film *Yellow Submarine*. The group members themselves didn't take part – Lance Percival and Paul Frees provided the voices – but their songs did feature, the titles – 'And Your Bird Can Sing', 'Good Day Sunshine', etc. – forming a loose basis for each story. Some episodes have since surfaced on British television but the series was not taken up during its original run. The Beatles themselves reportedly disliked the show but changed their minds in later years, even though they did their best to suppress it. In the nineties the rights to the series were acquired by Apple, the company that still handles their collective interests, which has resisted appeals to reissue it on remastered DVD. Poor quality episodes of the show can still be accessed on YouTube.

The other notable omission from the UK's schedules was *The Archie Show*, based on a cartoon strip about a bunch of teenagers and their band, the Archies, with vocals provided by Ron Dante and Andy Kim. Despite the show generating a huge UK number one hit – 'Sugar Sugar' – in 1969, there was strangely no interest from British broadcasters.

One semi-animated series that was seen on BBC1 was *The Banana Splits* (1970). This fondly remembered programme featured four actors dressed as animals who played in a band – dog Fleegle, gorilla Bingo, lion Drooper and an elephant called Snorky – although their music – apart from the catchy "tra la la" theme song – was almost an afterthought in the fast-moving package, secondary to buggy racing, cartoons, live-action adventure serials and an exhausting supply of wisecracks and catchphrases.

Kids could also enjoy the humour and music of *Whistle Stop* (1967–8), hosted by Roger Whittaker on BBC1. This featured comedy antics from Richard Hearne and, later, Jack Haig, plus Larry Parker and his Theodore Rabbit puppet, with female support from Dodie West and Dilys Watling. One pop act featured each week. Among those involved were Manfred Mann, the Fortunes and the Herd. A more dedicated music series was BBC1's *Monster Music Mash* (1969) – "Pop, Blues, Folk, and Whoopee!" – introduced in front of a young-adult audience by ex-Animal Alan Price, supported by comedy jazz from Bob Kerr's Whoopee Band. Refreshingly, the weekly guests had the freedom to perform a few numbers and not just their latest hit. First up were Fleetwood Mac, followed by, among others, Pentangle and the Moody Blues. There was also an early sighting of Slade. It was serious stuff to follow *Wacky Races* during children's hour but just one short series was produced.

ITV was still embracing pop music in its kids' shows, too. Rediffusion's *Five O'Clock Club* had finished in 1966 and its presenter, Muriel Young, then moved to Granada as a producer. Working with material she knew well, she first created *Discotheque* (1968–9), or *The Discotheque*, as it was sometimes billed. This was a half-hour showcase for chart hits and new releases hosted by Billy J. Kramer and his backing band – initially the Factory, then the Remo, or the Remo 4 as they had been known during their Merseybeat days. The Four Spots were the resident dance group and Dianne Greaves was the show's "Disc Dolly". After a few months, Kramer was replaced by singer Graham Bonney – best known for his 1966 hit 'Supergirl' – and Greaves later gave way to an up-and-coming vocalist named Ayshea. The guest list included the Idle Race, the Move, the Troggs, Amen Corner and Elton John (billed in the *TV Times* as "Elton Johns").

Discotheque, which lasted less than six months, was not fully networked by ITV but it was seen in most parts of the country, giving Granada an opportunity to show what it could do in this kind of programming, an opportunity it was to exploit more fully in the seventies.

★ ★ ★

Children's hour output aside, dedicated pop music shows were still rather slow coming in the late sixties. *Top Of The Pops* was going strong, of course, but both BBC and ITV struggled to find durable replacements for shows like *Juke Box Jury*, *Thank Your Lucky Stars* and *Ready, Steady, Go!*

Juke Box Jury had drawn to a close in December 1967 and the BBC was pinning its hopes on a replacement show starring Alan Freeman. *Pick A Pop With Freeman* – as the working title had it – attempted to recreate elements of the DJ's radio programmes on television and was based on his own idea. When it came to the screen, early on a Friday evening in January, *All Systems Freeman!* (1968) viewers were treated to the bizarre sight of the host, shirtsleeves rolled up, headphones on, sat behind a control panel, flamboyantly throwing switches and faders to bring in the next record or filmed feature. Alongside, guests sat ready to offer opinions on new releases, while bands performed in other parts of the studio. *All Systems Freeman!* was a brave and dynamic attempt to inject new life into the television pop format – ahead of its time, it perhaps turned Freeman into the first VJ (video jockey) – but it proved very short-lived and was gone from the screen before the end of March.[55]

ITV, on the other hand, had fallen back on some of its less glamorous programme providers for its pop output. A strong presence was Southern Television, where director/producer Mike Mansfield was busy turning out show after show. He put together a pop quiz hosted by Muriel Young called *Pop The Question* (1965–6), which was seen only in the South but evolved into another show called *Countdown* (1966) that was picked up by most of the ITV network. Muriel Young again asked the questions and Radio Luxembourg DJ Don Wardell "saw fair play" as various chart stars attempted to show off their musical knowledge. Mansfield followed this with the mostly networked *As You Like It* (1967), an early evening request programme that was hosted by Don Moss. Adam Faith – the programme's title being shared with one of his hits – featured in the first programme as a roving interviewer, taking a day trip to Amsterdam to discover what viewers wanted to see and hear on the show.

A year later, Mansfield contributed a short series called *A Tale Of Two Rivers* (1968), which was shown in a number of ITV areas. This was basically a device for bringing together British and French artists, the title referring to the Thames and the Seine, and filming taking place in both London and Paris. Adam Faith again featured, as did Sandie Shaw, Claude François and Petula Clark, plus the Gojos dance troupe.

Mansfield's biggest success at this time came with a programme called *Time For Blackburn!* (1968–9). This developed out of a partially networked series called *New Release* (1968), hosted by Tony Blackburn, who discussed the latest discs with the artists that made them. By this time, Blackburn was enjoying national celebrity, having been the first voice heard on Radio 1 when it launched in September 1967, so it made sense to capitalise on his fame by building his name into the title of a TV series. *Time For Blackburn!* – another early Saturday evening offering – was reasonably successful, with many of the ITV regions on board. It featured guest stars, interviews and, initially, a song a week from the host himself.

One other ITV region making a play for the pop market was Grampian. This small contractor produced a series called *Pop Scotch* (1969–70), which was hosted by former pirate DJs Jack McLaughlin and Cathy Spence, and, despite only being transmitted in its north of Scotland homeland, managed to get plenty of big names to travel to Aberdeen for recording.

★ ★ ★

If *Pop Scotch* was an example of the narrowest regional programming, *Our World* was its complete opposite. In autumn 1965, an idea was mooted within the BBC of putting on a show that would use television to circumnavigate the world. Satellite technology had advanced so far since the launch of Telstar in 1962 that it was now possible, also using microwaves and landlines, to link countries all around the globe for one audacious, ground-breaking simultaneous broadcast. *Our World* (1967) was the outcome, a pioneering collaboration between international broadcasters that took contributions from countries across the globe and packaged them, live, in one two-hour bundle.

The original plan was to broadcast the programme on June 21, the longest day in the northern hemisphere, hence the working title *The Longest Day – The Longest Way*. This was later changed to *Around The World In 80 Minutes*, to reflect the international diversity of the proposed input and the speed at which man could now, via the wonders of television, race around the globe, witnessing sunrise in one country as the sun was setting in another and take in any events happening in between.

It was agreed that participating countries would each submit a short feature item. These could not be "picture postcards": they had to tell a story, reflecting some aspect of life in their area, with humanity – the progress of mankind and the challenges it faces – at its core. There was to be no politics and heads of state were banned. Everything had to be generated live, with no pre-recordings permitted. The potential of the broadcast to become a global "happening" was obvious – up to 500 million people could be watching, all at the same time – but it took a year and a half of brainstorming, both within the BBC and among its international colleagues, to agree a suitable format. In the end, the "longest day" idea had to be shelved. Some countries would be seeing the show during their daytime when most people would be at work and so, to ensure the widest audience, the broadcast was shunted back four days to a Sunday.[56]

At 7.55 p.m. on June 25, 1967, *Our World* opened with a welcome from Cliff Michelmore. Eighteen broadcasters had finally agreed to take part, with other non-contributing countries also taking coverage, but the event had been somewhat derailed a few days before when military conflict between Israel and its Arab neighbours led to the Soviet Union and affiliated countries Hungary, East Germany, Poland and Czechoslovakia making a political statement and withdrawing. Nevertheless, 24 countries – around 170 million television sets – took the show, which began with footage of some of the Earth's newest inhabitants – babies that had just been born in Japan, Denmark, Mexico and Canada – and led into features that varied from monitoring the progress of a traffic jam in Paris to the bustle of a souk in Tunis.[57]

The BBC's input – apart from a report by Magnus Magnusson on the new town of Cumbernauld in Scotland – came in the form of a live performance by the Beatles – indicative of the band's importance to Britain internationally but also of how culturally integrated pop music was starting to become.

The Beatles saw the potential of the occasion and wanted to rise to it. In early discussions with the BBC, the group stressed that they were keen to take part but did not want to simply regurgitate an existing hit, so it was agreed that the item would show them in a studio making a new record. They began work on the number in May, conscious that the new song needed to be linguistically simple, for easy translation and comprehension, and a list of likely words was put forward for inclusion in the lyrics, "love" being one of them. Twenty-four days after the release of the *Sgt Pepper* album, the Beatles convened in Abbey Road's Studio One for the recording of 'All You Need Is Love', live, in front of the watching world.[58]

The Beatles' contribution came in a section of the programme entitled 'Artistic Excellence', closely following items on the filming of *Romeo And Juliet* by Franco Zeffirelli in Italy, rehearsals of Wagner's 'Lohengrin' in Bayreuth and Leonard Bernstein and Van Cliburn performing Rachmaninoff's 'Third Piano Concerto' at New York's Lincoln Centre. The segment was introduced by musician/critic Steve Race, who explained the process that was being followed to make the record. As well as producer George Martin and their usual entourage, the group was supported on this occasion by 13 other musicians – four violins, two cellos, two trumpets, two trombones, two tenor saxophones and an accordion – under the direction of Mike Vickers. The whole event was turned into a party as the band laid down what were declared to be the final stages of the song, bringing in the orchestra and John Lennon's lead vocal (much of the recording had been done in previous days and there was still a bit of tinkering to do after the TV show ended). Balloons, streamers and flowers littered a studio packed with friends, including Mick Jagger and Graham Nash, some displaying giant boards with the song's key words translated into various languages.

The Beatles – paid £5,000 for their work – were only on air for six minutes but pop music on television had never reached such an audience, and they weren't finished with television for that year, either.[59]

* * *

The appearance of the Beatles in a programme of such significance as *Our World* indicates that broadcasters were at last finding new levels to explore within the realms of popular music. That same year, a couple of serious documentaries were produced, digging beneath the skin of the developing music scene and its associated counter-culture, and what they came up with was unsettling for Middle England.

The films were made for *Man Alive*, the BBC2 current affairs series that set out to look at a changing world through the eyes of ordinary people. In April, the programme went behind the scenes of the '14-Hour Technicolor Dream', the psychedelic experience staged as a benefit for the recently busted *International Times* underground newspaper. The question *Man Alive* posed was: "What is a Happening?" and sent three film crews and their reporters to discover the answer. Shocked viewers in Tunbridge Wells and other self-respecting parts of the country were living-room witnesses as thousands of stoned youths mooched around London's Alexandra Palace, freaking out to a heady mix of film projections, loud music and vibrant light shows. Then, in June, an edition entitled 'The Ravers' turned the spotlight on groupies, interviewing teenage girls about their pursuit of artists and the intimate relationships that followed. It also took a view from the other side, courtesy of members of Simon Dupree & the Big Sound. The answers provided were surprisingly frank and the open permissiveness was disturbing to an older audience. It was pop music on television, but really not the jolliest take on the scene. Thankfully, there was more fun on the way.

* * *

In the autumn of 1967, Paul Fox, Controller of BBC1, had a problem. There was a gap in his schedule for Boxing Day, a prime-time slot at 8.35 p.m. that needed something big to fill it. Suddenly, along came the Beatles offering a TV special – a new movie, no less – and, like any right-minded television programmer, Fox grabbed it with both hands.

The Beatles, of course, were no strangers to the world of film. The success of *A Hard Day's Night* and *Help!* had encouraged them to continue with this diversion from making records. The difference this time around was that Dick Lester, who directed their first two movies, was not involved and the band had also just lost their guiding light, Brian Epstein, to a sleeping-pill overdose. It was left to the band members themselves to turn a basic idea, dreamed up by Paul McCartney, into a reality. With McCartney making most of the running, they fleshed out the concept of a coach trip around Britain, building in stops en route for added fun. Folding a generous dose of psychedelic fantasy into the mix, *Magical Mystery Tour* (1967) was born.

Working from a very loose – sometimes non-existent – script, the 52-minute film follows a brightly painted bus as it collects a motley crew of passengers – in fact a hastily assembled crowd of jobbing actors, off-beat speciality acts such as poet Ivor Cutler and veteran comedian Nat Jackley, and a few fans – and sets off for the West Country, ending up in

Newquay.* Dialogue is adlibbed, shooting seems ad hoc and the whole production, with its shaky camerawork and rough edits, falls somewhere between an elaborate home movie (George Harrison's words) and an art flick. The Beatles – as well as performing a number of original songs – loosely play themselves, offering typically oblique quips and sideways remarks, with Ringo, the most prominent, spending much of the journey bickering with his so-called Auntie Jessie. Surreal moments add to the eccentricity of the package – some wrestling midgets, a stripper supported by the Bonzo Dog Doo-Dah Band, John Lennon shovelling spaghetti onto a restaurant table – while other elements of the film seem to be inspired by childhood memories of happy charabanc outings. *Magical Mystery Tour* is, indeed, a very English film in its minutiae – bottles of ale and a sing-song on the bus, a stop for fish and chips, a big musical finale, complete with formation dancers – but these are combined with unsettling dream sequences to create a package that, for Boxing Night, was probably not quite what Paul Fox had imagined.[60]

Predictably, the film split the nation, although, if the BBC's audience survey can be relied upon, the overwhelming majority of viewers was not impressed. "Stupid, pretentious rubbish," sums up the negative response. Professional reaction was just as cruel, although Keith Dewhurst in the *Guardian* was somewhat kinder, calling it "an inspired freewheeling achievement".[61]

Paul McCartney, to his credit, fronted up to the criticism, conceding that "We tried to present something different for the viewers, but according to the newspapers it did not come off". Over time, however, the film has enjoyed a more positive appraisal, film director Martin Scorsese being one who admits to gaining inspiration from it. The fact that the film was initially screened only in black and white didn't help. *Magical Mystery Tour* was made in the year of flower power and Technicolor dreams. It was not designed for monochrome transmission.

---

* Much of the filming was done over a five-day period in the middle of September 1967, with the band and the rest of the cast and crew literally travelling from London to Cornwall and back, although a number of sequences were filmed a week later at an airfield in Kent.[62]

Only with a repeat in colour on BBC2 10 days later did viewers really see what the band had been trying to achieve.[63]

⋆ ⋆ ⋆

After the Beatles had presented their own television special, the Rolling Stones decided they wanted to make one, too. In 1968, former *Ready, Steady, Go!* director Michael Lindsay-Hogg was commissioned to put together some promo films for the Stones songs 'Jumpin' Jack Flash' and 'Child Of The Moon'. Mick Jagger then asked him to devise a one-off movie that could showcase the band along with some musical guests. Lindsay-Hogg's idea was *The Rolling Stones Rock And Roll Circus*, a series of performances set against the backdrop of a travelling circus, complete with the traditional troupe of clowns, fire eaters and trapeze artists. The original plan was for Brigitte Bardot to act as the ringmaster but, in the end, it was Jagger, in top hat and tails, who cracked the whip. Filming took place in a mock-up of a big top at Wembley Studios and saw an impressive line up of acts take to the ring – Taj Mahal, Marianne Faithfull, the Who, Jethro Tull and a one-off supergroup put together by John Lennon and featuring Eric Clapton, Keith Richards (on bass duty) and Jimi Hendrix's drummer, Mitch Mitchell. The Stones, of course, were due to headline but, as filming dragged on, they didn't make their entrance until after 2 a.m., when the long day had taken its toll. It wasn't their most impressive performance and when the footage was viewed back the decision was taken not to release the film, perhaps because the Who, match fit from recent US touring, far outplayed the Stones. There would be no TV special. The film remained unseen for 28 years until it premiered at the New York Film Festival in 1996. It was then broadcast for the first time on BBC2 on New Year's Eve that year.[64]

⋆ ⋆ ⋆

As the sixties progressed, it was becoming increasingly apparent that contemporary youth music had a value over and above its purpose as a commercial entity. The Beatles had shattered the myth that artists were incapable of writing and performing their own material, and now other stars of the pop world were beginning to be evaluated on their creative skills and musicianship and not just on how attractive they looked singing some Tin Pan Alley song, backed by a band of session players. Additionally, there was a growing realisation that this generation of musicians also had something important to say. The television offering that really nailed this change of attitude was *All My Loving* (1968), a film produced by a young BBC director/producer named Tony Palmer.

Palmer's introduction to the world of pop music came via an unexpected encounter in 1963. A student at Cambridge, dabbling in journalism through the university newspaper, *Varsity*, he was sent to cover a press conference for a concert by the Beatles at the city's Regal cinema. His failure to ask any questions piqued the interest of John Lennon who cornered him afterwards. When he learned Palmer was a student, Lennon asked for a tour of the colleges and, in return for a pleasant afternoon, gave him a phone number, telling him to call if ever he was in London.

A few years later, Tony Palmer, by now ensconced at the BBC, made that call, although he immediately realised it was unlikely to amount to very much. "It was perfectly clear from the sound of the girl on the end of the phone that I was the 400th person who'd rung up that morning to say: 'John Lennon said to call'. I thought I'd never hear anything back," he says. But he did. Half an hour later, Beatles press officer Derek Taylor phoned with a message from John. "Why has it taken you three-and-a-half years to call?" They agreed to meet for lunch at which Lennon, seizing on Palmer's possible position of influence, insisted that he had a "duty to do something about the state of pop music on the BBC". Lennon explained that many artists now no longer had the appetite to appear on *Top Of The Pops*, where they might be obscured by a group of gyrating dancers. They wanted, and deserved, more respect, he said. "Do a film."

Conveniently, after serving a general BBC traineeship, Palmer had graduated into film-making, working with Ken Russell on a project about Isadora Duncan and with Jonathan Miller on his version of *Alice In Wonderland*. He was then thrown in at the deep end to direct a film about Benjamin Britten, which turned out rather well, endearing him to the hierarchy at the BBC. Palmer had also fallen into writing a pop music column for the *Observer*, which led Huw Wheldon, the Controller of Programmes, to propose that he make a film on the subject for the BBC. This gave him an excuse to contact Lennon again and grant his wish.

Over another lunch, Lennon furnished Palmer with a list of names of musicians to feature. "I'll tell them to do it. You make the film," he said. So, towards the end of 1967, while also producing the comedy series *Twice A Fortnight*, Palmer set his mind to the project. A proposal entitled *The Greatest Ravers Of Them All* was prepared and detailed how the film could pan out. It would work on the understanding that the best of pop music was as interesting musically as anything else being composed at the time; that its lyrics offered mass satire and comment; that technologically it was bound up with what was likely to happen in the future. It would demonstrate how the medium had absorbed many other musical influences, how artists were now retreating from live performance in favour of creative time in the studio and how a visual dimension was increasingly important to their work. The film would reveal what pop music was all about. There would be no talk or sociology; no teenage opinion. It would be the musicians themselves who would speak and play. A tour of the US with Cream, a recording session with the Beatles and a cast of principal characters who explained it all, from Lennon and Jagger to Clapton and Zappa, were the devices on which the film would be constructed.[65]

The film that transpired did not exactly follow this pattern, but the general thrust was the same – let the music speak for itself and let the audience judge it accordingly – and the list of big hitters that Lennon – who also supplied the final title – had provided were still involved.

All My Loving opens with a quote from the Beatles' song 'Yellow Submarine': "As we live a life of ease". Next, Eddie Rogers, a former Tin Pan Alley publisher, talks scathingly about the music scene: "If it sells, who cares?", but his words are blown away when the action switches to Cream in full throttle. The next 55 minutes see arguments for and against the assertions made by Rogers as musicians, their associates and critics set out their stall, among them Eric Clapton, the Who's manager Kit Lambert, the Beatles, Manfred Mann, Frank Zappa, Pete Townshend, Donovan, Jimi Hendrix, Eric Burdon and writer Anthony Burgess. They discuss various aspects of the business, the art and technology of making music, the power it wields, the relevance of image, commerciality, morals, groupies and the use of drugs. Paul McCartney and Kit Lambert both equate pop to classical music, George Harrison's mum talks about fan mail and Pink Floyd perform in all their psychedelic glory. The Moody Blues pose for some album artwork while the Who trash their equipment in a show of mock violence. Zappa gets heavy, relating how he once performed with US marines who mutilated a girl doll to order, and Burdon speculates that Hendrix's "disturbed" music may be a symptom of America's racial tensions.

These sober interjections reflect a darker mood that is expressed visually from very early on in the film by the inclusion of some short, harrowing news clips of American police brutality on the streets and the shooting, point-blank in the head, of a young Asian man. There are grotesque scenes from a Nazi concentration camp and a Buddhist monk is engulfed in flames – the sort of images that, even today, are normally preceded by a viewer warning. Alongside the more trivial elements of the film, they provide a brutal contrast, one that is sharpened satirically by the final closing quip, that same refrain from 'Yellow Submarine': "As we live a life of ease". Rather than simply exploring the mechanics of pop music, the film delivers a graphic illustration of what the musicians of the day felt about their art and what they wanted to say about world around them.

Inevitably, *All My Loving* ruffled feathers. David Attenborough, later a close friend of Tony Palmer's but then his superior as Director of Television, was appalled and refused to show it. It sat on a shelf for months, with little hope of making it onto the screen until a new Head of Music & Arts was appointed. John Culshaw came from the world of classical music. As it happened, he and Palmer had crossed paths before and he was more sympathetic. He watched the film and was impressed, using his honeymoon period at the BBC to insist to Controller of BBC1 Paul Fox that it be shown. Fox, a blunt former sports reporter, demanded a compromise, but, much to Palmer's surprise, only in terms of the musicians' language, declaring: "You take out three fucks, you can have two pisses." Otherwise no changes were requested and the programme eventually went out as part of the arts series *Omnibus* on November 3, 1968.[66]

By that time, word had spread that this film was something different, something highly controversial. The *Radio Times* decided to warn the audience that it might not be easy viewing, claiming it was "as difficult and as startling as any film you are likely to see" before rather spoiling things by getting the wrong end of the stick and suggesting it was about "the love of a man for a woman". Despite such advance notice, the backlash after transmission was relentless. Critics such as Stanley Reynolds in the *Guardian* questioned whether, whatever the argument of the film, it was justified to incorporate such disturbing scenes. George Melly, in the *Observer*, took issue with the whole debate. "Serious but naïve" was how he described the artists' comments, adding again that the clips of atrocities could not be justified, although he did concede that the film "said more about pop than a year of 'Top of the Pops'".[67]

For balance, there was plenty of positive reaction, too, not least from Lennon who had achieved what he set out to do. "We have smashed down the door of the BBC, and rock'n'roll on television will never be the same again," he wrote to Palmer. The thoughts of Lennon, McCartney – who was one of the first people to be interviewed – and other musicians were very much in Palmer's mind as he put the film together and led to the inclusion of those violent scenes. Two issues in particular were dominant. "They were preoccupied about the fact that as musicians or as composers they were not being treated with the respect… that they deserved," the director explains. "They were perfectly articulate and perfectly coherent and they had something to say." Secondly, musicians like these wanted to "tell it like it is", in the world in which they lived. "So, if you've got Frank Zappa talking about the Vietnam War, you've got to show the Vietnam War. If you've got Eric Burdon talking about the things that Eric talks about in the film, you've got to show it. You can't not show it. I think that was what shocked the BBC when they saw the film the first time, when they put it on the shelf. They thought that pop music was sufficiently trivial that it couldn't deal with the really serious political issues of the day, which, of course, would have been deeply offensive to the people who had taken part in the film. It's not that I made promises to Eric and promises to Zappa that I would reflect what they were saying in terms of images but I was aware that that was part of my responsibility, that that is what, by implication, they were expecting me to do."

Palmer's own views he tried to keep hidden. The film's subtitle, 'a film *of* pop music', said a lot. It wasn't a film *about* pop music: it let pop music speak for itself. It didn't judge; it didn't offer an opinion. Palmer's aim, always he says, was to present the material and then let the viewer decide. "What I'm saying to the audience, which I say endlessly in the majority of films I've made subsequently, is 'You tell me. Here's the evidence. This is what they say. This is what they play. You make up your own mind'." While there is some narration in the film – provided by actor Patrick Allen – it was not intended to lead viewers to any particular conclusion. "Every single word was taken from what Anthony Burgess said in the big interview at the end," Palmer adds. "The interview with Anthony went on for 40 minutes and he said some wonderful things. I just lifted some of those phrases out."[68]

In response to the public outcry, Palmer pressed for a quick repeat, hoping to add a 15-minute introduction that would recognise the complexity of the programme and indicate which aspects of the film should be looked for. He also wanted a follow-up intellectual discussion immediately afterwards, taking on board all sides of the argument.[69]

"It wasn't that I felt the need to defend it but I felt the need to make some explanation of it," he says. "People had to grasp that these were extraordinary musicians. That's one of the things I would have said; that's one of the things I wanted to make absolutely clear. You may not like this music but you can't take away the fact that these are astonishing, technically gifted performers." In the film, this point is very subtly made by the soundtracks to the opening and closing sequences that feature pieces not by pop musicians but by Ralph Vaughan Williams – essentially conflating classical music with scenes of hell-for-leather improvisation by Cream and other examples of pop brilliance.

The second point Palmer would have made in support of his project was that the featured musicians wanted a parallel drawn between their music and the horrors of the time, not least the Vietnam War. "I wanted to make it clear that that was the intention and, again Dear Audience, you may not like that and you might find that deeply offensive, either to the people who had been killed in Vietnam or to anybody who's made that kind of soldierly sacrifice, but this is what they want. This is what they want us to think about. That's what I was going to say, certainly not to apologise for the film."[70]

A repeat showing did follow – six months later, in colour on BBC2 – but without the add-ons Palmer had requested. It's now been nearly 50 years since *All My Loving* was first seen and it still has the power to shock.

⋆ ⋆ ⋆

Tony Palmer continued to be a significant conduit between the worlds of pop music and television through the late sixties. After completing *All My Loving*, but before it was screened, he began producing an early-evening youth programme called *How It Is* (1968). This was an all-encompassing arts programme, covering everything from film, theatre and architecture to fashion, design and, of course, music. "It's about the world we live in from the point of view of young people," declared the promotional material, which went on to promise "a mixture of spiky opinion, good conversation and performance – Chopin to pop", adding "it will offend some, amuse others and stimulate everyone".[71]

The programme was scheduled for early Friday evenings, kicking off at 6 p.m. in London and the South-East with other BBC regions opting into the show for the last 20 minutes at 6.20, after their local news bulletins. Peter Asher (ex-Peter & Gordon) was installed as host but was edged out after a few weeks in favour of future novelist Angela Huth. A small studio audience was also in shot and Tony Palmer himself was seen as an interviewer. Initially, the programme was pre-recorded but it soon went live and it was for this reason that BBC1 Controller Paul Fox insisted that Palmer placed himself in front of the camera, knowing that he would be able to extricate the programme from anything awkward. "Given that it was live, they needed some sort of back-up," Palmer says. "I think, effectively, I was the safety net."[72]

Ever since the demise of *A Whole Scene Going* in 1966, the BBC had been looking for a young person's arts vehicle and had piloted a programme called *Sound And Picture City*, with Kenny Everett and Radio 1 DJ Chris Denning at the helm. This didn't work out and what eventually became *How It Is* took its place, after the working titles *Where The Action Is* and *My Generation* were dismissed. But the diktat from on high was that this was not to be just another pop music programme, hence a line-up of guests that began in the first show with Yoko Ono, Henry Moore, Alexis Korner and Victor Spinetti, and continued with the likes of Orson Welles, Tony Curtis, Leonard Bernstein, Kenneth Williams and Lord Snowdon. The pop music contribution came from such names as Joe Cocker, the Small Faces, Ginger Baker and the Nice, but the folk group the Spinners were resident and, tuning in, you might easily have stumbled across the Leicestershire Schools' Symphony Orchestra. "It mixed up classical music with pop music because there was no division between the two," recalls Palmer. "It made it absolutely plain that it didn't matter what aspect of the arts you were talking about. It related to the real world, the political world, with a small P. That was important for that generation."[73]

The show is also interesting for giving John Peel a good run on television. Peel was employed alongside *Oz* magazine editor Richard Neville to offer a weekly satirical take on some aspect of news or culture. The two would then be challenged by BBC announcer Ronald Fletcher who, effectively, provided the Establishment view. "I'd taken my cue for that straight out of *That Was The Week That Was* that used to have Bernard Levin, propped on a stool, giving his opinion," Palmer explains. "So we imitated that but we had Richard Neville, representing the underground, John Peel, representing all that was good and true about popular music, but in the middle Ronnie Fletcher, who was the voice of the BBC. He would just interrupt the other two." The routines were not scripted but they were very carefully discussed beforehand. "We'd pick a topic. Sometimes

Richard suggested it, sometimes John would suggest it, sometimes I suggested it and so the topic would then be discussed between these two with Ronnie being told to interrupt frequently and at any time, saying: 'Dear boy. I don't understand a word of that. Are you speaking English?', which worked wonderfully."[74]

Sadly, *How It Is* was destined to become yet another fleeting attempt to capture the mood of the nation's youth. After five months on air, the show was shunted to a time slot around 11 p.m., where it trundled along for another two months under the title *How Late It Is* (1969). Tony Palmer was no longer involved. He had already turned his attention to another project.

★ ★ ★

Frustrated at the BBC's decision to shelve *All My Loving*, Tony Palmer seized on another rare opportunity to show the "worth" of pop music to a disbelieving world. Through the course of his work, he had become friendly with Eric Clapton and was an early appreciator of Cream, Clapton's supergroup with Ginger Baker and Jack Bruce. By the end of 1968, after just two years together, the Cream experiment was coming to an end. There were plans for one final concert and Palmer was asked to film it.

The concert was scheduled for November 26, 1968, just over three weeks, it turned out, after *All My Loving* was eventually aired. Despite – or perhaps because of – the reaction to that film, Norman Swallow, the newly appointed editor of *Omnibus*, wanted the Cream farewell concert as another *Omnibus* film, slotted in among editions that year that covered such subjects as Kathleen Ferrier, Rossini, Graham Greene, Gaugin and sculptor Henry Moore. "That was the real achievement of *All My Loving*," reflects Palmer. "It was now thought okay to think of pop music in the same breath as Henry Moore. It wasn't to the detriment of either."

With his BBC hat on, Palmer also managed to secure the Royal Albert Hall as the venue for the concert, egged on by Cream manager Robert Stigwood who was having problems convincing the management that the venue was appropriate. There was one condition, however. The cameras could not be moved during the recording. Bearing in mind that early colour television cameras, which had only months before been acquired by the BBC, were enormous and hard to shift, this was not an impossible condition to agree to, but it did mean that the director's possibilities when recording were somewhat limited.

There were in fact two performances from Cream that night. The first Palmer treated as a camera rehearsal, which confirmed the difficulties he would face in capturing the band using just four static cameras, not least the problem of keeping the band members in the frame. "At the end of the first concert, I had a big row with Eric," he recalls. "I said: 'Eric. Your camera's here. Jack's camera's there. Ginger's camera's here. The only one I can guarantee is Ginger, because he can't move. Jack is being very well behaved. He knows where his camera is. All you do is turn your back on me and I can't do anything about it.' He was a little bit better behaved in the second concert."

The other technical hindrance came through the concert being videotaped rather than filmed. In those days, the editing of videotape was a haphazard affair. It had to be chopped like audiotape and all too often the cut would be clumsy and jarringly visible. For Palmer, this meant shooting the action as live, not risking any edits unless they were absolutely essential. But this had its benefits, explaining, to some degree, the raw energy that pervades the film.

"Jack [Bruce] always said that the fact that you couldn't edit – and it was therefore rough, to put it mildly, occasionally missing things – added to the impression that it was a) improvised, which indeed it was, and b) it was responding to the sensation of being there," Palmer says. "The energy mostly comes from them but also has come from the limitations that were imposed on us." The director did employ one fall-back: a collection of short interviews with the band members – actually left-over material from *All My Loving* – that could be cut into the concert footage to disguise what, otherwise, would be bad breaks. These were not universally appreciated by fans when they saw the finished programme, but they had a job to do. The same fans, in letters to the BBC, also expressed their dislike of the narration from Pete

Drummond, the alterations made to the show's running order, and the primitive special effects that Palmer, with the aid of Soft Machine's art director Mark Boyle, cobbled together, but the programme remains an important document in the history of popular music, a rare eyewitness to the end of something special.

The *Omnibus* presentation (1969) lasted 50 minutes. Longer versions of the concert have since been seen both theatrically and on video. These were commissioned by Robert Stigwood, who used left-over footage to fill out the original work. Palmer's time with Cream was not done, however. Again for *Omnibus*, he directed *Rope Ladder To The Moon* (1970), a film about Jack Bruce, who had just bought an island off the Scottish coast. It explored his deprived upbringing in Glasgow and his musical development. Palmer followed this with *Ginger Baker in Africa* (1973), relating how the drummer drove across the Sahara to Nigeria in search of new musical cultures. There was meant to be a third film, concerning Eric Clapton, but the guitarist was not in a good place. "By the time we got around to Eric, he was gone completely on the heroin and it just wasn't possible," Palmer recalls. "I went to see him and he wasn't making any sense at all. I had no idea what he was talking about. I thought, in fairness to Eric and his greatness as a musician, I'm not going to do that."[75]

★ ★ ★

The BBC wasn't the only broadcaster beginning to understand the growing significance of pop music. ATV, for instance, introduced a popular culture magazine called *Good Evening!* (1967–8), which about half the ITV regions showed, although not at the same time. The host was Jonathan King, freshly graduated from Cambridge and already himself a chart success through 'Everyone's Gone To The Moon' in 1965. Producer Tony Firth explained the premise: "It's for people who have done the teenage bit and want a bit more analytical approach to the pop scene. We'll be taking a look at pop music, books, films and theatre. A lot of the time we shall be criticising. This is going to be something of a controversial show." It was certainly that when the band the Love Affair admitted to King that they hadn't played on their big hit 'Everlasting Love'. The host suggested that this was just the tip of an iceberg: he knew of at least three records in that week's Top 20 that had been produced in a similar way. There was much heated discussion in the wider media as a result.[76]

Later, Granada turned out two notable specials that echoed Tony Palmer's work. *The Doors Are Open* (1968), produced by Jo Durden-Smith and directed by John Sheppard, was an hour-long film covering two concerts by the Doors at The Roundhouse, London, while attempting to explain, with the help of newsreel footage, the message that the band, and particularly lead singer Jim Morrison, were sending out to the world. Clips of public protest, street confrontations, US politicians and war graves were scattered through the band's set, and there were brief interviews with its members, including an apparently tripped-out Morrison.

The Stones In The Park (1969) was another rock milestone, capturing the heady day in July that year when the Rolling Stones gave a free concert in Hyde Park before a quarter of a million people. Using six camera units, co-directors Durden-Smith and Leslie Woodhead followed, dawn to dusk, the events of the day, from campers waking cold on the grass to litter pickers restoring the park to normality as darkness fell. Fans were shown arriving – old mods and rockers, new hippies – with Hell's Angels in Nazi helmets acting as security. Members of the group were interviewed. It was a difficult occasion for them, coming just two days after former Stone Brian Jones had been found dead in a swimming pool. Jagger recited Shelley as a tribute and a box of white butterflies were symbolically given their freedom as the concert opened but the solemn mood didn't last long once the band burst into life.[77]

⋆ ⋆ ⋆

As the decade drew to a close, the most significant new music series to arrive came via an unexpected route. With the launch of BBC2 in April 1964, the channel had introduced a 10-minute preview show called *Line-Up*. Scheduled at the start of the evening, it basically gave a plug to the programmes coming later. In September that year, the idea was expanded. *Line-Up* in its original form was discarded and, at the end of the evening, *Late Night Line-Up* (1964–72) took its place. This extended programme, broadcast live, provided reviews as well as previews, casting a critical eye over the latest arts projects – theatre, books, film and so on. A handful of studio guests contributed to lively discussions and interviewers such as Joan Bakewell and Denis Tuohy became familiar faces. Television itself came under scrutiny, with sometimes heated debates on programmes made not just by the BBC but by ITV, too.

The programme was produced by the BBC's Presentation department – the one that normally just dealt with announcements between programmes and other such matters. That seemed logical at the outset but looked a bit odd once *Late Night Line-Up* developed into a major part of the BBC2 output and even began to generate spin-off series. These included *Film Night*, with Tony Bilbow and Philip Jenkinson, and a rock music show, designed in part to draw attention to the BBC's new colour service, called *Colour Me Pop* (1968–9). The man behind *Late Night Line-Up* was editor Rowan Ayers. The fact that his son, Kevin, was a member of the band Soft Machine may have helped in the development of the new show.

Colour Me Pop began in June 1968 and, still billed under the *Late Night Line-Up* umbrella, was initially described as "a Friday diversion". It became a series in its own right five months later. Hosted by *Late Night Line-Up* reporter Michael Dean, the programme adopted a simple format. A psychedelic cartoon title sequence was followed by a studio or location performance. Usually, just one band/artist was featured in each half-hour edition, giving them time to perform more than just their latest numbers, either live or using pre-recorded backing tracks. The first band contributing was Manfred Mann; others included the Small Faces, Fleetwood, Mac, the Kinks, the Moody Blues, the Move, Caravan and Free.

Musically, the programme was a significant change of direction for the BBC. Despite its misleading title, it switched attention away from the singles chart and towards album music instead. Michael Appleton was a director and producer on *Late Night Line-Up*, and *Colour Me Pop*

k Jackson gets his teeth into another manic show.

'Teddy Boys' Pete Murray and Freddie Mills hang out with Jo Douglas.
EDWARD MILLER/KEYSTONE/GETTY IMAGES

A show within a show: Lonnie Donegan and band in the film *6.5 Special.*
HARRY TODD/FOX PHOTOS/GETTY IMAGES

›d advice: Jack Good with Joe Brown.
TED NEWS/POPPERFOTO/GETTY IMAGES

Cliff and Marty live on *Oh Boy!*
GAB ARCHIVE/REDFERNS

:le Miss Dynamite Brenda Lee rehearses in the street ahead of *Oh Boy!*
N FRANKS/GETTY IMAGES

Peggy Mount and Eric Sykes confirm *Juke Box Jury* is a hit with host David Jacobs.
POPPERFOTO/GETTY IMAGES

The Beatles, with road manager Neil Aspinall, arrive for *Juke Box Jury* service.
JOHN HOPPY HOPKINS/REDFERNS

ady, Steady, Go!: Cathy McGowan with Lulu.
PRESS/HULTON ARCHIVE/GETTY IMAGES

e Rolling Stones start the weekend on *Ready, Steady, Go!*
LIPPE LE TELLIER/PARIS MATCH VIA GETTY IMAGES

Greetings Pop Pickers!: Alan Freeman prepares to enter the studio.
HARRY HAMMOND/V&A IMAGES/GETTY IMAGES

Ayshea gets ready for *Lift Off*.
DOVE/DAILY EXPRESS/GETTY IMAGES

Getting *Whistle Test* on air: Bob Harris flanked by director Colin Strong (left) and producer Mike Appleton.
ALAN MESSER/REX/SHUTTERSTOCK

l Lynott and Friends (including Huey Lewis on harmonica) on *Whistle Test* duty.
ALKIE DAVIES/GETTY IMAGES

d Stewart works the stage on *Supersonic.*
/REX/SHUTTERSTOCK

So It Goes: Tony Wilson.
GEMS/REDFERNS

Heart throb with Heart Throb: Marc Bolan and dancers in *Marc*.
ITV/REX/SHUTTERSTOCK

provided his first flirtation with the world of album rock, a field he was to develop with great success in the seventies.

★ ★ ★

From being way down the pecking order at the start of the sixties, it was actually pop music that had the last word on the BBC as this tumultuous era drew to a close. Apart from a religious reflection by the Bishop of Stepney, the final programme of the decade on BBC1 was *Pop Go The 60s!* There was nothing exceptional about this one-off show, apart from the fact that it was a joint production with the West German television station ZDF, but its prominent scheduling reflects just how much pop music had helped shape the previous 10 years. The *Top Of The Pops*-like programme was hosted by Jimmy Savile and Germany's Elfie von Kalckreuth and featured an array of stars performing old hits, along with some repeated clips, including an extract from *The Beatles At Shea Stadium*.

The television highlight of 1969, however, was undoubtedly coverage of the first manned moon mission. The BBC devoted hours of live airtime to the occasion, but also sought to balance the science with a little art and culture half-way through the evening of lunar touchdown. After the excitement of the landing, and before the first moonwalk by astronauts Neil Armstrong and Buzz Aldrin, BBC1 slotted in an *Omnibus* presentation flippantly titled *So What If It's Just Green Cheese?* This one-hour "entertainment for moon night" featured a mish-mash of items, from literature read by Michael Horden, Ian McKellen, Roy Dotrice and Judi Dench to music from the Dudley Moore Trio and Marion Montgomery. The programme also included a jam from Pink Floyd.

The band's presence on such an occasion was only a small step in itself but it beautifully illustrated just how coverage of young people's music on television had taken one giant leap over the course of the previous 10 years.

THE SEVENTIES

Say Something Outrageous

There was a bit of a shock in store for Bob Harris when he turned up for his first day's work on *The Old Grey Whistle Test.* The job was not going to be quite as he envisaged. The 25-year-old Radio 1 presenter had been offered the role of front man for this strangely titled late-night programme when the original host Richard Williams decided to leave. Naïvely, Bob assumed that the job would mirror his radio experience, in which he played a full part in selecting the material for the show, "building" the programme himself. Not so. Series producer Michael Appleton had a very specific idea of what the presenter of *Whistle Test* was required to do.

The person needed to be a journalist, first and foremost, so that they wouldn't need briefing about guests and could prepare their own questions for interviews. Harris, having been a co-founder of London's events magazine *Time Out*, ticked this particular box. Otherwise, the presenter needed to be a broadcaster, someone who could just get on with anchoring the show, introducing whatever acts Appleton and his team had decided to book. Putting the show together was not part of the remit. The heavy bag loaded with albums that Bob had dragged in to the office was redundant.

"I assumed, when I went into *Whistle Test*, that he would want me to basically build the programmes, but of course that wasn't the case at all," Harris recalls. "I was the presenter of the programme and there was a quite specific division line between the building of the programme, and the choice of the people who were on it, and then the journalistic side of doing all the research for the interviews, writing the links, all that side. So it took a while before we got a balance where I began to have some genuine input into the content of the show. Gradually, Mike began to trust me and I began to trust him." And so began the most important relationship in music television of the 1970s.[1]

The Old Grey Whistle Test was first aired on BBC2 on September 21, 1971. In programme genealogical terms, it was a direct descendant of *Colour Me Pop*, that *Late Night Line-Up* spin-off that had introduced album music to television at the end of the sixties. When *Colour Me Pop* finished, it was succeeded by a show called *Disco 2* (1970–1), or *Line-Up's Disco 2*, as it was initially billed. Ambitiously, the new programme promised a package of "music past, present and future" and was introduced through its 18 months on air by Tommy Vance, Pete Drummond or Mike Harding, although their role was minimal and largely confined to radio-style voice overs. Day-to-day running of the show was in the hands of producers Granville Jenkins and Steve Turner but overseeing the project was *Late Night Line-Up* editor Rowan Ayers. Album sales had overtaken those of singles and artists no longer needed a chart hit in order to fill concert halls. *Disco 2* – despite what seems today to be a somewhat misleading title – set out to address this changing situation.

Ayers promised experimentation, both musically and visually. He offered to provide an outlet for "material which otherwise probably wouldn't get a hearing, like odd tracks from LPs". There would not be dancing girls but there would be film, including "old clips, and some new underground movies we've bought from America," he said. "The only criterion is excellence." Artists featured in the first show included Joe Cocker, Chicago, Lou Christie and Emile Ford, with later appearances by Procol Harum, Chicken Shack, the Strawbs, Yes, Juicy Lucy, Humble Pie, the Move, Fleetwood Mac and Elton John. What

Ayers didn't factor in was analysis or discussion. That changed once Mike Appleton became executive producer.[2]

One of Appleton's jobs on the show was to operate a device called a Telestrator, an electronic pen that allowed writing to be displayed on screen, and he used this to scribble the names of the artists for the benefit of viewers. It was all very arty and high tech. More importantly, he attempted to broaden the remit of the show, bringing in more talk to develop it into something of a music magazine. But his aims were only fully realised once *Disco 2* had come to an end and *The Old Grey Whistle Test* (1971–87) was born.

One of *Disco 2*'s guests had been James Taylor and it was precisely that artist that dictated the sort of show that Appleton planned next. "James Taylor came out with *Sweet Baby James* and that for me indicated where I was going," he reveals. "I decided this was what I wanted to do – this sort of music. That was the beginning of *Whistle Test*. It was specifically that album." He also wanted a beefed-up journalistic tone, to create a television equivalent of *NME*, *Sounds* and *Melody Maker* that, as well as telling people, could illustrate what was happening by having people in to play. "The idea was that it would be a magazine programme devoted to rock music," he says. "Occasionally pop stuff would come in, but basically it was rock music because I thought: 'There are a lot of rock musicians who take this seriously. Maybe television should take it seriously.'"[3]

This sense of "seriousness" about music had gradually developed during the late sixties, through the work of the BBC's Tony Palmer and the likes of Jo Durden-Smith at Granada. It was encapsulated very early on in the new decade when Thames Television devoted a short series of debates to the subject. Under the title *A Broad Look At Pop* (1970), each programme – lasting only 10–20 minutes and screened around midnight in the London area – asked: "Is there such a thing as a pop culture?" and, among other investigations, took a look at the role of popular music in the church.

The idea continued a year later, when BBC1 came up with a series called *Anatomy Of Pop* (1971). In this, Michael Parkinson tried to figure out how pop music successfully drew on other forms of music and how divisions between styles of music were becoming increasingly blurred. He also turned his attention to the recording process and the idea that artists were now able to control their own output. The last three programmes analysed to what extent record pluggers manipulated what the public listened to, the sub-cultures that were developing within the pop scene and, finally, what lasting value contemporary music might have. The analysis continued when ATV produced a one-off programme for ITV called *Whatever Happened To Tin Pan Alley?* (1972), which looked at the changing face of the pop music industry with the help of Mick Jagger, Paul Jones, Adam Faith, Pete Townshend and others.

By the time *The Old Grey Whistle Test* was underway, music on television had very definitely entered a new era. There was a new respect for pop musicians and a sense that the music maybe wasn't as transient as people had previously thought. It crossed Mike Appleton's mind that there were a lot of old blues guys still playing down in New Orleans, and that there was no reason why quality rock musicians might not prove just as durable. "If we take them seriously, we'll go along with them and see the development of rock music," he thought.

For the journalistic reasons outlined above, Appleton's first choice of host was Richard Williams, assistant editor of *Melody Maker.* Singer-actor Ian Whitcomb was inked in as a supporting presenter but a few weeks before the first live show, plans were thrown into disarray when Williams suddenly announced that he was about to get married and would be away on honeymoon just as *Whistle Test* was going on air. This clearly was not the start the show needed so Appleton came up with an idea to disguise Williams's absence, sending him to film some reports from a rock film festival being staged at the National Film Theatre that could be played into the show. He intended to temporarily promote Whitcomb to main presenter but disaster struck on the day of the first broadcast when, during rehearsal, Whitcomb developed a terrible stutter. He swore he would be word-perfect once actually on air but for Appleton it was too great a risk to take on a new show. The only answer was to step into the breach himself.

"With about an hour to go, we had to build a little cubby hole in the corner of the studio," he says. "I had to go in there and make all the announcements, out of vision." It may be that viewers thought the voice belonged to Richard Williams, as no one questioned the incongruity. Williams then returned, Whitcomb – whose live contributions had indeed proved stutter-free – dropped out and *Whistle Test* was up and running.[4]

The identity of the show was defined from the start by its modest budget and even more modest studio facilities. This being another programme produced by the BBC's Presentation department, it had to make do with one of the tiny presentation studios up on the fourth floor of Television Centre.

"It was really, really small," Bob Harris explains. "There was just enough room for three cameras but crucially there were only eight mike points available in the studio, so you couldn't have a full band playing. So we would have probably lead vocal, lead guitar live, playing over a backtrack, which would have been a supervised backtrack recording brought into the show." It wasn't perfect but it was a solution until other methods were developed to work around the issue. "Some of the bands would bring in their own sub-mixer, so they were able to sub-mix the sound for us and then feed that sound through to our desk, in which case everybody could play live."[5]

The same limitations accounted for the stripped-back look of the show. With space at a premium, there was no room for a cyclorama – a curtain backdrop – leaving the studio walls bare and exposed, but the team decided to embrace this visual austerity and use it to their advantage. "I always thought that, in those early days, when musicians hadn't been into television studios very much, they might be alienated by all the technology and everything going on," says Appleton. "Therefore, if you made it like a rehearsal room, they'd be that much more at ease. The things lying around on the floor were there because someone hadn't cleared them up more than anybody put them down to be artistic." The one concession to artwork was the show's "star kicker" logo – designed by the BBC's Roger Ferrin – that also found its way onto badges.

As for the weird programme name, that was generated during a conversation in the office. Mike Appleton had toyed with calling the show *The Florence Foster Jenkins Musical Emporium*, after the wealthy American heiress – played in a 2016 film by Meryl Streep – who was so deluded about her operatic talents that she funded her own recordings and even gave an unintentionally hilarious recital at New York's Carnegie Hall. Appleton thought it might provide an amusing title but is now very grateful that a far better option presented itself when assistant producer Gloria Wood mentioned the tale of how, in the days of Tin Pan Alley, songs were often played to the area's elderly janitors or delivery men to test their commerciality. If those guys ended up whistling a song, it was likely to become a hit. The "old greys' *Whistle Test*" was trimmed a little for television but proved an enigmatic and fairly timeless title. Similar longevity was hoped for from a theme tune, which led to the selection of the harmonica-driven 'Stone Fox Chase' by American band Area Code 615, a piece of quality music, says Appleton, but quirky in being hard to whistle or sing.

The first year of *Whistle Test* saw guests such as Lindisfarne, Wishbone Ash, Alice Cooper, Frank Zappa, Poco, David Bowie and Randy Newman establish the show as a must-see among discerning music fans. The late-night timeslot on a Tuesday was no deterrent. The format was nailed quite quickly but a change of host was soon needed when Richard Williams decided he'd rather remain a journalist and not become a TV star. "I loved working with Richard but he wasn't a natural in there," says Appleton. "He was writing his book *Out Of His Head*, about Phil Spector, and he was very involved in that and, in the end, said: 'I don't think I can do this. I enjoy it but my mind isn't concentrating on this'. That's when I got in touch with Bob."[6]

"He got me in first of all to do a guest spot as chairman of a discussion about the impending Night Assemblies Bill," Bob explains. This was a Parliamentary bill that had the potential to scupper music festivals or other events where groups of people gathered overnight. "I didn't know it at the time but that was my audition." It proved to be the start of a great friendship, despite that first-day misunderstanding over the precise duties of the presenter.[7]

* * *

While *Whistle Test* was finding its feet and growing into the number one rock show of the decade, other series also played to the knowledgeable music fan. BBC2's *In Concert* (1970–6) – the contents did what it said on the tin – saw Joni Mitchell as the first in a series of singer-songwriters to be given the chance to shine in front of an audience. She was followed in subsequent weeks by John Sebastian, Elton John, David Crosby & Graham Nash, and James Taylor, establishing a simple, lasting format that also had room for a spot of jazz, blues, folk or country from time to time. The series later evolved into *Sight And Sound In Concert* (1977–8; 1983–4), once the BBC's television and radio services had worked out a way to simultaneously broadcast vision and audio.

In similar fashion, Granada offered its regional viewers a studio-based rock show called *Doing Their Thing* (1970), a short series of individual showcases featuring the likes of Mungo Jerry, Free, Status Quo, Deep Purple and Family. The 25-minute programmes went out at teatime. Similar was another Granada local programme called *Out Front* (1971), except this was a late-night offering and mixed studio performances with location recordings, with the aim of showcasing styles of music that had minority appeal. Among the featured artists – sometimes more than one per week – were Cat Stevens, Fairport Convention, George Melly, the Alex Welsh Band and Jack Bruce & Friends. *Set Of Six* (1972) was another show just for Granada locals, channelling performances from one band a week in the early evening. Among the "six very different groups with six very different styles" were Badfinger, Slade and Pentangle.

By this time, too, Granada was bedding in as a producer of children's-hour pop shows. Encouraged by the relative success of *Discotheque* in 1969, producer Muriel Young gave the series a tweak and relaunched it under a new title. *Lift Off* (1969–74) featured the same hosts – Graham Bonney and Ayshea – although Bonney left after one series. This left Ayshea to run the show in the company of Muriel Young's own former *Five O'Clock Club* co-star, the puppet owl Ollie Beak, voiced by Wally Whyton (puppet dog Fred Barker was also seen in some later editions). By 1971, the show had morphed into *Lift Off With Ayshea*, as the actress-singer became the focal point, usually performing a couple of numbers each week as well as introducing chart names with their new releases. Early guests included Long John Baldry, Jimmy Cliff and David & Rozaa (a pairing of David Essex with "Miss Talent USA"). Later the show gave TV debuts to the Sweet and Wizzard, whose main man, Roy Wood, produced a record for Ayshea and roped her into performing backing vocals on the group's first number one, 'See My Baby Jive'. The relationship became even closer after that. "I was actually engaged to Roy for a year," she reveals. "What a strange couple we were."

Lift Off being a children's show, there was a lot of knock-about humour built in and the programme also strayed into playing clips from family movies at one point, but it did provide some useful chart coverage at a time when such a thing was a scarce commodity. At the outset, there was a resident band called the Pattern, who were managed by Chris Brough (son of ventriloquist Peter Brough), Ayshea's husband at the time. There was a resident dance troupe, too, initially the Ken Martyne Dancers and then Martyne's next creation, The Feet, whose members included future Hot Gossip choreographer Arlene Phillips.

The show was taped over the course of a day in Granada's studios in Manchester, with new backing tracks pre-recorded at the Strawberry Studios in Stockport to allow performers to mime on the show – although Ayshea always sang live. Most of the London-based performers travelled up and back by train, creating a party atmosphere. "We would all go up on the breakfast run from King's Cross," Ayshea recalls. "The entire cast of the show would be there and we'd all have breakfast together and then we all came back on the dinner train and, because we did it every week, the waiters would have all our favourite wines and foods laid out for us. It was like going to a restaurant."[8]

The series made a star out of Ayshea. She penned a weekly column for *Look-in* magazine ("the junior *TV Times*") and was always able to bag a good restaurant table in London, as waiters – not normally able to watch television because of their working hours – could catch her show between shifts. Building on acting experience she gained in series such as Gerry Anderson's *UFO*, she later moved to Hollywood, married CBS executive Michael Levy and featured in a couple of movies.

After five years, it was deemed that *Lift Off* had run its course and Muriel Young began to put together a successor show called *45* (1974–5), which was aimed at a slightly older audience. This began in just a few regions, with Ayshea again involved. By the time it had picked up national coverage – albeit shown on different days of the week by the ITV regions – Radio Luxembourg's Kid Jensen had been installed as host – his first British television job. "It was a great introduction for me to TV in this country," he says. "Muriel Young was wonderful, very kind, very generous and I loved working with her. Of course, a lot of younger viewers today wouldn't know what *45* meant but in those days everybody knew that it was singles."[9]

Ken Martyne was once again in charge of choreography for *45*, initially with an outfit called Stylus then with Zig Zag. In January 1975, the name was extended to *Rock On With 45* and some editions were recorded at the Hardrock discotheque in Stretford, Manchester. Featured artists varied from glam rock stars to bands such as the Troggs and the Hollies.

45 had pretensions to be more than a kids' show, as revealed by its 6.30 p.m. air time in its native Granada region, but, as soon as it ended, Muriel Young re-entrenched herself in children's television by launching *Look Alive* (1975–6). Hosted by Stephanie De Sykes and Gordon Bennett, this was her attempt to create a pop magazine show. Alongside guests such as Showaddywaddy, Labi Siffre and Hello, the hosts sang a few songs and then interviewed anyone from songwriter Barry Mason to DJ Johnnie Walker in a studio set colourfully dressed with big flowers and giant toadstools. Routines from the resident dancers Him And Us, made up of twins Lesley and Teri Scoble and their brother Michael, added to the mix. Features on other types of music – from Vivaldi to boogie-woogie – and a fortnightly teenage fashion parade completed the package.

* * *

During the early seventies, *Lift Off* and *45* were the only chart-related programmes that ITV could muster in response to the resilient *Top*

Of The Pops. The BBC's warhorse thundered into the new decade, emboldened by the arrival of colour television and given more space to breathe by a 20-minute programme extension. Although this was eroded away as the decade progressed, producer Mel Cornish was delighted with the added time, claiming that the show could now focus on the Top 30, rather than just the Top 20, and would be able to include more "Tips For The Top". "The new 45-minute formula has attracted even dollier birds and groovier dancers than before," trumpeted the *Radio Times*, revealing that the show had introduced prizes for the "best-dressed dolly" and the "best dancer". By early 1971, an "LP spot" had been added by new producer Stanley Dorfman, but that was phased out once founder-producer Johnnie Stewart eased back into the producer's chair later that year.

With Jimmy Savile and Tony Blackburn established as alternating hosts, Ed Stewart was the next DJ added to the roster of presenters. Noel Edmonds came on board in 1972, and Kenny Everett – a replacement for Stewart – and Dave Lee Travis both joined in 1973. Robin Nash became producer at the end of that year, overseeing the programme until 1976, a period that saw various DJs given a run out in front of the cameras – Johnnie Walker, Emperor Rosko, Greg Edwards and Paul Burnett – although things soon settled down into a regular presentation team of Savile, Blackburn, Travis and Edmonds in 1975, with David Hamilton joining them the next year.

The 500th edition of *Top Of The Pops* arrived in October 1973, by which time the series – now using a version of Led Zeppelin's 'Whole Lotta Love' by CCS as its theme music – had proved itself to be the perfect launch pad for glam rock in all its Technicolor glory.* Arguably, there would have been no glam without *Top Of The Pops*, which offered a weekly burst of colour and fun at a dark time of power shortages and industrial three-day weeks. The stars breaking through lapped up the

* Ironically, after a few unsatisfactory experiences at the start of their career, Led Zeppelin, arguably the biggest rock act of the seventies, made a policy decision never to perform live – let alone mime – on TV anywhere in the world.

exposure, Slade, Bolan, Glitter, Rod Stewart, the Sweet, Mud, Suzi Quatro and Wizzard all becoming regular performers.

To make the most of the opportunity, these tinsel-clad heroes were always ready to play to the crowd. The Faces kicked a football around the studio and roped in John Peel to strum a mandolin, Mud in their Teddy Boy drainpipes worked the stage with their 'Tiger Feet' dance, and Slade's Dave Hill even made his own band mates laugh with his bonkers outfits and six-inch platforms. And there was no more outrageous performance than that delivered by David Bowie on July 6, 1972. His rendition of 'Starman', flirting androgynously with guitarist Mick Ronson, has been written down in history as one of rock's landmark moments. But making an impression was easy on this show. Wizzard were masters of the art, helped by the fact that there were so many in the band. Viewers didn't know where to look next. While the focus may have been on Roy Wood's rainbow hair and greasepaint, in the background there might be a prowling gorilla or an angel on roller skates.

Pan's People, new to the show as the sixties ended, were by now an essential part of the package. Their weekly gyrations became the talk of classrooms and factories, particularly in the weeks where the skimpiest of outfits were employed. Choreographer Flick Colby's interpretation of a song's lyrics may have been risibly literal at times, but middle-aged dads and their teenage sons didn't care. With a couple of personnel changes – Cherry Gillespie for Andi Rutherford and Sue Menhenick for Louise Clarke – Pan's People remained with the show until 1976, when they were replaced by Colby's new ensemble, Ruby Flipper, that tried to adjust the gender balance by including three guys alongside a mostly-new quartet of girls. That didn't work and within five months it was an all-girl cast again, this time under the name of Legs & Co.

In due course, the role of the resident dance troupe was to be undermined by the creation of more promotional videos. The Beatles had been making these since the mid-sixties but they were still rarities, even on programmes such as *Top Of The Pops*, which was crying out for them to cover the all-too-regular instances when artists could not come into the studio. That all changed in November 1975 when

Queen, somewhat wisely, decided that the complexities of their new song 'Bohemian Rhapsody' made it unsuitable for the *Top Of The Pops* orchestra or even to subject to a rushed new backing track so they could mime. Instead, in just four hours, they put together a video to send to the BBC. When that film helped keep the disc at the top of the singles chart for nine weeks, the penny finally dropped in record company boardrooms.[10]

Once *Top Of The Pops* had stopped dallying with album tracks and returned to the ups and downs of the singles chart, the format of the show was so simple that – the usual time pressures notwithstanding – it was a straightforward programme to put together. Then punk arrived. The decision of whether or not to feature the aggressive new music in what was still very much a family show could have been awkward but, to some degree, it was taken out of the hands of the production team, when some bands – most notably the Clash – refused to appear. There was, however, controversy when the Sex Pistols very nearly topped the charts with 'God Save The Queen' at the time of the Queen's Silver Jubilee in June 1977 and there was no coverage on the show (the record having been banned by BBC Radio). Conspiracy theorists – among them Virgin Records boss Richard Branson – continue to claim that the record did reach number one and was massaged down into second place to avoid a scene. But *Top Of The Pops* that week did feature the Stranglers, and the Jam had already been on the show. Gradually other punks, or those affiliated to that scene, began to appear, starting with the Adverts and the Boomtown Rats. Even the Sex Pistols were eventually included, albeit on film. By the end of the decade, *Top Of The Pops* had integrated punk/new wave reasonably well into its output. It had to rub shoulders with everything from the Muppets to the Brighouse & Rastrick Brass Band, of course, but that was ever the *Top Of The Pops* way. The programme certainly didn't suffer the trials that would face *The Old Grey Whistle Test* during the same period.

The decade ended with a trio of producers – Stanley Appel, Brian Whitehouse and David G. Hillier – managing the show in turn and a new generation of excessively cheerful Radio 1 DJs – David (no longer "Kid") Jensen, Peter Powell, Mike Read and Simon Bates –

sharing the presentation duties as Blackburn was phased out and Savile's appearances became less frequent. Through the seventies, *Top Of The Pops* had built on its sixties' popularity and developed into a must-see Thursday-night, post-*Tomorrow's World* event attracting an audience of nearly 20 million. Its reputation for making or breaking new performers and for perpetuating or terminating careers was confirmed.

* * *

Like Granada over on ITV, the BBC also continued to see pop music as an ideal subject for children's programming. *Crackerjack* and *The Basil Brush Show* were still going strong, slotting in the latest chart stars among their corny quips, and there was also a show called *Ed And Zed!* (1970), a Saturday lunchtime mix of comedy, film clips and puzzles hosted by Ed Stewart and a robot assistant. Artists such as White Plains, Hot Chocolate and Mud added the music. Stewart brought pop to kids again a few years later when he hosted a lunchtime series made by Yorkshire Television for ITV called *Play It Again Stewpot* (1974). Taking a novel approach to the subject, this series saw guests rubbing shoulders with puppet versions of other pop stars, such as Cliff Richard, Elton John, Lulu and Elvis, with strings pulled by Roger Stevenson, who had previously created the puppet version of Ken Dodd's Diddymen for television.

The BBC also imported a new *Monkees*-for-the-seventies show from the US. *The Partridge Family* (1971–5) was loosely based on the true-life story of a family group called the Cowsills from Rhode Island. It starred Shirley Jones as mum Shirley Partridge who joins her kids' band, which comprises singer Keith (played by Jones's real-life stepson David Cassidy) and younger siblings Laurie (Susan Dey), Danny (Danny Bonaduce), Christopher (Jeremy Gelbwaks, replaced by Brian Forster) and Tracy (Suzanne Crough). Having somehow put together a hit record in their San Pueblo garage, the band takes to the road in a psychedelically painted school bus to score hit after hit under the cynical management of Reuben Kincaid (Dave Madden). Apart from vocals, the actors did not perform on the records.

The Partridge Family's first hit, 'I Think I Love You', broke into the UK charts a full seven months before the BBC actually screened the first episode, which suggests a degree of ambivalence about the series on behalf of the broadcaster, and that is echoed in the fact that only one part-series (12 episodes) was shown. But, when the hits kept coming, and particularly when Cassidy broke out of the band to become a massive teen idol, it must have been a no-brainer for the ITV companies to snap up the rights, showing the series – on various days of the week – over the following three years.

⋆ ⋆ ⋆

As in the sixties, the BBC continued to take full advantage of successful chart names, turning them into hosts of light entertainment shows for all the family. Joining the likes of Cliff, Lulu and Cilla, artists such as Bobbie Gentry and David Essex now gained their own series, although none was feted in quite the same way as the Osmonds, who featured for six consecutive days on BBC1 in August 1974. Noel Edmonds covered the family's visit to the UK through a series of diary pieces and they also hosted *Top Of The Pops*.

Meanwhile, at Granada, Muriel Young was developing her own line in star showcases. First in the frame were the Bay City Rollers, British pop's hottest property in the mid-seventies, for whom she created *Shang-A-Lang* (1975). Aimed firmly at a juvenile audience, this was recorded in a studio filled with screaming, swooning, scarf-waving girls. The Rollers performed in each edition, but wrapped around their contributions were appearances from guests like the Rubettes, Marc Bolan and Sparks, a look at the history of pop in a feature called 'Let's Roll Back', and lessons in guitar from top session man Big Jim Sullivan, helped by the band's Eric Faulkner and Stuart 'Woody' Wood. The resident dancers were Teri Scoble's Him And Us, as featured in *Look Alive*.

The next band benefiting from Muriel Young's attention was the Anglo-American trio Arrows. The format for *Arrows* (1976) was much the same as for *Shang-A-Lang*, with band members Alan Merrill, Jake

Hooker and Paul Varley performing tracks and welcoming guests. Him And Us – now augmented to Him And Us Plus One* and then extended further to Him And Us Plus Three – again did the hoofing. By the time of the second series, the band had gained a new member, Terry Taylor, but, for all the exposure the programme provided, Arrows never achieved another hit. Indeed, the last of their two chart successes had come a year before the first series was recorded.

The next year Muriel Young turned her attention to a more established star when she signed up Marc Bolan for *Marc* (1977). At this point in time, Bolan and his band T. Rex appeared to be past their peak. There hadn't been a Top 10 hit for four years and the lower reaches of the chart were the best they could manage. He clearly hoped for a bounce from the show, which bore many of the hallmarks of Granada kids' programmes – the elementary studio set, the Teri Scoble dance troupe, now known as Heart-Throb, and the star guests, who this time included the Jam, 10cc, the Boomtown Rats, Generation X and even David Bowie. Bolan himself was supported by a strong backing band that included Herbie Flowers, but the show did nothing to revive his fortunes. The latest T. Rex release – 'Celebrate Summer' – featured several times during the six-week run but the record failed to reach the Top 75 and, sadly, *Marc* proved to be Bolan's swan song. He was killed in a car crash with two editions of the series still to air.

Paul Nicholas was Young's next choice of leading man. She had earmarked him for a series in 1977 but he was tied up making the *Sgt Pepper's Lonely Hearts Club Band* movie so Nicholas was relieved to find the offer still on the table. *Paul* (1978), like *Marc*, was only a short series – just seven editions – but it was a handy profile-raiser for the singer/actor/dancer who had broken into the charts after time on the West End stage.

* * *

---

* The "One" was a certain Ken Warwick, later to become executive producer for *American Idol* in the USA.

While it was certainly leading the way, Granada was not the only ITV franchise holder looking at pop music and the most interesting entrant into the market at this time was Tyne Tees. This tiny station, serving the north-east of England, would become a major player during the eighties, but the foundations for that success were laid in a series known as *The Geordie Scene* (1974–6). Locally, the show was shown on Saturday mornings, but the handful of other regions that took it typically chose other days for broadcast. This was a gritty, sweaty show, as was emphasised in the title sequence made up of shots of urban and industrial Newcastle, with local dialect words like "Canny" and "Kidda" splashed on the screen to draw further attention to its regional accent. This was music in the round, with the audience viewing from all angles, and, while a number of bands that appeared were local, others were national names. Some mimed but braver guests – the Glitter Band and Dr Feelgood, for instance – performed live. Ex-Radio 1 DJ Dave Cash was one of the early presenters, along with local DJ Big Phil, Dave Lee Travis and then another former Radio 1 presenter, Dave Eager.

In a similar vein, *Jam* (1976–7) was a programme made by HTV in Cardiff as a showcase for Welsh rock bands. Although aimed at a Welsh audience, the series was later picked up as a school holiday filler by other ITV regions. A *Jam Special* at Christmas 1977 was almost networked, giving viewers around the UK a rare chance to see artists such as Sassafras, Racing Cars, Shakin' Stevens, Budgie and Man.

Given the influence of the biggest companies within ITV, there was predictably more success for LWT who, in 1975, gave former Southern Television director Mike Mansfield a chance to break the *Top Of The Pops* hegemony. Mansfield had been working with Muriel Young at Granada, directing editions of *Lift Off*, and he now threw himself into the heart of his new project. Not only did he run the gallery, he effectively also hosted the show as there was no studio presenter.

Supersonic (1975–7) was trialled with a one-off programme seen in London only in March 1975, after which it was deemed worthy of an extended run, starting in September of that year. The format impressed all the other ITV regions to buy into the project, although once again they somewhat diminished its impact by screening it on different days and at different times. In London, it was a Saturday morning show, designed to slot into a mix of adventure series, cartoons and competitions hosted by Sally James under the umbrella title of *Saturday Scene*. Indeed, for the last few months of its time on air, the whole package was re-labelled *Supersonic Saturday Scene*.

Supersonic took full advantage of the latest technical wizardry to offer a fast-moving package of contemporary pop, featuring a handful of stars in each half-hour show. Artists often performed more than one number, perhaps even a version of a hit from a couple of years earlier, working their way around a jet-black set that was furnished with gantries, scaffolding and a giant illuminated star. The silver-maned, pencil-waving Mansfield ruled the roost from behind the control desk, yelling instructions for the crew that doubled as intros to the performers: "Good luck everybody and roll *Supersonic*"; "Stand by Slade with 'Mama Weer All Crazee Now', cue music and take 2!". Cameras raced around the busy studio, shooting performers from above, below, in front and behind, as dry ice swirled across the floor and confetti showered from the ceiling. A small but enthusiastic audience was occasionally brought into view but generally kept well out of reach of their idols in raised seating. Andy Bown performed the upbeat theme song.

The show was created by Mansfield, he said at the time, to bring excitement and fun back to TV pop – in a sense echoing the work of Jack Good in the fifties. "I was sick of watching groups who seemed rooted in concrete," he claimed. "I wanted to contribute something visually." He favoured artists such as Rod Stewart and Marc Bolan, who had a relationship with the camera. "There is a serious, heavy side to pop, but with *Supersonic* I'm dealing with fun. I won't have anybody on the show who has a hit record but no act to offer".[11]

Visually, at least, *Supersonic* was different and the idea of making the programme director the hub of the show was a clever hook that attracted a lot of attention. It even inspired a sketch by comedian Benny Hill. The show returned for a one-off special shown on Channel 4 at Christmas 1983.

★ ★ ★

The seventies also saw some intriguing music documentaries. These included ATV's *James Paul McCartney* (1973), an hour-long, prime-time showcase for the former Beatle that blended performances of new and old material with an insight into his family life and an introduction to his latest band, Wings. There were scenes of a sing-song with family and friends in a packed Merseyside pub, arty sequences of Paul on horseback and even a Busby Berkeley-type song and dance routine. But, if this was an attempt to cast McCartney as a man of today and tomorrow, rather than of 'Yesterday', it seems to have backfired, as it wasn't well received. Alan Coren, writing in the *Times*, declared this to be not "the sort of programme you make a come-back with. It was the sort of programme you make a come-back after."[12]

More successful was *Cracked Actor* (1975), an *Omnibus* presentation that aimed to lift the mask off David Bowie. Shot in the US in 1974, the Alan Yentob-produced film followed the enigmatic star as he toured his *Diamond Dogs* show, having discarded the image of the Ziggy Stardust years. Drawing its title from a track on the album *Aladdin Sane*, the programme combined concert footage with close-up interviews, providing one of the first insights into the personality, character and techniques of the artist.

Pop also figured prominently in the work of arts broadcaster Melvyn Bragg. His BBC2 magazine show *2nd House* (1973–6) and its later incarnation *Lively Arts* (1976–8) included features on Mike Oldfield's *Tubular Bells*, the Irish band Horslips and songwriters Randy Newman and Dory Previn, for instance, and also dedicated whole editions to the Who (1974), the Kursaal Flyers (*So You Wanna Be A Rock'n'Roll Star*, 1976) and Rod Stewart (*Rod The Mod Has Come Of Age*, 1976).

Bragg then became editor of LWT's new arts showcase, *The South Bank Show* (1978–2010; 2012–), the first season of which saw one-hour profiles of such artistic giants as David Hockney, George Bernard Shaw, Harold Pinter, Herbert von Karajan and Ingmar Bergman. But it is revealing that the very first subject was Paul McCartney. This was a deliberate move by Bragg, whose focus was on creating a "popular" arts series and who felt that the choice of McCartney would show that he was serious about bringing pop culture into the arts fold.

Pop music, both technologically and intellectually, had reached a point where it could be enjoyed, appreciated and re-evaluated in posterity, just like Renaissance art, classic literature or the works of Beethoven. Bragg was determined to press that case. In subsequent years, Elvis Costello, Peter Gabriel, Jimi Hendrix, George Michael, the Pet Shop Boys, Stevie Wonder, kd lang, Blur, Moby, Nick Cave, Dusty Springfield, Jarvis Cocker, Coldplay and Elbow were just some of the many artists to feature on the programme, which has been broadcast on Sky Arts since 2012.[13]

The intellectualisation of pop music continued in other ways, too. At its most basic level, the idea that the history of the subject was now worthy of study and analysis, was manifested in a couple of television quiz programmes. In 1975, BBC1 ran a short series on Sunday afternoons called *Disco*. This was a flippant little quiz, played for laughs by team captains Tim Rice and Capital Radio DJ Roger Scott, aided by celebrity guests, and presided over by Terry Wogan. The name came from the fact that various discotheques around the country were used as venues. A far more competitive quiz arrived the year after in the form of *Pop Quest* (1975–8). Despite being a show for teenagers aged up to 17, and being screened during ITV's children's hour, this Yorkshire Television offering was a genuine test of music knowledge, past and present, and also included interviews with stars and features about the music industry. The first series was played in a team format, with three kids from each ITV region competing. It was hosted by former Radio 1 DJ Steve Merike. For the second series, *Pop Quest* became an individual event, a contest to find Britain's young pop *Mastermind* – the TV equivalent of Radio 1's *Quiz Kid* series. The dual hosts were Kid Jensen and Sally James. With Jensen subsequently tied into a weekday contract at Radio 1, the third and final series introduced Mike Read, newly installed at Radio Luxembourg, and singer Megg Nicol as the hosts. *Pop Quest* was the brainchild of producer/director Ian Bolt, who was genuinely surprised by the level of interest young people were showing in the detail of pop music. "We discovered that it was very 'in' to know such things as who the bass player was with The Byrds in 1969," he said at the time, "as well as to recognise 20-year-old songs after the first two bars".[14]

★ ★ ★

It wasn't all clever stuff, however. There remained a lot of uninspiring pop on television in the seventies as light entertainment bosses raked through the charts in attempts to build a family audience. Dougie Squires, who pioneered pop dancing on television back in the fifties with *Cool For Cats*, was still very active during the decade and his Second Generation troupe were given a summer Saturday night showcase – *2 'G's And The Pop People* (1972) – by LWT, in which they strutted their stuff to music old and new, helped by assorted DJs and guest artists such as Lulu, the Bee Gees, Argent and the Move. Similar fare came in BBC2's *They Sold A Million* (1973–4), hosted by Terry Wogan, which saw Vince Hill and the Young Generation dancers supporting artists such as Dusty Springfield, Neil Sedaka, Don McLean and the Supremes. Jack Jones and Slade appeared on the same show.

Fans of soul music might have been excited to see BBC2 develop a series called *Colour My Soul* (1973–4) but were probably a little confused to find it swinging between gospel songs one week and warmed-over tunes for the chicken-in-a-basket brigade the next. Madeline Bell, Jimmy Helms, Doris Troy and Freda Payne were among those somewhat wasting their talents, Helms in one show entertaining the clientele at Cesar's Palace – the one in Luton, not Vegas.

In 1976, Johnnie Hamp at Granada came up with a novel take on the pop scene when he put together *The International Pop Proms* (1976–7) for ITV. Intended to be the pop equivalent of the BBC's *The Proms* from the Royal Albert Hall, Hamp's series promised a mixture of pop and classics, everything from "Bizet to Bacharach, ragtime to rock'n'roll", performed by guests such as Marty Wilde, Demis Roussos, Duane Eddy, Johnny Mathis, Georgie Fame, Buddy Greco and Roy Orbison. The stars were supported by the International Pop Proms Orchestra that included a string section brought in from the Hallé Orchestra and was conducted by Les Reed or a guest conductor – George Martin, Tony Hatch and Elmer Bernstein all waved the baton. Most of the shows were recorded in front of a 4,000-strong audience at the King's Hall, Belle Vue, Manchester. But the place had seen better days. The summer of 1975, when the shows were recorded, was hot and, at times, wet. Temperatures topped 37°C (100°F) at one point, warping the instruments; on another occasion, rain poured in and caused the ink dots on the sheet music to run. "The hall was falling to pieces," remembers Hamp. "There were holes in the roof and the girls were shoving the violins up their skirts to keep the rain off." Two later editions, shown in 1977, came from the more secure location of the Guildhall, Preston. One was dedicated to the music of the fifties and the other to the music of the sixties.[15]

Hits old and new were also the basis for the *BBC's Pop At The Mill* (1977), an extension of the lunchtime magazine programme *Pebble Mill At One*, which was recorded on the lawns of the BBC's Birmingham studios and shown on Saturday evenings. Described as a weekly "pop festival", it was about as close to the middle of the road that the BBC could have driven, with Pete Murray as host and guests including the Rubettes, Helen Shapiro, Billy J. Kramer, Joe Brown, John Miles, Mud and Paul Nicholas. A year later, BBC2 came up with *Sounds Like Friday* (1978), a showcase for singers such as Kris Kristofferson and Rita Coolidge, Marion Montgomery, Madeline Bell, Elkie Brooks and guests, with Leo Sayer taking over the later editions.

Still chasing that family audience, television also returned to the idea of awards ceremonies. *The British Rock And Pop Awards* (1977; 1979–84) was an initiative of the *Daily Mirror*, whose readers voted for the winners. ITV broadcast a highlights package of the inaugural ceremony, which was hosted by Maurice Kinn, a concert promoter who had launched the *New Musical Express* in 1952 and was responsible for that paper's annual awards in the sixties. After a fallow year in 1978, the BBC then picked up the event and bolted it onto its early evening magazine show, *Nationwide*. Bob Wellings and Kid Jensen hosted the coverage. As well as the usual Best Male Singer, Best Group, etc., there were three "special" awards – the Radio 1 Disc Jockeys' Award for outstanding contribution to British pop music, the Mirror Readers' Award for outstanding pop personality and, somewhat inevitably, the Nationwide Golden Award for the artist or group with the most family appeal. The *Observer*'s TV critic Clive James dismissed the occasion as having "the lasting importance of someone breaking wind in the middle of a hurricane". Still, the awards returned, running until 1984, after which the BBC turned its attention instead to *The British Record Industry Awards*, later to be known as *The Brit Awards.*[16]

Meanwhile, that perennial family favourite, the *Eurovision Song Contest*, continued to defy musical reality. From Dana's triumph in 1970 to Israel's 1979 winner Milk & Honey, the event stubbornly declined to reflect what was happening in the real world, with just the odd exception, most notably Abba's glam rock triumph in 1974 that introduced the now legendary Swedish group to the world at large. The UK's only success during the decade was with the Brotherhood Of Man's novelty song 'Save Your Kisses For Me' in 1976 – the year that punk rock arrived.

★ ★ ★

A new direction for pop music in the seventies came through religion. The BBC was the first to see the potential in mixing pop with the pulpit in the series *See You Sunday* (1973–5). Clumsily described as "a weekly reflection of the religious world of a new generation", the show was hosted by Alex Dolphin and Alastair Pirrie (later to front the series *Razzamatazz* in the eighties) and combined performances by the likes of Cat Stevens, 10cc, Medicine Head, Colin Blunstone and Randy Newman with discussions about the Children Of God movement, transcendental meditation and Young Methodists. Four years later, ITV picked up on the idea with *Pop Gospel* (1979–80). "Why does the Devil have all the best tunes?", asked the *TV Times*, quoting Salvation Army founder William Booth, and this children's-hour series – fronted by *Opportunity Knocks* discovery Berni Flint – set out to prove that he didn't, with the help of guests like Cliff Richard and regular performers Nutshell, Parchment, Bryn Haworth and Garth Hewitt, who became co-host in the second series. *Pop Gospel* was another Muriel Young production at Granada and, apart from the religious slant, was cosily familiar, including routines from the TSDs (Teri Scoble Dancers). Directing some of the early editions was former Monkee Micky Dolenz, before he went on to produce and direct the comedy series *Metal Mickey*.

The BBC was to return to the religious idea in the eighties when it launched *The Rock Gospel Show* (1984–7), in which former missionary Sheila Walsh and her later co-host Alvin Stardust introduced acts such as Amy Grant, Cliff Richard, Paul Jones, Jimmy Ruffin, Mike & the Mechanics and Huey Lewis & the News, alongside gospel choirs and American gospel rock stars. Walsh also interviewed artists such as Kajagoogoo about their Christian beliefs.

⋆ ⋆ ⋆

Pop Gospel aside, Muriel Young remained active with regular music shows. In summer 1978, she produced *Breakers*, a showcase for up-and-coming artists, who were given a whole programme to prove their worth. Radio Luxembourg's Rob Jones introduced Child, Jim & Ady, Rosetta Stone, Alfalpha, the Pleasers and Linda Fletcher. Fletcher – who had been discovered on the talent show *New Faces* – was then involved in a more successful programme for Young called *Get It Together* (1977–81), hosting with former Basil Brush straight man Roy North. The pair contributed songs of their own, and there were music quizzes. *Get It Together* attracted many significant performers as the decade drew to a close and the eighties arrived, including Shakin' Stevens, Darts, Abba, the Boomtown Rats, ELO, the Pretenders, Squeeze, Elvis Costello and U2. Mike Moran was the musical director, the TSDs provided the dance and puppet Ollie Beak made a return in the last two series, for which former *Pop Quest* presenter Megg Nicol replaced Fletcher.

Over at the BBC, pop was turned into a game show, courtesy of *Cheggers Plays Pop* (1978–86). The effervescent Keith Chegwin had come to fame as the roving reporter on *Multi-Coloured Swap Shop* (1976–82), which itself offered a sprinkling of pop artists each Saturday morning, usually being interviewed down the phone by viewers. Music was not its *raison d'être* but it definitely had a light pop flavour, although this was not as strong as in its anarchic ITV rival, *Tiswas* (1974–82). *Cheggers Plays Pop* built on that by presenting a number of fast-moving quizzes and *It's A Knockout*-style games themed around music. Two teams – the Reds and the Yellows – representing schools, Scout troops or youth clubs, competed each week. In and around the fun, guest artists did their thing, among them Dexy's Midnight Runners, Bad Manners, Martha & the Muffins, Duran Duran, Bananarama, ABC and Spandau Ballet. *Top Of The Pops* founder Johnnie Stewart directed the early shows.*

While the BBC was turning pop into slapstick, somewhat unusually ITV adopted a more elevated tone through the programme *Fanfare* (1977–8). This saw members of Flintlock, Thames Television's favourite pop band, learning about other types of music from studio guests.† These included a boy chorister, an African drum specialist, a concert pianist and a Spanish guitarist, with the likes of Nigel Kennedy, James Galway, George Melly and Julian Lloyd-Webber also explaining their art. *Fanfare* ran for two series – the band Rosetta Stone replacing Flintlock on a couple of occasions – and then developed into *Fanfare For Young Musicians* (1978–82), an annual musical competition for talented children under the age of 13, where the emphasis was rarely on pop.

★ ★ ★

The "fun" aspect of pop/rock was extended to grown-ups when Ray Davies of the Kinks starred in a mini rock opera called *Starmaker* (1974). Made by Granada, this aired as part of a series of plays entitled *Late Night Drama* and gave Davies the opportunity to build on an earlier TV appearance. In 1970, he had taken the lead role in a BBC *Play For Today* called *The Long-Distance Piano Player*, written by Alan Sharp, starring as a musician attempting to break a world piano-playing record in a municipal hall in the north of England. Davies contributed two new

---

* Lorne Alastair Stewart, better known as Johnnie, was so closely associated with *Top Of The Pops* that he even had his own image – a silhouette of a man on a stool with a jacket slung over his shoulder – superimposed at the end of many editions. He died, aged 87, in 2005.[17]

† Flintlock appeared in many Thames shows at the time. The teenage line-up included drummer Mike Holoway, who was given a major role in the sci-fi series *The Tomorrow People*, and singer/saxophonist Derek Pascoe, whose daughter is stand-up comedian Sara Pascoe.

songs for that play but his involvement in *Starmaker* was total, writing the script and the whole score.

The 35-minute fantasy focused on an arrogant, vain rock star who assumes the life of one Norman Gray, a dull 36-year-old accountant, in order to gain inspiration for new songs. The star invades all aspects of Norman's mundane existence but eventually finds himself overtaken by it and the lives of the two men become confusingly blurred. Perhaps the star is actually no more than a figment of Norman's imagination. June Ritchie appeared as Norman's wife and a team of dancers, directed by Dougie Squires, provided support as the action meandered around the open studio with cameras and audience always in shot. The Kinks provided the backing music, which was later released on an album called *The Kinks Present A Soap Opera.*

The dramatisation of pop came to a head a couple of years later with the very successful *Rock Follies* (1976–7), written for Thames Television by American writer Howard Schuman. The story of a girl vocal trio known as the Little Ladies, the series starred Rula Lenska, Charlotte Cornwell and Julie Covington in the roles of Q, Anna and Dee, watching their rise through the industry in the hands of dodgy manager Derek Huggin, played by Emlyn Price. Exploitation – financial and sexual – lurks around every corner as the girls struggle to achieve credibility and battle their way to the top. The grim realities of trying to make a name in a music business dominated by men are contrasted by optimistic, Broadway-inspired fantasy sequences. With this adventurous package, *Rock Follies* won a BAFTA award for Best Drama Series, ahead of such programmes as *I, Claudius*, *The Duchess Of Duke Street*, *When The Boat Comes In* and *The Glittering Prizes*. For the second series, entitled *Rock Follies Of '77*, Sue Jones-Davies joined as fourth group member Rox, as the group gains a new pushy American agent named Kitty Schreiber, played by Beth Porter. Andy Mackay of Roxy Music was responsible for the series' music content, with an album of music from the show, re-recorded in stereo, going straight into the chart at number one in 1976. The following year a single called 'OK?', also reached the chart.

Another band fabricated for television was the mighty Rutles. First glimpsed as part of the BBC2 comedy series *Rutland Weekend Television*

(1975–6) – a collection of programme parodies put together by Eric Idle, Neil Innes and others, masquerading as "Britain's smallest television network" – the "Pre-fab Four" burst out into their own TV movie entitled *The Rutles In All You Need Is Cash* (1978). In this, Idle and Innes play Dirk McQuickly and Ron Nasty, two members of a world-conquering, Beatle-esque group completed by Ricky Fataar as Stig O'Hara and John Halsey as Barry Wom. Held together by uncannily authentic tunes composed by Innes – 'Hold My Hand', 'Get Up And Go', 'Ouch!' and more – the programme looks at the career of the legendary group, inter-cutting spoof interviews with the likes of Mick Jagger and Paul Simon with scenes of the lads in action at the height of Rutlemania. George Harrison lent his support to the project by playing an interviewer and a single release, 'I Must Be In Love', was a minor UK hit. "Any resemblance to another famous pop group success story," said *Radio Times*, "is of course entirely intentional."

★ ★ ★

Having been responsible to a large degree for the intellectualisation of popular music on television during the sixties, Tony Palmer still had more to say and in the seventies his major contribution was an exhaustive history of the whole subject. As with the film *All My Loving*, the inspiration came from John Lennon, whom Palmer bumped into, just by chance, on a Manhattan street in autumn 1972.

Over lunch, the ever-demanding Lennon asked if he was "doing anything useful" as the conversation drifted on to the epic documentary series that were all the rage at the time, such as Kenneth Clark's *Civilisation* and Alastair Cooke's *America*. Didn't Palmer think that the history of popular music was worthy of similar treatment? In terms of the social and cultural development, Lennon certainly thought so, and he promptly started drawing up a list of topics to be covered. "Blues: what's that? Ragtime: what's that? Swing: what's that? I think we wrote down about 20 names and I whittled it down to 16," Palmer recalls. "Then he had to go. He got to the door of the café, turned round and said: 'I've got the perfect title for you. Call it *All You Need Is Love*.'"

So began the first major television insight into the origins of popular music, one that attempted to look beyond the commerciality of the business to champion the people whose artistry fed the voracious and cynical industry. By Palmer's own admission, there was a socialistic slant to the project, fostered by the experience of meeting people of real talent who felt their art form was being bastardised and betrayed. He believed it was time to understand where this music had come from and what these people were trying to say.

With the support of his old boss Paul Fox, then at Yorkshire Television, Palmer, who had by now left the BBC, sweet-talked ITV into commissioning the programme. Sixteen episodes were planned, one for each of the names on that Lennon-inspired list. It was a monumental undertaking and, faced with a mountain of research, Palmer enlisted some help. He contacted acknowledged specialists in every field – among them George Melly, Stephen Sondheim, Humphrey Lyttelton, Jack Good and rock journalist Charlie Gillett – and asked them, for a fee, to write a 2,000-word essay to explain what jazz, country, the musical – whatever – meant to them. These essays then provided a loose basis for each episode, with a "script" credit to acknowledge the essay provider, although they were not actually scripts in the accepted sense. The essays also worked as a basis for an accompanying book.

The next step was to track down people that needed to be filmed, people whose own words could relate the story of each musical style. Palmer took to the road and, over five months, in around 40 countries, assisted by researcher Annunziata Asquith*, filled reel after reel of film with interviews and performances courtesy of some of the most important names in music history – Dizzy Gillespie, Ray Charles, Hoagy Carmichael, Richard Rodgers, Bing Crosby, Cab Calloway, Artie Shaw, B.B. King, Pete Seeger and virtually everyone – Presley aside – who mattered from rock'n'roll onwards. Some were harder to track down than others. Jerry Lee Lewis was discovered playing piano in the lobby of a Holiday Inn and Muddy Waters entertaining a pitifully small audience in a Chicago blues club. But the effort paid off.

---

* Great-granddaughter of Prime Minister Herbert Asquith.

All You Need Is Love (1977) is a remarkable catalogue of the great and the good of twentieth-century music, one that astonishes even the director in retrospect. "I occasionally look at bits of it for one reason or another and I can't believe that I met these people," Palmer says. It was perhaps even more amazing that they all agreed to get involved, given the project's low budget. Palmer has Paul McCartney to thank for that. Hearing his financial predicament, McCartney told him: "This is what you do. Whatever fee I agree with you, you tell everybody that this is what I've agreed and everybody has to have the same. How about that?" The agreed fee was $500. "So we paid everybody $500," says Palmer. "Whoever it was, they got exactly the same."

It's not just the people that make *All You Need Is Love* such a valid historical document. It's the places, too, the music venues where it all happened. Many are now long gone so, in a sense, the series offers a final look at this lost heritage. While much of the film is original, Palmer and Asquith also managed to unearth rare existing footage and obtain material secreted away in private collections. It was thought, for example, that no film existed of Arlo Guthrie, but the series found some.

The first episode begins in Africa with tribesmen beating drums and explores how this music was transported to America where it blended with white musical traditions. Subsequent episodes tell the story of ragtime, jazz, blues, vaudeville, Tin Pan Alley, the musical, swing, rhythm & blues, country, protest, rock'n'roll, the Beatles, "sour rock" (Rolling Stones, Hendrix, Zappa, etc.), "glitter rock" (seventies glam) and finally "new directions" (from Tangerine Dream to Electric Light Orchestra).

When the series came to air, these 16 chapters were preceded by an introductory episode that spelled out what viewers could expect in the coming weeks. As an idea, this was a late addition and a clever one, because it encouraged people to watch the whole work and not just dip in and out when their favoured genre was featured, or even perhaps to give up on the series if the first few episodes failed to inspire. Palmer also wanted to add one further episode but was thwarted by his financial backers, who were headed by one of the old-time theatrical impresarios.

"By the time we were editing, punk had started," he explains. "I went back to Bernie Delfont, who was the head of EMI entertainment, which was one of the principal financial supporters, and begged him for more money to do another episode about the punk explosion. Of course, thinking about it, Bernie Delfont and punk? I don't think so. The whole 17 hours cost less than a million quid – not considerably less: it was just over £900,000, I think – and Bernie said: 'You've had enough money, thank you'. By the time the thing was shown on television, punk was everywhere. It was the next thing that was happening and I should have filmed it but I didn't."[18]

★ ★ ★

Tony Palmer intended *All You Need Is Love* to be his last major input into the filmed appreciation of popular music. "That was my attempt to put a line in the sand," he says. "There were other people who were doing it much better, with much better equipment and more resources at their disposal." It was time to move back to other arts subjects but not before he was persuaded by Granada to contribute a music-related film to the company's *This England* series of documentaries. The subject was to be the strange success of Wigan's Casino nightclub, the home of so-called northern soul. Hundreds of young people would congregate here on Saturdays for an all-night event, kicking off at 12.30 a.m. There was no alcohol on sale; the kids just came for the music. It was their form of escapism in an industrial town that had sunk into grave decline.

When Palmer first approached the youth committee that ran the event, he found himself viewed with suspicion. "When I turned up, they were being hounded by the police who were determined to find drugs and all kinds of iniquities going on," he recalls. "And they thought, Granada Television, from Manchester, was going to do an exposé." That was just one problem the director faced. Another was technical. How could the gloomy dance hall be filmed without using lights that would kill the whole atmosphere and probably send dancers scuttling for the shadows. In the end, with the kids on his side, Palmer was able to film using just one camera and one light.

In the documentary, the soul music is secondary, or even further down the pecking order. The real story is the role the club plays in the lives of local people – and many from further afield – who have little to look forward to elsewhere. Gritty shots of Wigan's past and present industrial landscape, with sobering background folk music, provide a contrast to the exuberance of club nights and there are interviews with local people young and old who reveal all about the town's industrial and social decline. "The story was: here's a place that had been an industrial centre. All the cotton mills had closed, huge unemployment, the town was derelict," Palmer says. Local youths needed a distraction. "The one moment in their life was the all-nighter up the road at the Casino."

After transmission, *Wigan Casino* (1977) lay forgotten in the vaults at Granada for more than 30 years until Palmer restored it for DVD release. In 2009, it received a well-attended ceremonial screening in Wigan, a town by this time somewhat rejuvenated. "We projected it onto the wall, which is now in a supermarket where the Wigan Casino had been," the director says. "It was packed."[19]

* * *

With Bob Harris installed as presenter, *The Old Grey Whistle Test* continued to build a following through the early seventies. The format was simple, a couple of bands or artists would perform each week, there'd be a bit of industry and gig news and Bob would chat with an interview guest. Films of bands in concert were thrown into the mix and there was also a clever way of illustrating tracks for which no bands or footage were available: vintage film shorts – usually bearing little thematic resemblance to the music – were dusted off and cut to the sound.

The man responsible for melding together old film and fresh music was Philip Jenkinson, whom Mike Appleton had worked with on *Late Night Line-Up*. The archive of old footage and the synchronising skills he brought to the idea made this feature of the programme an attraction in its own right and there were some inspired creations. The marriage of Mike Oldfield's 'Tubular Bells' with a monochrome skiing film directed by Leni Riefenstahl, the famous director of Nazi rally films, lingers in Appleton's memory, as does the Paris cabaret dance sequences used to illustrate Led Zeppelin's 'Trampled Underfoot'. "We found that there were lots of art students that were watching, not for the music but for the film clips," he says. "In a funny sort of way, I think we almost started videos".

These films fed into a *Whistle Test* show that was always presented live. Because of the limitations of the studio, one of the bands was usually pre-recorded earlier in the day, but the rest of the show went out as it happened late at night. "To a certain extent, it wasn't too difficult because you were following a pattern – unless something special happened," says Appleton. Such an occasion came when Bob had flown to New York to interview John Lennon. Lennon enjoyed the experience so much that he offered to film some new tracks for the show. It was such a big event that Appleton booked only one band for that edition but the clock ticked on and the Lennon film still hadn't arrived. It would have been embarrassing to say the least if the film had not arrived or was simply not good enough. It eventually turned up only a matter of hours before the show was due to go out. "It was almost the first time we'd seen it when it went on air," he says. "It was a close thing. But if John Lennon's doing something, you know there will be something in it that makes it worthwhile."

Once the success of the show had led to a move downstairs to one of Television Centre's larger studios, the pre-record and backing-track days were mostly over. The show became an essential appointment-to-view programme on a Tuesday night, a mellow, respectful wallow in the top musicianship of the era, enhanced by measured introductions from the laid-back Harris, who soon gained the nickname "Whispering Bob". Singer-songwriters fared very well, with names such as Jackson Browne, Elton John, Judee Sill, John Martyn, Bonnie Raitt, Tom Waits and Tim Buckley all enjoying valuable *Whistle Test* exposure. They also benefited from the strangely sterile studio atmosphere, where there was no audience to cause a stir.

Bands on the other hand often preferred to have the edge that only an audience could provide, but nevertheless there were many who did themselves justice and made a name for themselves on the show – the Edgar Winter Group, Little Feat, Dr Feelgood, Lynyrd Skynyrd, Focus and Bob Marley & the Wailers just some of those that caught the eye in the early seventies.

In its time, the show introduced many new or seldom-seen bands to a British audience, although one important television debut very nearly didn't happen. This followed the arrival of a mysterious, unidentified album in the *Whistle Test* office.

"There's a thing called a white label, which is a very early pressing put out for promotional reasons," Appleton explains. "We had one arrive one lunchtime but whoever brought it in hadn't put any indication on it what record company it was from or who it was." Appleton played the record and was impressed. He decided to include one track from it in the show and sent it to Philip Jenkinson to match up with a film. Jenkinson cut to it an old cartoon that had been made for one of Roosevelt's American election campaigns and featured the president's head as the front of a train. The film went out with the admission that the team didn't have the foggiest idea of the identity of the performers and with a request that someone please let them know. "The next day EMI were in touch with us straight away," he says. The track was 'Keep Yourself Alive', the first single by Queen.

On a later occasion, Appleton discovered a new star while attending a music publishers' festival in the south of France. "There was a crowd round one of the stands so I pushed my way to the front and there was this amazing video with this large gentleman singing and riding motorbikes." It was Meat Loaf. "I don't think anybody, apart from the people who were associated with him, knew anything about him. I said: 'I've got to have a copy of that.' We slotted it in the programme and all hell broke loose."[20]

Most of the artists selected for *Whistle Test* were mutually appreciated by Appleton and Harris, although occasionally something would jar, as was evident when Bob introduced a new band called Roxy Music with less than his customary enthusiasm. "I'd seen them about three weeks earlier," he explains. "They did the *Radio 1 In Concert* at the Paris Theatre, which I'd introduced, and I'd spent some time in the control room with them. At the time, they were so arrogant. It was outrageous how arrogant they were. This was even before the release of 'Virginia Plain'. I took an aversion to them, which I then took onto the screen with me". A similar fury erupted when the New York Dolls played in the studio. A clearly unimpressed Harris back-announced the track, describing it as "mock rock". "I was sarcastic about it and sarcasm is never particularly attractive but what I was saying, actually, I still hold to, because they were mock rock. They were the Stones translated 10 years into a new generation. David Johansen was Mick Jagger. People were so outraged that I'd made these comments about them."[21]

Bob also encountered some difficulties with interviews. Most guests were well behaved and in good form, but there were a few that caused stress levels to rise. "We had Van Morrison in," remembers Appleton, calling up one notorious example. "He wouldn't say anything so we had to quickly start talking to his bass player." Harris has similar memories. "There was just a fabulous moment with Lou Reed, who appeared in the doorway of the studio with two massive great minders, one on either side of him." These guys were not there for protection: they were there for physical support. "I noticed that Lou's feet were dragging along. They sort of arranged him in the seat and there he was sitting next to me, basically kind of nodding off. It looked to me like his left eye was shut completely and I really did think he'd fallen asleep. It was like somebody had put a key into his back and then started winding because he just came to life in front of me. It was so funny."[22]

The series also ventured out of the studio, in a couple of ways. Firstly, an annual summer excursion to the US was instigated as an answer to the perennial question of how to get American bands on the show when they weren't touring the UK. The films that were made were then played into the subsequent series. Secondly, the show began to cover live concerts. This introduced the possibility of simultaneous radio and television broadcasts, allowing viewers to turn down their televisions, with their limited mono speakers, and turn up their FM hi-fis to get the sound in stereo.

The first experiment along these lines was a recording of a Van Morrison concert made in July 1973, which went out simultaneously on *The Old Grey Whistle Test* and Bob Harris's Monday night Radio 1 programme in May 1974. By the end of the year Appleton and his team were emboldened enough to stage their own Christmas Eve concert in conjunction with Radio 1, something that became a minor tradition. First up was Elton John live from the Hammersmith Odeon. The following year it was Queen at the same venue, with Rod Stewart at London's Olympia in 1976 and the Kinks at the Rainbow in 1977. In a slight deviation, the 10cc concert at Wembley Conference Centre in 1978 had been pre-recorded earlier in the week, while 1979's concert, while live, was shunted to New Year's Eve, with Blondie performing at the Apollo, Glasgow.

Mike Appleton says he developed the live Christmas concerts "to show a bit of solidarity with our viewers". Nearly all BBC programmes at Christmas were pre-recorded and edited. "There weren't going to be any surprises,' he says. "So I thought: Right. We will make an effort and do a live programme each Christmas Eve. That's our contribution. We can then go away and get pissed or whatever. That will be live and it will have an atmosphere."

While the simultaneous broadcast – "simulcast" – seems obvious in hindsight, it was not an easy concept to bring to fruition. For a start, BBC Radio and BBC Television operated independently and, while Radio 1 might be championing the same sort of music as *Whistle Test* (at least for part of the day), there was little communication between the two. There was also a technological vacuum that needed to be filled. It wasn't possible to easily edit the video and keep it synchronised with the stereo audio track, or vice versa. "If you could just start at the beginning and go all the way through, it was a piece of cake – just take the tape and the video tape, put them on the machine in sync and off they'd go," explains Appleton. "But, if you had to edit it, it became really, really complicated and sometimes you had to go back to the beginning and start again." When the idea was rolled out into the series called *Sight And Sound In Concert*, there were times when an insurmountable problem occurred during recording and the concert had to be restarted.* [23]

Such technical glitches aside, by the mid-seventies everything at *Whistle Test* was going swimmingly. Bob was well entrenched, whispering his introductions and rocking in his chair to the live sounds in the new, bigger studio. The show was a must-see for all serious music fans – the one show that really took album music seriously. But trouble lay just around the corner and it all kicked off at the end of 1976.

* * *

Major changes took place at ITV in 1968. Some of the well-established regional companies had lost their franchises to broadcast on the channel, two of which being London's service providers, Rediffusion and ATV. ATV was allowed to continue its work in the Midlands, indeed was given the whole week to fill rather than just weekdays, but Rediffusion was told by the ITV regulator, the ITA, to merge with ABC, which had previously broadcast to the Midlands and the North at weekends, in order to create a new contractor for London's weekdays (with a new company, London Weekend Television, awarded the weekends). The newly amalgamated company was christened Thames Television and took to the air on July 30, 1968, launching on the same day a new early-evening current affairs magazine called *Today*. *Today* remained a fixture in the Thames schedules for nearly nine years but its name meant nothing to viewers outside the capital until one day towards the end of its time on air.

On December 1, 1976, the programme was due to feature an appearance by Queen. When the band pulled out at the last minute, a replacement needed to be found and a 90-second interview was awarded instead to a new band called the Sex Pistols who had been causing a bit

---

* "For the best effect viewers with Stereo Radio 1 should turn off TV sound and position their speakers on either side of the screen, but a few feet away. Stereo headphones provide a suitable alternative." – *Radio Times* advice for viewers of *Sight And Sound In Concert*.

of a stir. The band had appeared on television a few times already, so perhaps the Thames researchers felt comfortable about booking them onto the show but it was a confidence that proved to be sadly misplaced. Members of the band and a few hangers on made their way into the studio for the live broadcast, where interviewer Bill Grundy was ready to ask the questions. Regrettably for Grundy, and luckily for the Pistols, it all went horribly wrong. Affronted by their aggressive swagger, and seemingly by the fact that they'd just received a £30,000 advance from a record company, Grundy was not a sympathetic host. When Johnny Rotten uttered a mild expletive, he attempted to humiliate the singer by asking him to repeat it. He then challenged the lads to "say something outrageous", prompting a couple of F words from Steve Jones. "I hope I'm not seeing you again," Grundy quipped as he signed off.

As TV interviews go, it was brief but explosive. The station switchboard lit up as viewers jammed it with complaints. One claimed to have been so incensed that he had kicked in the screen of his new set. Thames broadcast an apology later that evening and Grundy was suspended for two weeks, but the reputation of the Pistols had been cemented. Initially, their manager Malcolm McLaren was distraught, believing all the work he had put into shaping the band had just been thrown away and, when a number of venues for their up-coming concert tour pulled out, it seemed he had good reason to feel let down. But the publicity that followed was sensational. From that moment, the Sex Pistols and punk rock in general were hardly out of the newspapers. A movement that had been building slowly all year suddenly exploded. Within a couple of weeks the Pistols' first hit, 'Anarchy In The UK', had broken into the charts and by summer of 1977 punk had gone mainstream – with serious repercussions for the coverage of music on television.[24]

* * *

The Sex Pistols' appearance on *Today* may have been the slap across the face that rudely alerted the wider British nation to punk rock, but the new movement had already begun to seep into the consciousness of music followers, thanks to a more welcoming television outlet. The first programme to see the way the wind was blowing was *So It Goes* (1976–7).

In 1975, Granada asked a 25-year-old journalist by the name of Tony Wilson, a reporter on its evening magazine *Granada Reports*, to put together an idea for a new music programme. Wilson didn't have the confidence in the quality of the music around at the time to make it a straight musical offering so he brought in Clive James to add some wry monologues and fiddled around with bits of cartoon, odd video clips and some adult puppetry. If the music didn't really stand up, Wilson felt, then let's have a bit of a laugh with it. By the time of the second series, a year later, punk was in its prime. James was no longer required as there was much more for *So It Goes* to get its teeth into.[25]

That first series featured such artists as Thin Lizzy, the Chieftains, Tom Waits, Graham Parker & the Rumour and Kiss, but the significant booking, in the final programme of the series, was the Sex Pistols, who made their television debut performing 'Anarchy In The UK'. Next time around, punk/new wave was all over the show and the Buzzcocks, Elvis Costello, Ian Dury, Iggy Pop, the Jam, the Stranglers, Magazine and the Clash all featured. Wilson hosted the show from a swivel chair in front of a bank of television monitors, his velvet voice brimming with an enthusiasm for the spiky new music that was somewhat out of place with his trendy college-lecturer fashions – all leather jacket, denim shirts and flares. The first series was seen late on a Saturday night in Granadaland and a few other ITV regions, with London catching up a day later. For the second series, the pattern was reversed. London went for Saturday with Granada and others switching to Sunday, but neither series was fully networked. Even fewer viewers caught the spin-off series, *So It Goes Concert*, that Granada broadcast only to its own region in spring 1977, but punk fans would not have been interested in a line-up that offered the likes of Andy Fairweather Low, Sad Café and Asleep At The Wheel.

So It Goes' time on air may have been limited, but it stands out in broadcasting history as new wave's first champion, and Tony Wilson's work wasn't over. Factory Records – the label that brought us Joy Division, New Order and the Happy Mondays – was a later project, and then there was the club he opened, the Hacienda, helping to reinvent "Madchester" as a vibrant music hub while continuing his work as a serious broadcaster.*

★ ★ ★

The natural successor to *So It Goes* came from ATV. At the time, the Midlands ITV company was responsible for the talent show *New Faces*, employing as one of its judges the record producer Mickie Most, who now worked with them to develop *Revolver* (1978). For Most, music on television was a problem waiting to be solved. He felt that putting rock bands into a TV studio was an alien concept. "The music becomes flabby – half the time it's faked anyway – because it has to compromise with the pictures," he said. In this new series, the cameras that usually inhibited the talent would be incidental.

To achieve this effect, Most devised a fictional setting for the show – a rundown ballroom in the Midlands that had lost its traditional revenue streams and had turned to rock music as a way of staying afloat: it was either that or bingo. He even created a bow-tied ballroom manager, played by comedian Peter Cook, to curmudgeonly and confrontationally introduce the acts. Rather than intrude upon the stage, Cook appeared from the manager's office via a large video screen, looking down on the audience in more than one sense. He was helped on the ballroom floor by his "assistant manager", Birmingham DJ Les Ross, who offered news and gems of rock'n'roll trivia as he flipped some burgers. To gee the audience up, DJ Chris Hill was involved as a professional heckler.

In retrospect, *Revolver* sounds rather too much like a rock version of Granada's *Wheeltappers' And Shunters' Social Club* variety show, but it was thankfully redeemed by the excitement of the acts, which included the Lurkers, the Stranglers, the Vibrators, Ian Dury & the Blockheads, the Buzzcocks, the Rezillos, Nick Lowe, Elvis Costello, X-Ray Specs

* Celebrated in the film *24 Hour Party People*, with Steve Coogan as the man himself, Tony Wilson – a divisive figure known for his enormous ego as much as his musical and other achievements – died in 2007.

and the Only Ones, many of whom were just breaking through. "We're not playing safe by going for established names," declared Most. "We're going for bands who are about to make it."[26]

To ensure that the show crackled right from the off, each edition opened with an act in full throttle, playing out the final seconds of a number, with the audience – who had been specially selected and invited after a trawl of Midlands clubs – already bouncing and vocal. Split-screen technology was then used throughout the performances to keep things lively and interesting for viewers at home.

At the launch of the series, the *TV Times* felt the need to explain the concept of new wave to its readership, with features on the bands, the fashions and the dances likely to be seen on the show. In reality, the music was actually a bit more wide-ranging than some viewers probably wanted, with the likes of Darts, Bonnie Tyler and Suzi Quatro also featured, along with up-and-coming acts such as Dire Straits, Whitesnake and the Tourists. And it wasn't all new either, with a weekly "Reviver Spot" offering archive footage of such greats as the Stones, the Animals, the Kinks, Julie Driscoll and Otis Redding.

Although piloted in an early-evening slot, the 45-minute series, which, like *So It Goes*, suffered from not being fully networked, ended up confined to late Saturday night, ideally timed for pub leavers perhaps but clearly not attractive enough for most viewers because just one series was produced.

Around this time, fans of the new music could also tune in to a ground-breaking series on BBC2. *Something Else* (1978–82), as its name suggests, was an attempt to do things differently. Rather than the BBC just making a programme for young people, young people were allowed to make it themselves, with the help of the BBC's Community Programme Unit.

Something Else was a wide-ranging, early-evening magazine/ discussion show for the under-20s that laid the foundations for later youth programming. It was broadcast from a different location around the UK each time (initially monthly, later weekly) and covered issues of interest and relevance to its audience – anything from single parenthood, Rastafarianism and glue-sniffing to alcoholism, video games and arranged marriages. The music input came from the Jam, the Specials, Siouxsie & the Banshees, the Undertones, the Skids, the Revillos, Secret Affair, Stiff Little Fingers and others, with usually a couple of acts featuring in every show. The political message of new wave was evident in the very first programme, which saw the Clash give a rare television interview. One programme in 1981 was made by Paul Weller and some friends.

★ ★ ★

Other programmes may have welcomed punk/new wave with open arms but it was a different story at *The Old Grey Whistle Test.* As bands like the Pistols, the Clash, the Damned and the Jam began to attract huge followings, they remained notably absent from the BBC2 show, which sailed serenely onwards, still wedded to Nils Lofgren, Dr Hook, Joan Armatrading and the like. But the fact that the nation's number one music programme seemed to be ignoring what was happening in the clubs and increasingly in the charts did not go unnoticed. Followers of the new music were incensed and their outcry grew louder and louder until it exploded in a brutal act of violence against the host of the programme.

"There was a resentment that began to build up towards us and it surfaced in this specific hostility from the punk movement towards myself, which even to this day I can kind of understand," explains Bob Harris. "You know: 30-year-old hippie, long-haired, white, middle-class, BBC, stadium-rock-loving – how many boxes do you want me to tick? But the hostility was just outrageous and came right at me, particularly the famous night at The Speakeasy with the Sex Pistols."

This was an occasion in March 1977 when Bob and his friend George Nicholson called into the West End club for a nightcap after a day in the recording studio. It was an unfortunate move as the Sex Pistols and their entourage were in the building, celebrating their new record deal with A&M. Trouble kicked off when one of the hangers on challenged Bob, demanding to know when they would be on *Whistle Test.* A brawl broke out and Bob found himself in an ugly situation, cornered by punks clutching broken glass. Only the intervention of the Procol

Harum road crew and some other guys saved him from grievous injury but George Nicholson was not so lucky, being glassed in the head and requiring 14 stitches.

Understandably shaken, Bob was left questioning his position. "There was a huge hostility from nowhere towards the programme," he says. "Journalists, who, literally, six months before had been writing how absolutely amazing we were, had suddenly become so hostile towards us. And yet we hadn't done anything wrong. It was not like the programme had put up a barrier."

All *Whistle Test* had done was to follow its own rules. While punk may not have particularly appealed to Harris and producer Mike Appleton, it was not a matter of taste that led to its exclusion. It was simply because *Whistle Test* was an album show and punk bands, to that point, had not issued any albums.

"It was the specific condition of the programme existing that *Top Of The Pops* was the singles show and *Whistle Test* was the album show," says Harris. "That was the rule. Of course, punk and new wave happened completely via singles and independent labels. I was the first person on radio to play Dr Feelgood. I'd seen them at the Hope & Anchor. I thought: 'This new burst of energy is just what we need.' Things really had got overblown. We all knew that. Massive stadium concerts; bands out-dry icing each other. It just got so indulgent. Punk and new wave came along to remind us that, actually, the way that rock'n'roll was always recorded was floor to tape – Elvis, 'Heartbreak Hotel', bam, three minutes you've captured the energy, that's it. We, all of us, endorsed that idea totally. Where it turned round on us, but me in particular, was the fact that clearly the programme was not reflecting this new movement, because, until they arrived on album, we couldn't."[27]

"It was fairly alien, but it also didn't fit into the format," confirms Appleton. "I wasn't going to discard albums. If I'd had a bigger unit then I would have probably done a singles programme or a programme that concentrated weekly on punk music but I wasn't going to sacrifice *Whistle Test* and the people who appeared on it to the great god Punk. As soon as they started bringing albums out, we had them on. But they had to have gone – as all the other bands before had gone – to that level."[28]

That condition was met in February 1978, when the Adverts became the first British punk band to appear on the show, 18 months after the Sex Pistols had been seen on *So It Goes*. The frustration long felt by the punk movement was vocalised rather drily at the time by TV Smith, the Adverts' lead singer, when he opened the set declaring: "At last the 1978 show" (a pun on a comedy series from the sixties called *At Last The 1948 Show*). After that, new wave bands raced through the doors – XTC, Radio Stars, the Jam, the Only Ones, Magazine, Siouxsie & the Banshees. *Whistle Test* may have been anathema to many in the new wave movement but plenty of its exponents were happy to be on the show.

A similar problem arose with a *Whistle Test* spin-off series called *Rock Goes To College* (1978–81) that Mike Appleton created to solve a log jam at the BBC. He had been granted a budget for some *Whistle Test* "in concert" shows but he wasn't allocated a venue in which to record them and didn't have the money to pay for one. Inspiration came from his jazz-loving days. He recalled an album by Dave Brubeck called *Jazz Goes To College* and that set his mind in motion. If there were a *Rock Goes To College*, the concerts could be staged at universities and colleges, which would provide the facilities and audience in return for a free gig. The first band in the frame were the Boomtown Rats, recorded at Middlesex Polytechnic, and there followed a mixed bag of talent from the Climax Blues Band (City of Birmingham Poly), AC/DC (Essex University) and the Cars (University of Sussex) to Rory Gallagher (Middlesex Poly), Police (Hatfield Poly) and Tom Petty (Oxford Poly).

The politics of punk raised its head this time around when the Stranglers were booked to play the University of Surrey, in their adopted home town of Guildford. After a few numbers, the band began to abuse the student audience. "You lot are the most boring people I've ever seen in my fucking life," ranted Hugh Cornwell. "Have you all got your *Crackerjack* pencils? Stick them up your arses then!" After declaring "we hate playing to elitist audiences", the group stormed off, leaving compere Pete Drummond embarrassed and floundering. Amid scenes of chaos, he promised: "Next time we come, we'll bring a professional band."

The Stranglers claimed to be upset that people from the town hadn't been allowed into the gig. "It was all set up," recalls a sceptical Appleton. The band argues otherwise, stating that the venue and the BBC had agreed to allow wider access than the student base but then reneged, going so far as to throw out a number of fans that the band tried to smuggle in. Whatever the facts, the Stranglers made the national papers and the BBC was left without a show for transmission the following week so hasty arrangements were made to double up at the next engagement, which was scheduled to feature Rich Kids at the University of Reading. Consequently, students there were treated to two free concerts in one evening, with John Martyn brought in to record an early show and Rich Kids playing later. The Martyn show then went out in place of the Stranglers' gig.[29]

For Bob Harris, this was a troubled time. The punk experience had diminished his enthusiasm for presenting music on television. "From then on, it was much more difficult to be objective about this new music and each individual band," he says. "And one of the things that I most resented was the fact that, by this hostility coming at me, it was now beginning to prevent me from doing what I most loved to do and that was go to venues and watch bands. So life just got very much more difficult all of a sudden."

Reluctantly, Bob decided to leave *Whistle Test* and a replacement was found in Radio 1's Anne Nightingale – another journalist-broadcaster in Mike Appleton's desired mould. "I just thought everything needs freshening up," Bob explains. "The thing is, when you're presenting the one music programme on TV – there were others that came and went but basically *Whistle Test* was it – eventually everybody gets to see it and you become so recognised. In my autobiography, I refer to myself as having become the Ken Barlow of rock. I thought I'd become so stamped with this identity and yet it was only a part of a wider life. I felt it was important to get away from that kind of typecasting and just start to live my life with a bit more freedom again."

Harris's last show was the 1979 New Year's Eve concert given by Blondie in Glasgow. "I wanted to leave at the end of the series before but Mike persuaded me to stay on for one more series as a sort of cross-over between myself and Annie, but I didn't really enjoy that last series." Overall, though, Harris treasures his *Whistle Test* years. "As time goes on, you begin to look back a bit more objectively and I'm so proud of what the programme did and the legacy of the programme. To be right in the middle of it all was just such an incredible experience. I was very, very lucky."[30]

As Debbie Harry belted out her last note, an era in rock music came to an end. *Whistle Test* was still on air. It had finally embraced changing musical times but, without Bob, could it survive into the eighties? Britain's most revered music show faced an uncertain future in a decade that was to see music television explode into life with the launch of an exciting new series on a brand new channel.

THE EIGHTIES

It's 12 Noon In London

The 1980s saw the biggest shake-up in British broadcasting since the arrival of ITV in 1955. It was a decade of seismic change that saw the introduction of a new commercial channel, the start of breakfast television, the extension of daytime output and the expansion of cable networks, leading to the start of satellite broadcasting. Not surprisingly, the opportunities such outlets provided meant that music on television was about to undergo a radical overhaul, with new productions bursting onto the screen and the need for existing programmes to re-examine where they were coming from and, more importantly, where they were heading.

During the seventies, the future of broadcasting in the UK had come under intense scrutiny when the Government appointed a panel of worthies – politicians, businessmen, academics and broadcasters – under the guidance of Lord Annan, to analyse the status quo and to come up with proposals for the way forward. While Annan's substantial report, issued in 1977, was not adopted wholesale, some key elements were picked up, the most significant being the decision to create a new fourth television channel.

It was decided that the new channel would be regulated by the IBA, as the ITA had now become, and would operate on commercial lines.

It would not make its own programmes but buy in from outside providers. The money for this would come from the various ITV companies who would regionally sell the advertisements. A key part of the remit was to be innovative. In some respects, the new channel would act as ITV's version of BBC2. Channel 4 took to the air on November 2, 1982, preceded the day before by S4C, the new fourth-channel service for Wales that, while predominantly Welsh-language based, also screened many of Channel 4's English-language programmes, although not necessarily in peak hours.

The potential the new channel offered for small production companies was immediately grasped by the savvier members of that fraternity, and none were savvier than the folk at little Tyne Tees, the ITV service provider for the North-East. The company had branched out into music programming with *The Geordie Scene* in the seventies and had built on the relative success of that experiment by launching a more adventurous show called *Alright Now* (1979–80). The brains behind the new programme was former teacher Malcolm Gerrie, who had joined Tyne Tees as a trainee researcher after staging a nationally acclaimed school production of the Who's rock opera *Tommy*. His plans for *Alright Now* were ambitious: he wanted to address the new-music deficiency that existed on television and he hoped the show would be networked across the ITV regions. His superiors at Tyne Tees were less optimistic but gave him the chance to see if it could work.

"The problem that Tyne Tees had, which all of the regional ITV stations had, was basically there was a cartel within ITV," Gerrie recalls. "So the big companies *de facto* got their shows on the network. They had a lot of power and that meant more money, more revenue and obviously more people watching. Companies like Tyne Tees struggled to get any of their big entertainment shows on the ITV network." They were always the poor relation of the "Big Five", he says, referring to Thames, LWT, Granada, ATV and Yorkshire. "If you look at the history of music on Tyne Tees and a lot of the regional stations up until Channel 4 was invented, it's nearly always regional, it's nearly always late night and it's nearly always relatively short runs. So things like *The Geordie Scene* were never networked fully." This inevitably had a knock-on effect when it came to booking artists, as record companies would almost always favour the likes of *Ready, Steady, Go!* or *Top Of The Pops* over shows with less exposure. The smaller companies lost out on every front.

That last point, Tyne Tees believed, was the key to breaking out of this vicious circle. Gerrie was told by station head Andy Allan that, if he could get the right acts on the new show, he would fight for it to be given a networked slot. That was the deal.

Gerrie was given the green light and put together the first shows. While he was editing the recordings, a summons came from Andy Allan's office. It didn't sound promising. "I go up and he's writing away, didn't lift his head off his desk, and he said: 'Malcolm, you remember that conversation we had about *Alright Now*? You said you could deliver the talent and I would do my best to get this on the network? How do you expect me to book this show when you insist on booking no-account talent? I'm not even going to take that to the network committee meeting'." Gerrie looked at him in disbelief. The two acts Allan was referring to were the Police and Dire Straits. This was early 1979 and neither had yet made an impression on the world, despite Gerrie's confidence that they were destined to be big.

Alright Now never did secure its place on the network but it was seen in several ITV regions. The first series was hosted by Den Hegarty of Darts, aided and abetted by a group of local youngsters called the Krazy Koffee Bar Kidz, as the show combined music with youth access programming ideas. The outcome was successful enough for the show to be granted a second series, with this time guest hosts, including Billy Connolly and Mickie Most, replacing Hegarty. A smokier, more clubby atmosphere pervaded the new run.

"The reception we got was fabulous, both from the music industry and from the press, especially the second series. Everybody we wanted did the show," says Gerrie, reeling off names such as the Pretenders, the Jam, Thin Lizzy and Elvis Costello. But the band he really hoped for was the Clash, who famously didn't do much television, so he was stunned to take a call from Joe Strummer. "Joe rings me up and says: 'We watch your show. We love the fact that you won't allow anybody to mime. We love the fact that there's a live audience and we love the fact that you said you could play as long as you want. Tell us when you want us to do it and we'll be there.' And they were so good and so nice to deal with. We had more trouble from Lindisfarne!"

Tyne Tees had clearly done something right with *Alright Now* because the company's next foray into pop music did get a network screening, albeit during children's hour, this being a typical concession to the little guys from the big companies. The series was called *Razzmatazz* (1981–7) and it became one of the longest running music shows of the decade.

Unlike *Alright Now*, *Razzmatazz* was solid kids' fare, playing to a studio audience of around 300 noisy teenagers and packed with jokes, competitions and youth-related features that covered everything from American football to yo-yoing. There were regular games and tongue-twisting contests based around the character of Peggy Babcock, a lady pirate; you could learn all about disco dancing or take a music workshop with Stewart Copeland (drums) or Rick Wakeman (keyboards). Alastair Pirrie was the male host (subsequently also the show's editor), joined initially by Lyn Spencer, with later presenters including Suzanne Dando and a young Lisa Stansfield, as well as Zoe Brown, David Jensen and Annabel Giles. There were plenty of headline guests, too, from Adam Ant, Go West and Madness to Paul McCartney, the Police and Eddy Grant, some given whole editions to themselves.

Razzmatazz was a big success for Tyne Tees but it was hugely overshadowed by the music series that the company decided to produce next. The imminent arrival of Channel 4 was like a carrot dangling in front of Malcolm Gerrie and his boss, Andrea Wonfor. The promise made by Jeremy Isaacs, the new channel's chief executive, rang in their ears. All of the shows were going to be networked (there being no regional options), regardless of who made them or where they came from, and they would be properly funded. "This is an opportunity and a half', was the thinking at Tyne Tees and minds turned to new proposals. "We cooked up this thing called *Jamming*," says Gerrie. "I think it was eight half-hours. Basically, it was a version of *Alright Now* but with collaborations. Nobody was doing collaborations in those days." The idea was submitted and the team carried on with *Razzmatazz*, building up to a New Year's special at the start of 1982 that was due to feature Abba. Gerrie went to Sweden to make the show but his trip was unexpectedly and suddenly cut short.

"I'm in Stockholm, about to have dinner with Bjorn and Benny and all the guys before the big shoot, and I get a call in the bar," he remembers. The call is from Andrea with news from Channel 4. "I've just spoken to Jeremy Isaacs," she said. "It's bad news and good news. The bad news is they don't want *Jamming*. They're not interested in eight half-hours. What they do want is 20 one-hour-45-minute shows, starting on the Friday the channel goes to air, completely live. The budget is seven figures. You need to get your arse here for lunch tomorrow with Jeremy."

Cue panic at the Abba dinner table where "the schnapps and vodkas are going down like there's no tomorrow". The next day, a worse-for-wear Malcolm Gerrie staggered into the arranged meeting at an Italian restaurant in London, having spent the flight over working out what the show was going to be about. "I'm jet lagged, I'm hung over, I'm stressed. I haven't a clue what I'm going to talk about, apart from some headlines," he says. The tension builds when Jeremy Isaacs doesn't show. "He was due to meet us at one o'clock. Two o'clock: let's have the main course. Three o'clock: no Jeremy. We're literally on the coffees, thinking he's just forgotten, or he's changed his mind. Suddenly, the doors open and in comes Jeremy. He had this big greatcoat, mane of hair, his coat was flying around. He looked like Batman." Apologising profusely, Isaacs downed Gerrie's glass of wine and declared: "It's good news anyway, isn't it? We're going to make this show, Malcolm, and I trust you completely. Two things I want to say to you: it's got to be live and give it balls. Right. Got to go. Have fun." And that was it.

A week later, a West End theatre was the venue for the grand press launch of Channel 4. Having had more time to work on the format of the show, Gerrie was a key speaker but, before he could spell out the detail, the programme was already under fire when a journalist stood up and had a pop at Jeremy. "Why is this show coming from Newcastle? You'll never get the talent. Why isn't it coming from London's trendy

West End, where everything is happening and where you'll get the talent?" A riled Jeremy turned on the questioner. "The reason it's not coming from London's West End is precisely because of people like you and what you just said. I'm not interested in London's trendy West End. That's why it's coming from Newcastle." It was quite a put down, especially as the journalist was none other than Elkan Allan, the man who had helped create the idea of Swinging London when he devised *Ready, Steady, Go!* in the sixties. The world of music television had been turned on its head. From the time that Gerrie's new show, *The Tube*, took to the air in November 1982, Newcastle, not London, was the place to be.[1]

⋆ ⋆ ⋆

While preparations were underway for *The Tube*, there were significant changes taking place at the UK's longest-running music show. *Top Of The Pops* entered the decade with a new broom when Michael Hurll took over as executive producer in the middle of 1980. That was a year of considerable change for the programme, defined in the summer by a Musicians' Union strike that led to some cancelled editions after the BBC decided to scrap five of its 11 orchestras. By the time the dispute was finally resolved, Hurll had concluded that *Top Of The Pops*' own orchestra was no longer required. This may have presented problems given the Union's continuing miming ban but this stricture had gradually become looser. At a time when the rights of trade unions were coming under attack from the Thatcher government, this restrictive practice seems to have been quietly and conveniently forgotten about and had disappeared by the end of the decade.

Hurll also set about revamping the show in other ways. The audience was doubled in size and pushed around the back and the sides of performers, as well as in front, and dual presenters were introduced. Along with celebrity hosts that included Elton John, Kevin Keegan and Michael Palin, the DJ roster now included the names Steve Wright, Tommy Vance and Richard Skinner. In 1981, Hurll took things further, purging the audience of moping teenagers and installing professional cheerleaders and dancers to really raise the roof. There were acrobatics on the studio floor and even the odd fire-eater. Streamers, balloons, rara skirts, shoulder pads and big hair became the visual motifs. "There was a lot of energy in the studio and, as we rolled into the eighties, it became more and more like a New Year's Eve party," says presenter David Jensen.[2]

The show's theme music was changed again to bring it in line with the sounds of the new decade. Phil Lynott's 'Yellow Pearl' now opened the show as part of a title sequence that featured brightly coloured vinyl discs bursting out of clouds. Hand-held cameras and crane shots added yet more dynamism to each production, as did a new 20-strong mixed dance troupe called Zoo – a bunch of street dancers and similar athletes who took over from the predictable Legs & Co, whose appeal had waned, despite their increasingly skimpy outfits. A live show – one of an increasing number of live shows during this period – celebrated the programme's 900th edition. The 1,000th edition then arrived in 1983 and was simultaneously broadcast in stereo on Radio 1. Around this time, regular reports on the American music scene from Jonathan King were added to the package.

Further changes were prompted by the rise of the music video industry, with artists and record labels increasingly investing in slickly made promotional films that *Top Of The Pops* eagerly incorporated. Ultravox, Duran Duran and David Bowie were among the first to grasp the merits of the concept. Videos even had their own chart rundown on the show for a while and soon ousted Zoo as the main alternative to studio performances, bringing the days of dance groups on *Top Of The Pops* to an end.

Of the musicians that did appear in the studio, some proved more telegenic than others. There wasn't much action from the static synthesizer bands, but at least the New Romantics camped it up. This was also the era of what is often thought to be *Top Of The Pops*' biggest faux-pas – that giant photograph of darts player Jocky Wilson behind Dexy's Midnight Runners as they performed 'Jackie Wilson Said' – although Dexy's Kevin Rowland later explained that the choice of image had been entirely intentional, brought in just for a laugh.[3]

Someone else having a laugh was the latest DJ to join the presentation rota. The unlikeliest candidate, John Peel had been given one shot at the job back in 1968 (when he forgot the name of Amen Corner), then happily retired to the relative anonymity of late-night radio. Oddly, from 1982, he became a regular member of the *Top Of The Pops* team, even if his preferred style was flippancy and dry sarcasm rather than the excessive enthusiasm of most of his peers. David Jensen worked on the show for eight years, but it was his time co-hosting with Peel that he found the most rewarding. "Peel and I, who were working in the evenings together on Radio 1, used to have a lot of fun doing *Top Of The Pops*," he says. "He was very sardonic in his delivery, very dead pan. A lot of the *Top Of The Pops* we did, for some reason, were live; most of the other guys were recorded. They had the luxury of a safety net, if you like, for doing links, but we always did live *Top Of The Pops* and so, when he said something, it went out." On one occasion, Peel introduced Queen as "those Sun City boys", referring to the band's recent performances at the apartheid-regime entertainment complex in South Africa. "People were boycotting that area and that's why he said that, which they didn't particularly like," Jensen explains. "There was never a dull moment. I can't remember who instigated the dressing up in silly costumes but we started doing that and that added to the merriment." Although Peel's presence on the show seemed somewhat out of place, Jensen says that the late DJ quietly took pleasure in the more frivolous side of the pop world. "I was glad when he did do it because he used to secretly like that sort of thing. It didn't suit him to be chatting about the Bay City Rollers on his late-night show. Nonetheless, I think he quite enjoyed being in that kind of mainstream."[4]

Soon the DJ roster was expanded to include Mike Smith, Janice Long (the first regular female presenter), Gary Davies, Pat Sharp, Andy Peebles, Bruno Brookes, Dixie Peach, Paul Jordan and Simon Mayo. There was also another new theme tune from 1986: 'The Wizard' by Paul Hardcastle.

★ ★ ★

Elsewhere at the BBC, music on television at the start of the eighties largely meant recorded concert footage, beginning with *Rock Week Concert* (1980), a five-day sequence of performances featuring Joni Mitchell, the Kinks, Cream (Tony Palmer's last concert film again), Rainbow and Randy Newman. Following on was *Late Night In Concert* (1982–8), hosted by Anne Nightingale, which pulled together gigs from around the world featuring the likes of AC/DC, U2, Barclay James Harvest, the Style Council, INXS and Aswad. There was also *Pop Carnival* (1982–3), two series of recorded open-air concerts from parks in Fulham and Liverpool, as well as Brunel University, shown on consecutive weekday evenings and featuring such names as Echo & the Bunnymen, Nick Heyward, Big Country and Tears For Fears. The BBC then offered coverage of the annual *Montreux Rock Festival* in Switzerland from 1984 to 1988, breaking up highlights over three or four programmes.

The *Rock Goes To College* idea was kept alive in Northern Ireland, where the local BBC put on *Campus Rock* (1982). One edition featured the Moondogs at Coleraine University. It was the trio's last concert until they reformed in 2000 and capped a disappointing year that had promised much, not least because they were the final artists to be granted their own ITV kids' series by Muriel Young at Granada. *The Moondogs Matinee* (1981) saw the band supported by guests such as Slade, Chas & Dave and Elton John, but the exposure never translated into chart success, suggesting that kids who watched at 4.20 p.m. had other priorities for their pocket money than buying discs.

Still on ITV, *Rockstage* (1981) was another late-night performance show. Recorded by ATV at the Theatre Royal, Nottingham, this was shown across some ITV regions, including London, where it was stupidly scheduled against *The Old Grey Whistle Test*. Among those contributing were the Average White Band, Motörhead, Madness, Hazel O'Connor and the Stranglers. ITV, otherwise, was still trading in pop nostalgia, after the revival of *Oh Boy!* in 1979. *Greatest Hits* (1983), a Saturday evening family show hosted by Mike Smith, adopted a tighter format, each programme reviving hits from a given year between 1964 and 1981 with the original artists trying to rekindle the old magic with the aid of archive footage, a look back at the fashions of the time and clips from vintage TV programmes.

The channel was also still keen on pop fun and games, producing, via Granada, its own equivalent of *Cheggers Plays Pop* called *Hold Tight!* (1982–7). This contest for school teams was staged at Alton Towers theme park. Among the treasure hunts, giant snakes and ladders, attempts at breaking records and comic sketches, there were two musical items each week, with the likes of Depeche Mode, Dexy's Midnight Runners, the Housemartins and Deacon Blue getting involved. Bad Manners provided the theme music and the Selector's Pauline Black (who admits to hating every minute of it) co-hosted the first series. ITV also broadcast a new kids' pop quiz called *Poparound* (1985–6), a follow-up to the game show *Runaround*, hosted by Capital Radio's Gary Crowley.[5]

Local music shows continued in some ITV regions. In 1980, Yorkshire Television offered *Calendar Goes Pop*, a short series spun off its evening news magazine, *Calendar*, hosted by a fresh-faced Richard Madeley. The same year saw the start of a Scottish Television series called *Hear Here* (1980–4) that presented an eclectic mix of music, encompassing everything from Simple Minds to Andy Stewart. After airing on its own turf, the show was picked up by a number of other ITV regions. And Tyne Tees, despite being preoccupied with *Razzamatazz* and *The Tube*, also continued to think of its local viewers. It created *Rock Around Midnight* (1983), which saw Radio 1 DJ Mark Page welcome guests such as Kate Bush, Rory Gallagher and Thin Lizzy, and then another late-night regional music show called *TX 45* (1985–7). This was usually fronted by a local youngster named Chris Cowey, who had previously co-hosted a youth affairs show with a musical slant called *Check It Out* (1979–82), which was primarily local but did have a short run across ITV in summer 1980.

Such youth programming was also firmly on the minds of executives at the BBC. *Something Else* was still on air and then came the launch of *Oxford Road Show* (1981–5), taking its name from the location of the BBC's studios in Manchester. Described as a "live and lucid look at some aspects of the week gone by or the week to come", the show was aimed at viewers aged 15–25 and filled its studio with 150 young people ready to ask questions of guests or sound off an opinion. Rob Rohrer was the first host, helped by Martin Bergman, Paula Yates (delivering pop world gossip) and Jackie Spreckley. For the second series, Robert Elms joined the team and, by series three, the show had gained a Radio 1 connection with Peter Powell as presenter. After this, the programme title was abbreviated to *ORS 84* and *ORS 85*. Throughout its run, the music side was provided by established bands performing in the studio and up-and-coming acts pre-recorded on video. Those appearing included Japan, Tears For Fears, Duran Duran, the Alarm and the Smiths.

The BBC added another young music-and-arts programme when it created *Riverside* (1982–3). This took its name from the fact that it was broadcast from the Riverside Studios in Hammersmith, although the third series actually came from a converted warehouse/pumping station close to the Thames. Mike Appleton's *Whistle Test* team, headed by producer John Burrowes, put the show together. Mike Andrews, Steve Blacknell, Nicky Picasso and later Debbi Voller introduced features on fashion, film and poetry, although about two-thirds of the show was dedicated to music, looking to bridge the gap between the singles-oriented format of *Top Of The Pops* and the album-based *Old Grey Whistle Test*. Burrowes hoped to introduce a number of bands that had not enjoyed television exposure before, some even without recording contracts, but among the bigger names featured were New Order, Bow Wow Wow, Killing Joke and Big Country. There were interviews with the likes of Steve Strange, Lemmy and Marc Almond; Ian Birch, journalist with *Smash Hits* magazine, provided news and reports; and the pastimes of various musicians were explored – Stewart Copeland's amateur film-making, for example. Some stars were even roped in for a bit of cross-culture work – Neil Arthur from Blancmange road-tested the latest video equipment, while the Cure danced with Nicholas Dixon of the Royal Ballet.[6]

But, for the music purist, arguably the two most interesting new programmes from the BBC in the early eighties were *Eight Days A Week* (1983–4) and *Rockschool* (1983–4; 1987). The former was another product of Mike Appleton's Network Features department (as Presentation had become) and promised to be "the television equivalent of a music paper", effectively picking up on the idea Appleton had had all those years earlier while working on *Disco 2*, although the credit for this new series was given to former *Melody Maker* assistant editor Michael Watts, who pitched the proposal to the BBC under the working title of *Music Week*. That was dismissed because there was already a print magazine with that name and the Beatles-inspired alternative was adopted instead. *Newsnight* and *Guardian* journalist Robin Denselow was installed as host and the format saw him joined by three guests each week – musicians, video-producers, DJs – to discuss new releases, gigs, TV programmes, music books and so on. One show featured the combined talents of Neil Arthur, Jools Holland and Bill Wyman; another brought together Tony Blackburn, George Michael and Morrissey. With the latest music news, studio performances and interviews with informed guests about hot issues, the series – broadcast live in the early evening – broke a little new ground for music on television.[7]

Rockschool was shown on BBC2, but repeat showings quickly followed on BBC1. The eight programmes were designed to help aspiring musicians, with hints and tips about performing in a band. This wasn't a series for beginners: it was taken as read that anyone watching would know the basics but would want to move things forward. With the aid of clips of bands in action, and filmed reports from places like guitar factories, tuition came from Deirdre Cartwright (guitar), Henry Thomas (bass) and Geoff Nicholls (drums) and, in a somewhat dry fashion, they covered everything from the choice of equipment to how to play different styles of music – heavy metal, funk, blues, reggae and more. Rock names such as Carl Palmer, Ian Paice and Wilko Johnson offered their own advice and a live roadshow was put together, giving audience members a chance to ask questions and provide feedback. A second series, broadcast a few years later, expanded the coverage to vocals and keyboards (through additional presenter Alastair Gavin), with contributions from Tony Banks, Graham Bonnet, Vince Clarke, Jan Hammer and others.

* * *

The advent of the music video was clearly a boon to *Top Of The Pops* but the real potential of these promotional mini-movies was realised on the other side of the Atlantic. It has been argued that the first music videos date back almost to the birth of cinema. Eisenstein's films in the twenties and Disney's *Fantasia* are cited as just two examples of how music dictated image on the silver screen. As a means of directly promoting music, perhaps jazz musicians led the way in the forties with their "soundies" – short films made for coin-operated projection machines in clubs and bars. By the sixties, the Beatles, the Stones, Dylan and others were already playing around with music films to cover their absence from the television studio, paving the way for the game-changing 'Bohemian Rhapsody' from Queen in 1975. As the seventies turned into the eighties, videos became more sophisticated, telling stories rather than just providing moving wallpaper. Few benefited more from the medium than Abba who devised simple but thoughtful videos that often featured close-ups of their two girl singers. These not only cemented their image worldwide but precluded the need for touring, never a high priority for the group. The Boomtown Rats came up with the dramatic 'I Don't Like Mondays' and then Ultravox went all arty with 'Vienna'. Bands, managers and record companies now saw the marketing value of a classy video. There were even enough in existence – just about – to open a dedicated TV channel.

On August 1, 1981, MTV – a creation of Warner Amex Satellite Entertainment – took to the air in the USA. For the founders, there was only one film with which to open – the Buggles' hopefully prophetic 'Video Killed The Radio Star', and this was followed by Pat Benatar's 'You Better Run' and Rod Stewart's 'She Won't Dance With Me'. But the number of videos available at the time – estimates put the figure in MTV's catalogue at around a couple of hundred – was so limited that the artists who had been ahead of the game richly reaped the rewards, Rod himself picking up numerous plays during the first 24 hours.

Those early days for MTV were difficult. Broadcast only via cable, its audience was minuscule compared with the big US TV networks, and attracting advertisers was a struggle. Nevertheless, the channel struck a chord in more ways than one and quickly became essential viewing for a certain sector of America's youth and, while the advertising didn't yet pay the bills, the channel did at least support itself in another way. Because it provided a ready outlet for music videos, it encouraged the industry to supply even more, and to spend greater sums of money on them. Consequently, the music video as an art form really took off.

Initially, some record companies wanted to charge MTV for the right to screen the films but they soon realised the amazing promotion the channel provided. In those early days, as Rod Stewart discovered, British acts fared particularly well because they had been actively making movies while American performers were slow off the mark, but the indigenous talent soon woke up. Michael Jackson's 'Thriller' would not have been such a phenomenal success without the stunning extended video, shot by film director John Landis, and the airtime it received on MTV – which, ironically, up to that point had been criticised for its lack of black artists. 'Thriller', first shown in December 1983, was a landmark for the channel and helped it turn a financial corner and expand. Less than a year later, MTV was established enough to launch its own music awards and over time diversified into specialist music programming. Sister channels followed. VH-1, for the more mature audience, was launched in 1985. The whole package was then sold to Viacom and MTV continued to broaden its base from the simple music video into all kinds of youth programming, introducing comedy, game shows, fashion, soap opera, animation, talk shows, documentaries, dating and so-called reality drama.[8]

MTV didn't come to the UK until 1987 when MTV Europe was launched* but there was always an awareness of this strange beast across the Atlantic and even some attempts to emulate it, but in a country where there were only three (soon to be four) television channels

---

* The first video on MTV Europe was Dire Straits' 'Money For Nothing', with its guest vocal line from Sting – "I want my MTV" – echoing the channel's early advertising slogan.

available, this seemed an unlikely possibility, until, as in the USA, a potential solution eventually arrived through cable and satellite.

* * *

While Mike Appleton's team were increasingly involved in new projects such as *Riverside*, the bedrock of the department, *The Old Grey Whistle Test*, entered the eighties looking to put the difficulties of the punk explosion behind it. With Bob Harris now retired from the show, Anne Nightingale was left in the presentation hot seat. In 1981, she was joined by *Smash Hits* editor David Hepworth, who had been contributing reports to the programme, and the duo oversaw the show's move to Riverside Studios in November that year, the programme having temporarily relocated from Television Centre to Shepperton Studios.

In another diversion, in August 1982, the *Whistle Test* team put together a mini-marathon of music called *Bank Holiday Rock*. Kicking off at 1 p.m., it offered more than three hours of film and performance, starting with the Elvis movie *Jailhouse Rock* and continuing with a *Rock Goes To College* repeat featuring the Specials, a documentary about Mick Fleetwood and an old *Whistle Test* recording of Genesis at London's Lyceum. The package was hosted by Hepworth with *Smash Hits* colleague Mark Ellen who, a couple of weeks later, took over from Nightingale as Hepworth's partner on *Whistle Test* itself.

The front of house team had been refreshed and now it was time for the show's name to reflect the new era, too. Something old and grey sent out the wrong message in the colourful electronic eighties. It was felt that just shortening the title to *Whistle Test* – which is what most people called it anyway – would signify that the show had been given a bit of a facelift. Consequently, June 1983 saw the last *Old Grey Whistle Test*. In the following November, the programme returned as a series of six shows entitled *Whistle Test – On The Road*, covering concerts at different venues in the *Rock Goes To College* fashion, but this time mostly in clubs. When the series proper came back in January 1984, it was just as the pared-down *Whistle Test*. There were other changes, too. The "star kicker" image had been pushed aside and the studio had gained a more obvious stage, rather than having bands perform on the wire-strewn floor. 'Stone Fox Chase' was deemed to have had its day as a theme and was replaced by a new electronic track, and the presenters introduced acts from a set that looked like a cross between an art deco living room and a home office, complete with Venetian blinds. When a later titles sequence introduced the show's new figurehead – a strange futuristic mannekin – the transformation was complete.

All these radical developments were the result of fundamental changes that had taken place behind the scenes. Mike Appleton had been promoted to head of the Network Features department, leaving him less time for the show. He remained as executive producer but the day-to-day running was placed in the hands of two producers. John Burrowes had previously shared directing duties on the show with the long-serving Tom Corcoran and had recently been producer of *Riverside*; Trevor Dann was an assistant producer who had arrived in television from BBC Radio and now gained a promotion.

"Mike's original idea was that John would book the bands and I would book the other content – the films, the journalism," Dann explains. "John and I said we didn't want to do that, because we both wanted to do both." Appleton then suggested they produce alternate shows, which is how things progressed, although the system, says Dann, didn't really work. "I didn't think there was any continuity and it also led, absolutely inevitably, to competition. I'm sorry to say this because it sounds so catty but I think we did talk to record companies and say: 'Can you give me that for one of my shows?'" There was also a difference of musical taste. Burrowes, Dann says, was very keen on new bands. "He'd come from *Riverside* and he brought that to it. I was more interested in the traditional *Whistle Test* values of rock and albums. For me, doing a film about Ry Cooder or showing a Frank Zappa video was still relevant. John was much more interested in Roddy Frame. I think a mixture of those two would have probably been better."[9]

The new look, the new presenters, the two-tier approach to programming – all these changes were meant to make *Whistle Test* more robust and more pertinent to the look, the feel and particularly the sound of the eighties. And they came as a response to the startling work being done at Tyne Tees.

⋆ ⋆ ⋆

Having won the commission from Channel 4 for a new music programme, Tyne Tees needed to rise to the occasion. "Give it balls," Jeremy Isaacs had said, so Malcolm Gerrie, Andrea Wonfor and the team sat down to work out how to do that. The result was *The Tube* (1982–7), the most exciting music programme of the decade.

The team knew that, if the new show was going to work, a lot depended on the presenters, but the *Whistle Test* idea of having journalists as hosts didn't appeal, nor did the thought of handing the show over to popular DJs like *Top Of The Pops*.

"*The Old Grey Whistle Test* brought in David and Mark to try and spice it up a bit but, even then, you could see where their own personal bias was, and it certainly didn't feel like to me what was happening out there," says Gerrie. "I wasn't sure about having two journalists curating the only decent music show on television and nor was I keen on having a squeaky-clean Radio 1 DJ presenting the biggest pop show on TV. It just seemed neither did the job really. I love Mark and I love David. I've massive respect for them but I thought this was so bland and dull. Nobody was pushing the medium."

Backed by his superiors, Gerrie decided on a different approach. "There was a magazine which I just adored, called *The Face*. So we took an ad, just a little box saying: 'Wanted: a face for the space' – no mention of TV – and a telephone number. That was it. We held auditions all around the country to find new talent. If you were an established name, you could rock up, but you had to go to one of these sessions."

It proved to be an eventful process, most memorable for the auditions held in London. "In a church hall somewhere in Camden, we had stacks of people lined up, because the word had got out," Gerrie recalls. "The doors opened and this girl came in with the full bridal gear on – the veil, the train, the whole thing." Thinking she'd come to the wrong room, they were about to redirect her down the corridor when the veil was lifted and it became clear that there was no mistake. "It was Boy George. He sat down and we all had a giggle. He just blew us away. Andrea and I just fell in love with him. He was sharp, he was erudite, he was quite rigorous about his music... just a brilliant, wicked, mischievous sense of humour." The gig would have been his, except for the fact that his band secured a recording contract the following week.

With George out of the picture, the auditions failed to come up with any ideal presenters but the process had confirmed that it would be right for the show to be fronted by a mix of new and established people, although definitely not an old-school presenter type. Ideally, one would be a musician. "I thought if we get a musician who can present, then it's credible," says Gerrie. "If they're going to talk to another musician, they'll know what the hell they're on about and there's a bit of mutual respect, as against somebody who's just going to ask them about their new record or tour dates." That said, no name stood out but the other half of the presentation equation was solved when gossip columnist Paula Yates was booked. Gerrie had met her while working on *Razzmatazz*. "I thought she was fabulous: a journalist, knew everybody in town – which was not unhelpful – stunning, sexy." He thought she was great but who the hell could he put with her?

Malcolm really struggled to find the right guy until, one night at home, he sat down to watch a documentary about the Police recording an album in Montserrat.* The film was presented by Jools Holland, who had just left Squeeze. Gerrie was particularly amused by a section where Jools interviewed guitarist Andy Summers and asked him to play a few riffs. "It's pretty boring and, on camera, Jools leans over and unplugs his guitar and says: 'I think that's enough of that, don't you?' That takes some balls. I was on the floor laughing. I loved his irreverence. Also, he looked great because he was in the middle of Montserrat, looking pretty cool."

There was only the matter of persuading Jools to join the show. He was not enthusiastic but he did agree to take part in an audition with Paula. It's a screen test that has gone down in television folklore, "an

* *The Police – Montserrat 81* was shown on BBC1 in December 1981.

absolute, unmitigated disaster, just a shambles", according to Gerrie. "They were obviously both really nervous. Paula was in Jools's lap, rubbing his breast and rubbing his crotch, but there was something there, an absolute chemistry, which was just brilliant. The pair of them together looked amazing and the repartee was hilarious." Bravely, Tyne Tees decided to make a pilot episode. "I think I must have lost a stone in the gallery that night," reveals Gerrie. "It was just awful. They missed their cues but again what came over was the energy." Channel 4 surprisingly remained positive and it was decided to give them a chance.[10]

With the team in place, plans progressed to the opening night – November 5, 1982, just three days after Channel 4 had taken to the air. The first edition – live, at 5.15 p.m. – saw Holland kick things off in front of the perspex awning ("the tube") that marked the entrance to Tyne Tees' new Studio 5. Waving a Bonfire Night sparkler, he, not too convincingly, declared: "We're going to do something now that's going to go in the anals (sic) of television history". Typical as this was of Holland's throw-away humour, it nevertheless proved to be a prescient introduction. *The Tube* was on its way to becoming the dominant music show of the decade and really hit the ground running.

The pace was frantic from the start. That inaugural night, after the first airing of the show's swirling theme music,* Paula Yates, dressed like a fairy from the top of a Christmas tree, led the camera inside the building, introducing viewers to the dark studio with coloured tube lighting where this exciting new show was going to happen. Bands would perform on the three live stages but they might also be encountered in the foyer, in the green room, in the lifts or in their dressing rooms – every inch of the Tyne Tees complex was going to be in use. The place was buzzing and totally anarchic.

That first show featured Heaven 17, Bananarama, Duran Duran and – first up – Sunderland band the Toy Dolls, but the real bonus was having the Jam who used the occasion to surprise the nation by declaring they were splitting up. Grabbing the music headlines in this way instantly

* A version of Jeff Beck's 'Star Cycle', produced by Trevor Horn.

proved that the show was relevant and on the button. And so the pace continued as *The Tube* consolidated its position, racing noisily into the mid-eighties and piling pressure on its more sedate rival, *Whistle Test*, although the team at the BBC was soon to prove that it still held the upper hand in some respects.

★ ★ ★

The Tube was the first and by far the most important music show Channel 4 introduced, but it wasn't the only programme up the new broadcaster's sleeve. The same evening that *The Tube* began, the channel offered the first instalment in a six-part documentary series called *Deep Roots Music* (1982) that, with Mikey Dread at the helm, looked at the history and development of Jamaican music, from slavery to ska and reggae. Later that week, there was something for the nostalgic viewer when Alan Freeman introduced the first edition of *Unforgettable* (1982–3). Like the later *Greatest Hits* on ITV, this was a chance to discover what pop stars of the past – anywhere between the fifties and mid-seventies – looked like in the early eighties as they reprised a couple of their old hits. Among those appearing were Freddie & the Dreamers, Lonnie Donegan, Mungo Jerry, Gerry & the Pacemakers, Helen Shapiro, the Glitter Band and Chicory Tip. Archive footage was also used.

Another early offering was *Whatever You Want* (1982–3), presented by comedian Keith Allen from the Brixton ACE venue in London. This was a mixture of live music, comedy and discussion – raising subjects requested by its audience, such as apartheid and community policing. Among the bands appearing were Killing Joke, the Dead Kennedys and the Undertones. To round off the series, a handful of programmes entitled *Whatever You Didn't Get* pulled together more of the performances that had been recorded for the show. Channel 4 then replaced this with a package of live music, comedy, arts and gossip that went out under the title *Loose Talk* (1983). Anchored by Steve Taylor, who was assisted by guest hosts such as Ian Hislop and Muriel Gray, it came from the Albany Theatre in Deptford and featured artists like Aztec Camera, Tenpole

Tudor and Jo Boxers. The first series was broadcast in the early evening and the second late at night.

The channel's commitment to music continued when it launched two programmes that alternated weekly in the same time slot. First up was *The Other Side Of The Tracks* (1983–5) in which Paul Gambaccini looked at the careers of performers old and new, mixing specially recorded performances and concert footage with location interviews to build a deeper understanding of what the musicians were all about. The first show focused on Phil Collins and EMI's latest big hope, Kajagoogoo; later editions, over three series, homed in on such names as Joe Jackson, Joan Armatrading, the Police, Robert Plant, Culture Club and Bryan Ferry.

The alternating show was *GasTank* (1983). Hosted by Rick Wakeman and Tony Ashton (of Ashton, Gardner & Dyke), this provided an opportunity for artists to play material of their own choosing with the two hosts and the house band, and to discuss their work in a relaxed, smoky, night club-like atmosphere, with Wakeman conducting chatty interviews over a drink at the bar. Several artists featured in each edition and among those taking part were Rick Parfitt, Eric Burdon, Alvin Lee, Steve Hackett and Roy Wood. Just six programmes were made.

Not such a good idea was *Mini Pops* (1983) in which precocious kids, made up like pop stars, sang saccharine versions of chart hits. The children, aged between seven and ten, had been chosen through a Channel 4 talent show called *Don't Do It Mrs Worthington*. Their music was nauseating enough, but what was perceived as the cynical sexualisation of pre-pubescents, encouraging them to preen and to pose for the camera, really caused a stir. Although the idea came from a 1981 hit album, and the motives were innocent, this was one of director Mike Mansfield's more misguided productions and, faced with intense criticism, it quickly bit the dust.

* * *

As executive producer of *Top Of The Pops* through most of the eighties, Michael Hurll was aided by producers Brian Whitehouse, Gordon Elsbury,

Stanley Appel and Paul Ciani, but his control of the programme – and the strong light entertainment gloss he applied to it – was always evident. Hurll's background was firmly in variety, working on programmes such as *The Little & Large Show* and *Seaside Special*. He wasn't there to be at the cutting edge of music, whatever was happening on other channels, and he wasn't alone in that respect at the BBC as light entertainment remained the Corporation's default route for much of its coverage of pop music at this time.

A summer show called *Six Fifty-Five Special* (1981–3), with its reference back to Jack Good's formative programme of the fifties, teased those expecting musical excitement but instead they were treated to a *Pebble Mill*-style early-evening magazine, with just a little musical in-fill, and not always pop. At around the same time, BBC1 launched *Pop Quiz* (1981–4; 1994), a celebrity panel game for Saturday evenings, fronted by Mike Read who had developed a niche as a pop music maven, to the point where listeners to his radio show could phone in and try to catch him out. The series ran for three years before being revived with Chris Tarrant in the chair 10 years later. It fared a lot better than *Pop The Question* (1986), another light-hearted celebrity gig, devised by Jeremy Beadle and radio producer Phil "the Collector" Swern for TVS, the company that had taken over the ITV franchise previously held by Southern Television. The series – hosted by Lee Peck, with team captains Chris Tarrant and David Hamilton – aired locally on ITV in 1985 but was then repeated nationally by Channel 4 the following year.*

Further Saturday evening family fun was ensured by *1 On The Road* (1984). This short series aimed to capitalise on the success of the long-running *Radio 1 Roadshow*, which saw the station's DJs touring the country each summer. Hosted by Peter Powell from a different venue each week, the package saw Radio 1 producer John Walters out and about meeting local characters, various presenters tackling the "DJ Challenge" and bands such as Frankie Goes To Hollywood, Spandau Ballet and the Human League providing the music.

* The BBC returned to the theme two decades later when Jamie Theakston hosted *A Question Of Pop* (2000–1), with team captains Suggs and Noddy Holder.

The *Eurovision Song Contest* was another light entertainment highlight, of course, if that is the right word, and there was renewed enthusiasm for the event in the UK after Bucks Fizz's skirt-ripping win with 'Making Your Mind Up' in 1981. But the British entries through most of the decade – even those that were laden with synthesizers and drum machines like Ryder's 'Runner In The Night' in 1986 and Rikki's 'Only The Light' in 1987 – could easily have come from 10 years earlier. With the exception of Scott Fitzgerald and Live Report's even older-sounding ballads – 'Go' and 'Why Do I Always Get It Wrong' – that narrowly came second in 1988 and 1989, UK songs didn't really trouble the scorers too much.* The decade's real Eurovision stars both came from Ireland. Johnny Logan single-handedly won two of the contests, while Terry Wogan began adding his playfully acerbic commentaries for British television in 1980.

Music awards formed another part of the light entertainment equation, firstly *The British Rock & Pop Awards* that ran over from the previous decade and then *The British Record Industry Awards*, later known as *The Brit Awards* (1985–). This annual shindig has secured its place in the annals of broadcasting history, and not always for the right reasons, but when the event was inaugurated in 1977, to commemorate 100 years of recorded music, it was a classy black-tie affair. Five years later, the idea was exhumed and became an annual jamboree, although it was only televised from 1985 when the BBC took it on with Michael Hurll as producer and Noel Edmonds as presenter. With the exception of 1987, when Jonathan King hosted, Edmonds remained host until 1989 when the name was shortened to *The Brit Awards* and all hell broke loose. But more of that anon. The BBC also decided to add the *Smash Hits Poll*

---

* Arguably more relevant was the *International Battle Of The Pop Bands* (1983), in which Sugar Ray Five from Orpington, winners of a domestic heat earlier in the year, represented the UK. Other countries taking part were the Netherlands, France, Finland, Spain and Germany, with bands judged on content, performance and potential by a panel comprising Paul Gambaccini, Kim Wilde, Robin Gibb, Tony Visconti and Carlene Carter. There was an earlier UK-only event in 1982 but no international final.

Winners' Party (1988–2002; 2004–5) to its schedule. This was a far less controversial affair, screened during Sunday afternoons from the Royal Albert Hall and then the Docklands Arena, hosted initially by Phillip Schofield.

⋆ ⋆ ⋆

It is hard to imagine today just what an impact the video had on televised music during the eighties. The arrival of the latest production from one of the major artists was quite an event at the time – much like the premiere of a film – and with record companies now ploughing serious money into these promotional vehicles, many turned out to be little works of art. Jonathan King's series *Entertainment USA* (1983–8) made good use of them, unveiling the latest American releases alongside Hollywood gossip and features on American life and leisure. They also featured prominently in King's next venture, a youth programme called *No Limits* (1985–7), which saw new young faces given the chance to be presenters. Out of some 4,000 applications, Jeremy Legg and Lisa Maxwell were chosen to host the first series, and Jenny Powell and Tony Baker the second, with the help of some regional presenters as the show toured the UK. "The world's fastest rock show", the *Radio Times* called it, although it was just as much a travelogue, in a cheesy, superficial, "let's be wacky" sort of way. King also appeared from time to time but mainly contributed behind the scenes.

By this time, the BBC had decided that the music video was such a good idea that it created a strange programme called *The Golden Oldie Picture Show* (1985–8), in which Dave Lee Travis introduced new films specially made to accompany hits from years gone by. Such videos, had they been authentic, would have been useful additions to *The Rock'n'Roll Years* (1985–7; 1994), a nostalgic wallow in the events of the years 1956 to 1979 (one year per show) that played hits of the time over footage of the headline news. The idea was based on a Radio 1 series called *25 Years Of Rock* (subsequently remade and expanded as *Sounds Of The 20th Century* for Radio 2) and was piloted in 1984 with a one-off programme on the year 1966. Each edition was skilfully put together, cleverly tying in the lyrics of songs with the subject of the news clips. There was no narrator, just superimposed text to provide the ongoing story of the year. The series returned in 1994 to update coverage to the end of the eighties, but that's where the story seems to have ended as this style of the programme seems too dated now to be revived.

Further evidence that the music video was an audience-puller came when Channel 4 launched *The Max Headroom Show* (1985–7), an innovative production using the computer-enhanced character Max – modelled on and played by actor Matt Frewer – to introduce the latest video releases. Pre-dating the days of home PCs, the character, with its deliberately staccato delivery and movement, gained a cult following.

Appreciation of the video then soared to new heights when the BBC devoted an extended *Omnibus* programme to it. *Video Jukebox* (1986), kicking off at 9.30 p.m. on a Friday night and running through to 2 a.m., in the capable hands of John Peel and John Walters, charted the history of the genre. Some of the early Beatles, Stones and Dylan promos were shown and adding comment were film-makers such as Ken Russell, Dick Lester and John Landis, as well as video specialist musicians like Kevin Godley and Lol Creme, David Bowie, Madness and David Byrne.

* * *

Video Jukebox was not the only *Omnibus* presentation to focus on popular music during the eighties. *Johnny Be Good* (1980) was a film about the career of Chuck Berry and *Stevie Wonder: Inner Visions* (1981) followed the Motown star on a US tour. There were also programmes on Roger Daltrey (1983), Ray Charles (1986), Aretha Franklin (1987), Leonard Cohen (1988) and Paul Simon (1988). D.A. Pennebaker's film about Bob Dylan, *Don't Look Back*, also premiered on British television under the *Omnibus* umbrella in 1986 and this was followed a year later by *Getting To Dylan*, a film about the musician at work as an actor in the film *Hearts Of Fire*.

The BBC's other major arts strand, *Arena*, offered some equally interesting documentaries and performances, including the Brian Eno film *Double Vision* (1980), *Beat This! A Hip Hop History* (1984) and Jonathan Demme's *Stop Making Sense*, about Talking Heads (1987). An *Arena* documentary on the hundredth birthday of the juke box then provided the platform for a revival of *Juke Box Jury* in 1989 and the strand was also responsible for one of the few rock drama productions of the decade. Described as a "musical for the 80s", David Leland's film *Ligmalion* (1985), was a part-fantasy, part-documentary directed by Nigel Finch. It told the story of Gordon Shilling, played by Jason Carter, a Lincolnshire lad living homeless in London who is taught how to "lig" – that very music industry concept of eating and drinking for nothing by showing up at promo events – by the mysterious Eden Rothwell (Tim Curry) and makes his way through life blagging accordingly. Along the way, he bumps into a succession of weird characters, including John Bull (Alexei Sayle) and Machiavelli (Sting). Music was provided by Working Week.

The other noteworthy rock drama of the eighties was *Body Contact* (1987), a BBC film written by Lee Drysdale and directed by Bernard Rose. This was set in a slightly warped version of north London and starred Ricco Ross as taxi driver Smiley who gets caught up in a Mafia vendetta when he helps out a client called Dominique, played by Joely Richardson. Other members of the cast included Timothy Spall, Miriam Margolyes and Jack Shepherd. The music was composed by 10cc guitarist Rick Fenn.

★ ★ ★

It was important that the first edition of *The Tube* made an impact as the stakes were high. The *TV Times*, in trailing the programme, billed it as "the hottest TV rock magazine since *Ready, Steady, Go!*" and the ante was upped further by having Pete Townshend on the first show, claiming there had never been enough space for music on television. He harboured "real high hopes for this programme". Thankfully, it didn't disappoint.

Former *Check It Out* presenter Chris Cowey, who was now a researcher on the show, explains how Tyne Tees drew on a big, diverse pool of talent to make it so successful. "*The Tube*, by today's standards, had a huge production team," he says. "We'd all go out and see bands and listen to a lot of music and talk about it collectively, and we'd champion different bands. Chris Phipps, one of the researchers, was a big heavy metal fan, so he'd always be banging on about these heavy metal bands. I was a bit of a soul boy, so I booked people like Cameo and Grandmaster Flash and that kind of thing, although I also loved guitar bands. I was big on the Big Country, U2, Bunnymen, that kind of area as well. There was also quite an age range on *The Tube*. I was the baby. I had my 21st birthday on *The Tube* and some of the production team were in their forties and fifties, so it was quite a diverse bunch of people."[11]

As a result, *The Tube* was always willing to showcase new sounds like hip hop and unearthed loads of fledgling talent who had never seen the inside of a television studio before, from the Fine Young Cannibals to the Housemartins, not forgetting Frankie Goes To Hollywood, whose filmed appearance performing 'Relax' caused quite a stir and directly led to their first recording contract.

"The team went down and shot this amazing film, I think it was in the Liverpool ballroom," says producer Malcolm Gerrie. "We first saw them above a pub and they were wearing all the bondage stuff … it was pretty outrageous and the song was obviously risqué because of the lyrics. Anyway, we put it out and it just lit up the switchboard. Both up in Newcastle and at Channel 4, you couldn't touch the switchboard because it was white hot."[12]

The programme also recorded Madonna when she was so low on the list of priorities of her record label that Tyne Tees had to foot the bill to bring her to the Hacienda in Manchester for filming. Many of the big rock names – Elton John, Paul McCartney, Little Richard, James Brown and more – featured as well, which proves that *The Tube* had little trouble enticing bands out of London, contrary to the view expressed by Elkan Allan at that Channel 4 press launch. Indeed, the very fact that the show required travel to Newcastle proved to be a big plus in attracting the talent.

"The bands absolutely loved doing it because it got them out of London, away from the record companies," says Cowey. "They'd arrive on Thursday, do a bit of a sound check and then rehearse and do it on Friday. If we got on well with them, we'd take them out to a couple of nightclubs around Newcastle on Thursday night. I remember some amazing times with Paul Young in a nightclub called Julie's on the Quayside, borrowing the DJ's microphone to sing some old Sam Cooke and Otis Redding songs. I don't suppose it had to be Newcastle, although Newcastle is quite a rock'n'roll place and very warm and friendly. I suppose it could have been anywhere, as long as they couldn't get back to London that night and they couldn't be doing interviews with Capital and Radio 1 in the afternoon. That was a real benefit. They were totally, totally focused on doing *The Tube.*"[13]

But 105 minutes of live television every Friday (or 90 minutes, as it later became) took some filling, so the programme wasn't just focused on music. "People forget *The Tube* was actually only 70 per cent music," says Malcolm Gerrie. "The rest was comedy and reportage and magazine stuff from around the world." There were topical contributions from punk poet Mark Miwurdz (real name Mark Hurst) and features on anything from hairdressing and portrait artists to theatrical suitmakers and the Troubles in Northern Ireland. Director Geoff Wonfor (husband of Andrea) had a budget to roam the world and bring back classy features – the Cannes Film Festival, the Bahamas to see Robert Palmer, Culture Club in Japan. On the comedy side, Vic Reeves made his television debut on the show, hosting a spoof game show called "Square Celebrities". Harry Enfield was another debutant and Rik Mayall inspired a volley of complaints by pretending to be drunk and vomiting on air. Stephen Fry, Robbie Coltrane, Alexei Sayle and French & Saunders were all semi-regulars, along with a lunatic comedian called Foffo Spearjig, aka "The Hard", a Geordie tough man, who appeared in filmed inserts. Dressed in a black-and-white hooped sweater – padded in the muscle areas – he endured extreme physical torments each week, but never admitted to any pain ("Felt Nowt!").[14]

All of this played out in front of an invited audience that included a nucleus of 20 or 30 regulars who looked good and had plenty of life. Artist performances were almost always live, but there were a few exceptions. "Occasionally, there were things that just wouldn't or couldn't work live but, by and large, the policy was for it to be live," says Chris Cowey. "When we had Dead or Alive, who had just got to number one singing 'You Spin Me Round (Like A Record)', they weren't going to do it live because it was a Stock Aitken Waterman thing. Pete Waterman said: 'We spent months, years, perfecting this backing track. We're not going to let a band go to Newcastle and do it badly live.'"

Attempting to hold things together – because *The Tube* was never a streamlined show – Jools Holland and Paula Yates were joined by TV newcomers such as Nick Laird-Clowes, Michel Cremona, Gary James and Tony Fletcher. While Yates went off on maternity leave, actress Leslie Ash temporarily took her place, and the team was bolstered permanently later with the arrival of Muriel Gray. But keeping order was never easy, not helped by the fact that neither of the two main hosts seemingly really cared if they were there or not. Programmes were edgy, some of the presenters were nervy and interviews were prone to the odd, usually unintentional, profanity. That, in itself, made the show compelling viewing, as disaster, the viewer felt, might strike at any moment. At a time, when television was still heavily scripted and rehearsed, such unpredictability was fresh and exciting.

"We used to almost build in, by not over-rehearsing and not over-planning, those moments where you didn't quite know what was going to happen," says Chris Cowey. "*The Tube* started in 1982 so there was still the afterglow of post-punk and it was a case of expect the unexpected. There were moments when nobody really knew what was going to happen and that was great because it was sometimes car-crash television. You'd close your eyes and grit your teeth and hope it was going to be alright and occasionally it would go horribly wrong and occasionally it would make for the most joyous moments. You had some really brilliant musical moments and chunks of *The Tube* are things that people won't forget."[15]

★ ★ ★

A show of the nature and duration of *The Tube* could not run 52 weeks of the year, so Channel 4 offered other music show producers the chance to fill the gaps when the programme took a break. The first vacation was taken over by another live show called *Switch* (1983), a very youthful set-up presented by TV newcomer Yvonne French (aged 21) and actor Graham Fletcher-Cook (19), with three music editors all aged under 25 choosing the artists. *The Tube* had raced off the blocks by having Paul Weller exclusively announce the demise of the Jam in the first show. *Switch* clearly hoped for a similar bounce by booking Weller for the first live television appearance of his new band, the Style Council. Three acts performed each week and there were features from around the country from reporter Mark Issue.

Channel 4 next filled *The Tube*'s absence with *High Band* (1984), a series of recorded concerts of varying vintage. Featured artists included the Thompson Twins, Ultravox, Thomas Dolby, Kate Bush and Siouxsie & the Banshees. A year later, the channel was more adventurous and created two new programmes for specialist audiences while *The Tube* was away. First up was *ECT* (1985), which was dedicated to the heavy rock and metal market. Motörhead featured in the first programme and other performers included Warrior, Hawkwind, Phil Lynott and Hanoi Rocks, playing live in front of a moshing crowd. There was a dance group, too, called Beauxartz, choreographed by Kevan Allen. Watching a full-on rock show at 5.30 in the afternoon did seem a bit weird, though.

The letters "ECT" were said to stand for "Extra Celestial Transmission", a seemingly contrived way of fitting the show into a weekly strand called *Friday Zone* that was linked by clips from the fifties TV serial *Space Patrol*. Also in the strand was a 10-minute interlude called *Paintbox*, that combined new music with thought-provoking visuals, and the second of Channel 4's major new music programmes, *Soul Train* (1985).

Inspired by the long-running US series of the same name, *Soul Train* combined studio performances with the latest videos and classics from the archives. A young Jonathan Ross was a member of the production team. Among the featured artists welcomed by host Jeffrey Daniel – who had danced on the original US series –were Millie Jackson, Marvin

Gaye, Ike & Tina Turner and Rose Royce. After the first year, the *Top Of The Pops*-like show evolved into *Solid Soul* (1986–7), hosted by singer Juliet Roberts and Capital Radio DJ Chris Forbes but on-screen presenters were later abandoned and guests were just introduced using captions.* Channel 4 completed the *Tube* in-fill with edited highlights of *Ready, Steady, Go!* from the sixties and another new series, produced by Janet Street-Porter for Border Television. *Bliss* (1985) was a short-lived, 50-minute magazine hosted by Muriel Gray that, as with several television offerings around this time, attempted to blend music with fashion and style.

The next year saw the debut of one of commercial television's longest-running music shows. *The Chart Show* (1986–98) was a programme without presenters or studio performers that simply focused on videos, some of them labelled "exclusive". Alongside the main chart (which was not the official BBC chart), the show counted down a number of specialist charts, including indie, dance, heavy metal and reggae, showing clips from each entry and pausing for longer extracts from selected videos.

Much was made of emerging computer graphics to fill the titles sequences with colourful cartoon images of funfairs, popping balloons, rockets and spaceships, while video recorder instructions such as REWIND, FFWD and PLAY flashed onto the screen whenever a chart was going to be paused or jumps were needed to another section. In the absence of presenters, information about the artists was loaded into superimposed text boxes.

The Chart Show ran on Channel 4 for two years before being taken over by ITV (and retitled *The ITV Chart Show*), where it stayed on air for another nine years, moving from Friday evening to Saturday lunchtime and also going out in the middle of the night in some regions.†

---

* With three series in all, *Soul Train/Solid Soul* was more successful than an earlier Channel 4 foray into black music. *Rockers Roadshow* (1983) was an altogether earthier production that saw Mikey Dread hosting reggae, soul and funk from clubs and music hot spots in cities around the UK.

† Channel 4 exhumed the show in January 2003, running it daily for a couple of weeks in the morning while the breakfast magazine *RI:SE* was being revamped.

★ ★ ★

Having dabbled in rock marathons with 1982's *Bank Holiday Rock*, Mike Appleton and his *Whistle Test* crew were inspired to go for a more substantial offering the following year. On the Saturday of August Bank Holiday weekend 1983, BBC2 presented *Rock Around The Clock* (1983–4; 1986), 15 hours of non-stop music, starting at 3.15 in the afternoon. It was certainly something different, not least because television channels at that time normally closed down around midnight. David Hepworth, Mark Ellen, Anne Nightingale and Steve Blacknell hosted this mixed package that featured recorded concert footage of Ultravox, Robert Palmer, Duran Duran, Spandau Ballet and Eric Clapton, plus two live shows from the Regal Theatre in Hitchin featuring Roman Holliday and 10cc. Documentaries on Bob Marley, Jimi Hendrix, the music scene in Australia and an American rock radio station, plus a repeat showing of a film Nightingale had made covering the Police tour of the Far East, completed the line-up, along with the movies *All This And World War II*, *American Graffiti* and *Deadman's Curve*.

The concept was repeated a year later when the same team presented Simple Minds and the Pretenders, recorded the night before in Germany; a 1973 concert by Van Morrison at the Rainbow; a repeat of Jools Holland's 1981 film with the Police in Montserrat; live music from New Order, Aztec Camera and the Cure; and various features and movies. There was also a rock look-alike competition and – a touch of innovation – viewers were able to phone in and vote for videos to be shown through the day as well as a whole music programme that would be screened towards the end of the evening.

A slightly pared-down version of *Rock Around The Clock* was broadcast two years later. This included a new feature, 'Battle Of The Giants', where the audience could decide who was greater: Madonna or Prince, Springsteen or Queen, Simple Minds or U2 and, inevitably, the Beatles or the Stones. Concert footage this time came from A-ha, Dire Straits and the Damned, with live performances from the Town and Country Club in Kentish Town by W.A.S.P. and Cameo. Mark Ellen, Andy Kershaw, Janice Long and Ro Newton were the hosts.

The eagle-eyed will have noticed that there was no *Rock Around The Clock* in 1985. Plans had been put in place for the programme but it was all blown out of the water by a little something called *Live Aid*.

* * *

It's possible that *Live Aid* might never have happened had it not been for *Rock Around The Clock*.The simple fact that Mike Appleton had a budget to spend on a summer music showcase set the ball rolling. Instead of using the money for the TV marathon, it would go towards covering this huge concert that Bob Geldof was planning, on the back of the success of the charity single 'Do They Know It's Christmas?', in order to help combat famine in Africa.

The idea was that the concert would be staged at two venues – Wembley Stadium in London and the JFK Stadium in Philadelphia – and Geldof set his ambitions high. He wanted the biggest stars to take part and to this end cajoled, coaxed and embarrassed artists into agreeing to perform, going so far as to announce names to the media without consulting them first, knowing they were unlikely to pull out and face the bad press. When word of the concert first filtered into the BBC offices, the immediate thoughts were that, because of Geldof's relationship with Paula Yates, *The Tube* team at Tyne Tees would be asked to produce the television side, but this was quickly recognised as infeasible.

"In reality, *The Tube* couldn't have done it. It was much too big an event and the best place it could have gone was the BBC," says Appleton, whose available budget made it possible for him to persuade the BBC hierarchy to come on board, although the magnitude of the task had not hit home at that point. "I didn't realise, to be honest, what it was going to become," he says. "It was a bit like a snowball going down a mountainside, getting bigger and bigger and bigger as it went along. It happened so quickly." Fortunately, the BBC had the resources Appleton could call on. It was equipped with its own outside broadcast units and, of course, there was a team at *Whistle Test* already in place, so production staff wouldn't need to be corralled from other areas.[16]

"The great unsung hero of *Live Aid* is Michael Grade," says producer Trevor Dann. Grade, then the BBC's Director of Television, gave the project his full backing, committing resources to make it work and clearing the schedules to accommodate the broadcast. That said, it was still an enormous undertaking. "Mark Ellen quotes me in his book, saying it was like asking BBC Radio Cambridgeshire to cover a general election nationally," Dann says. "And it kind of was because we were so ill-equipped to do this. The idea that people like me and John [Burrowes] and others could produce 16 hours of live television was insane. And, my God, it's creaky. If you watch it back, there's a lot of stuff we should be deeply ashamed of. It was not very good but the event made it happen. The bands, many of them, were just sensational and I think the spirit of the moment took it where it went."[17]

Despite its shortcomings, the fact that *Live Aid* made it on air at all was remarkable, given the size of the task, the time available and the technology of the time. When the BBC developed the idea of *Our World* in the sixties, it took nearly two years of planning to bring all the international broadcasters on board and set up all the technical links. Appleton and his team had a matter of weeks, with limited means of communication. "There were no faxes then," he says. "There were no mobile phones, just telexes, and it was a 24-hour operation because gradually Australia came in, Japan came in, Russia came in, the West Coast of America, the whole of Europe. I'd never worked so hard in my life." And it wasn't just keeping all the broadcasters on side; the musicians, too, needed organising. With two venues having to be linked by satellite, timing was crucial. Performers could not simply play to the crowd and run over. They were allocated either 12- or 20-minute slots, depending on their importance, and, to their credit, the artists largely played ball.

"I mostly found at the time I was dealing with rock stars, however sassy they were, if you actually gave them responsibility, they'd take it," says Appleton. "If you try and make them do something, they'll rebel against it, but say that the only way this can work is if you do this, they will usually do it. I still to this day can't work out quite how well it worked in terms of time. The first time we went to Philadelphia, we were there within 90 seconds of the time we should have been there, which is outrageous."[18]

When the big day arrived – July 13, 1985 – there were inevitably nerves and tension in the production crew, not helped when the scheduled opening to the event had to be changed at the very last minute. Trevor Dann and John Burrowes had been given the job of producing the programming that slotted in between the bands on stage – a mix of interviews, fund-raising appeals, reaction, etc. – which came from what was normally a football presentation box suspended high in one of the Wembley stands. It was hot, at times unbearably hot, which added to the discomfort as the seconds ticked down to the show getting underway. The introduction to the day was due to be handled on the stage with the arrival of the guests of honour, the Prince and Princess of Wales. Unfortunately, the royal party was held up and plans had to be hastily changed. The introduction now had to be made in the programming box. As well as going out on television, it would be relayed to the whole stadium. Richard Skinner was ready to do the link but there was obviously no prepared script.

"My mind went back to *Two-Way Family Favourites* on the old Light Programme," says Dann. "It always used to start: 'It's 12 noon in London, one o'clock in Cologne, Germany, and, at home and away, it's time for *Two-Way Family Favourites*', so I just grabbed this bit of paper and wrote in block caps: 'It's 12 noon in London, 7 a.m. in Philadelphia and around the world it's time for *Live Aid*...' and just gave it to Richard. At the point we were cued, he just had to read it and he got about four words into it when they suddenly switched the stadium PA on. Boom! As he was saying the words, the whole thing was shaking. Then Tommy Vance said something on stage and then Quo started." At this point the pressure and the emotion took their toll. "Richard and I were standing in the box and we embraced each other and cried because it was the most stressful thing either of us had ever done. It was such a wonderful thing to think: 'We've actually done this. It's on. It's bloody rockin' all over the world.'"[19]

Following Status Quo onto the Wembley stage were artists such as Style Council, the Boomtown Rats, Spandau Ballet, Elvis Costello, Sting,

Howard Jones, Bryan Ferry, U2, David Bowie, the Who, Queen, Elton John and Paul McCartney. Over in Philadelphia performers included the Beach Boys, Simple Minds, Nile Rodgers, Madonna, Tom Petty, Neil Young, Eric Clapton, Led Zeppelin (Page, Plant and Jones playing together – somewhat shakily – for the first time since the death of John Bonham in 1980), the Temptations, Mick Jagger, Tina Turner and, finally, Bob Dylan, accompanied by Keith Richards and Ronnie Wood, neither of whom seemed to know what Dylan was playing. Phil Collins, winging across the Atlantic on Concorde, played at both gigs, on his own and, in the USA, as one of two guest drummers with Led Zeppelin. The two shows climaxed with all-star British and US ensembles singing their respective "Feed the World" anthems. The biggest rock event ever to be staged over one day, it raised more than £40 million in the UK for famine relief in Africa, helped by Geldof imploring viewers to not go to the pub but to give their money to "Feed the World" instead. Joining Richard Skinner in the BBC presentation team were Janice Long, David Hepworth, Andy Batten-Foster, Mike Smith, Mark Ellen, Andy Kershaw, Paul Gambaccini and Steve Blacknell. More than a hundred countries took coverage of the event.

★ ★ ★

While all this excitement was going on, back in the day-to-day world, the BBC team was struggling to retain *Whistle Test*'s importance in a post-*Tube* world. Although the sets and the presenters had changed, and the show had become increasingly flippant and playful – some way from the hushed reverence of the Bob Harris years – it was still felt that the show needed yet more rejuvenation. There was no better place to start than with the presentation team again so, in 1984, Trevor Dann was charged with finding a younger colleague to freshen up what Mark Ellen and David Hepworth brought to the show. "Mark looked a lot younger than Dave but the two of them together just said 'rock' in an old-fashioned way," he says. "Initially, the plan had been to try to move Dave on and bring in somebody new with Mark but then it was felt that, actually, having three might be better."

Dann had encountered a young lad from Rochdale, via Leeds University, called Andy Kershaw, who was working as a roadie for Billy Bragg. Impressed by his musical knowledge and loquacious powers of persuasion, Dann asked if he'd like to do a screen test, alongside a few other potential presenters. "He was far and away the best. He had no television training. In many ways, technically, he wasn't very good at it but he had such a spirit about him." Kershaw became part of the team but, just as Bob Harris had discovered in the seventies, not all the music featured was going to be to his taste and, Dann says, it showed. "Little did we know that actually he really didn't like a lot of the music he was going to be asked to introduce, so you got a very up-and-down performance from Andy. If he was introducing Elvis Costello or the Smiths or somebody he liked, he was very enthusiastic. But if he had to introduce Tears For Fears or Howard Jones, you could tell it was being done through gritted teeth."

Andy Kershaw was not the last recruit. Radio 1's Richard Skinner began adding reports and in 1985 Ro Newton added some female balance as David Hepworth became less involved. But, despite these changes, after 16 years on air, *Whistle Test* appeared to be running out of steam, not helped by the trimming of the running time from 50 to 30 minutes and some bizarre scheduling decisions.

"It had always been a late-night show and it knew what it was when it was there," explains Dann. "It was a show that was a bit alternative, if it needed to be, wasn't required to have a big audience and was quite grown up. It wasn't *The Tube*. It wasn't full of people mooning and sticking their tongues out. Then Graeme McDonald, who was the Controller of BBC2, decided to bring it forward in the schedules and, for one season, it ran at 7.30, which was a bit too early, but we could live with it and it did really well. Then BBC1 launched a new soap opera called *EastEnders* on the same night, which just killed it completely." The scheduler's response was not to move *Whistle Test* back into the safety of late night, but to move it even further forward. Some programmes went out as early as 6 p.m. and that spelt the beginning of the end for the show. "It was really insanely early so it was not going to be watched by anybody who liked it. They took us away from the place where our audience was and deployed us to do a different job, which we didn't have either the skill or frankly the format to achieve."

With its regular studio out of commission, for its final series *Whistle Test* was rendered prematurely homeless, so the decision was made to take the show around the BBC regions. Apart from a few subsequent specials, the series bowed out in March 1987. "It was felt that the battle against *The Tube* had been lost and so a new idea was needed," recalls Dann. "John and I went away and made two pilots. John's was called *Hip Pop* and was very youthful, very stylish in that pop video way of that period of music. It was studio based with a live audience. I made a pilot for a show called *FMTV*, which was presented by Johnnie Walker. It was different because it was not shot in a studio at all. We went out and we filmed Lloyd Cole & the Commotions somewhere and a weird old group called I, Ludicrous doing something, so it was more of a reportage than a straightforward studio thing. We submitted these two pilots for consideration by the network and I went off to make a documentary about Fleetwood Mac."

While Trevor was in Los Angeles, a record company executive called him with some disturbing news. "I don't want to worry you but I've just been up to your office and all your stuff is in a skip in the corridor. I wondered if anybody had told you." When Trevor checked things out he discovered that Janet Street-Porter had arrived to run "yoof" TV, claiming both the office space and the budget. "*Whistle Test* was a gonner and so were both our new pilots because all the budget was being put into that strand that was going to be called *DEF II*. We were, effectively, out of work."[20]

At this point, too, Mike Appleton left the BBC to work for Landscape, a music-based satellite channel, as the Network Features department was being wound up, and he admits not battling to keep *Whistle Test* on air. "It had been going 16 years, so it was difficult to keep it fresh anyway and let's say I didn't put up a fight for it," he says. "It came to a conclusion, which was probably as well. If it had gone on any longer, it would have probably dragged on. Certainly, I wouldn't have been there and it was my baby so I didn't really want any nannies looking after it."[21]

The cancellation of *Whistle Test* left a serious music void in the BBC schedules, one that took a number of years to fill. "It was a great tragedy for the whole of the BBC, in my view," says Trevor Dann. "With *Whistle Test* out of the picture, there was nothing else until *Later*."[22]

★ ★ ★

The Tube was very much a child of its time. The early eighties was a period of social upheaval, marked by riots, unemployment and industrial strife. Young people were kicking-back against the Establishment, Thatcherism and the generally accepted way of doing things. *The Tube*'s relaxed approach to the conventions of television and its run-ins with the regulator, the IBA, mirrored all this, although ironically the programme was itself accused of prurience on one occasion when a band called the Redskins smuggled a striking miner on stage to give a speech. His microphone wasn't live and so viewers never heard a word. A technical cock-up said the producers; censorship, claimed the miners' supporters.

The show certainly touched a nerve and it was always bold. In 1984, an extended edition – five hours long – was broadcast under the title *A Midsummer Night's Tube*; in 1985, a continental collaboration produced the five-and-a-half-hour *Europe A Go Go* across 13 countries; and in 1987, one of the last ever editions was based around a clever spoof of the sixties cult TV series *The Prisoner*, with Jools Holland being hounded, just like Patrick McGoohan in the original, for having the temerity to resign from the programme.

The Tube was a show that had a major influence on the music scene of the eighties and the way music television subsequently evolved, but it also had quite an impact on its home city. "The effect on Newcastle was profound," says Malcolm Gerrie. "On a Thursday and Friday night, you could not get a hotel room. You had all the bands, all the roadies, all the managers, all the record labels, all the PR guys, all the hangers-on. It was just sensational. British Airways changed the flight of the last plane so people could get back. The last plane was like half-past six and we were on air. So Elton John and people were either having to be limo'd back or they were on the train, getting hassled. We made a fuss about it and they changed the flight. When *The Tube* finished, the local taxi company laid off over a hundred drivers."

The reason often cited for the show's eventual cancellation is a run-in that Jools Holland had with the regulator. In a live trailer shown on ITV, the presenter encouraged viewers to watch *The Tube* or be "a completely ungroovy fucker". It was not the best choice of language for children's hour. Holland was immediately repentant for the slip, which he put down to tiredness, but was suspended from the show for six weeks. By this point, however, the decision had already been taken to bring *The Tube* off air.

"The apocryphal version of events as to why it ended was because of Jools's bad language and us getting into trouble with the IBA," says Malcolm Gerrie. "It had nothing to do with that at all. It was basically down to two factors. One was the changing regime at Channel 4, coupled with a change of management and an economic squeeze at Tyne Tees."

At Tyne Tees, head man Andy Allan had left and been replaced by David Reay, whose approach to the job changed the atmosphere in the building. "He was a very different beast, and he was tasked with making economies and trying to squeeze bigger margins out of what we already had," says Gerrie. "Therefore, we started to see all sorts of unrest within the station. In fact, an entire *Midsummer Night's Tube* – I think it was called *The Big Tube* – got cancelled with all the artists booked. Five hours of live TV. The union went on strike that week so we were in this dreadful situation of having to contact all the management and the artists and stand everything down. That was when I realised that there was a tectonic plate shift, if you like. Andrea Wonfor was at the sharp end of that because she was controller of programmes and was being asked to make serious editorial and creative sacrifices."

The change taking place at Channel 4, Gerrie says, was quite extraordinary. "We had a junior researcher working on the show by the name of John Cummins, who Andrea had recommended. He was 24 when he joined the show and incredibly posh. I was struck by his affability. He came on board as a trainee researcher and very quickly forged a bond with Jools and Paula and Geoff Wonfor. He was superb in his job – very efficient, great with talent, good initiative." Amazingly, a couple of years later, Cummins was appointed commissioning editor for youth programmes at Channel 4. "He became my boss," says Gerrie. "I'm very fond of John. He's a lovely guy, a dear friend who's made a very successful career for himself in business consultancy. Sadly, he was a much better researcher than he was a commissioning editor. By his own admission, he didn't have the experience, or perhaps a way of persuading people to do things." When this development was combined with the changes on the top floor of Tyne Tees, says Gerrie, "it felt like a very different place all of a sudden," and it led to departures.[23]

Faced with continuous industrial unrest and budget squeezes, Andrea Wonfor quit to join the independent production company Zenith.* Soon after, she encouraged Gerrie to join her. With the loss of these leading figures, and Jools Holland's enthusiasm diminishing, Channel 4 decided to cancel the show. In April 1987, Studio 5 at Tyne Tees closed its doors. *The Tube* was no more.† By the end of that year, both *The Tube* and *Whistle Test* – two of the main pillars of music on television – had disappeared.

★ ★ ★

★ Andrea Wonfor later became Controller of Arts and Entertainment at Channel 4 and Director of Programmes at Granada. Among the many programmes she worked on or championed were *Byker Grove*, *The Big Breakfast*, *This Morning* and *Loose Women*. She was awarded an OBE in 2003 and died, aged 60, in 2004.[24]

† It wasn't quite the end for *The Tube*. In November 1999, Malcolm Gerrie – then working for the independent company Initial – revived the show as a three-hour special for Sky 1. *Apocalypse Tube* was hosted by Radio 1's Chris Moyles and MTV presenter Donna Air. A co-production with Sky and Tyne Tees, the show was recorded in its original home of Studio 5 but was deliberately contemporary and not a nostalgia fest. Paula Yates and Jools Holland made guest appearances and the featured artists included Travis, Robbie Williams, Beverley Knight, Paul McCartney, Macy Gray and Paul Weller. Channel 4 repeated the show in two parts early in 2000. There was talk of a weekly revival but it didn't transpire.

Television had not seen the end of Jools Holland, however. Despite his ups and downs on *The Tube*, the musician was increasingly in demand during the eighties. Having initially impressed in the film about the Police in Montserrat, he was now wanted for other music/travel projects, which led to *Walking To New Orleans* (1985) for Channel 4. The resultant, semi-comic film, directed by Geoff Wonfor, featured artists such as Fats Domino, Lee Dorsey, Allen Toussaint, the Neville Brothers and Johnnie Allen. It was narrated by Stephen Fry and, in parts filmed in London, there was music from Sting and George Melly. Holland was also seen in an unusual offering called *Rebellious Jukebox* (1985). This was a late-night music show with comedy sketches, made primarily for the Showtime cable network in the USA. The setting was the fictitious Rebellious Jukebox nightclub, with Holland playing the manager and Mari Wilson the cloakroom attendant. Kevin Godley and Lol Creme – who had left 10cc and refocused on music video production – were the show's directors but only two editions were shown in the UK.

Holland also laid the groundwork for the BBC's *Hootenanny* shows that started in the nineties with a New Year's Eve "party" called *Come Dancing With Jools Holland* in 1986. Again, this was produced in Newcastle by Tyne Tees and combined comedy and music, with guests such as Go West and Jimmy Ruffin. Holland was notching up the credits and really beginning to establish himself as the face of music on television.

⋆ ⋆ ⋆

With the demise of *The Tube*, Channel 4's reputation for successful and innovative youth programming came under scrutiny. Its response was to bring in producers Janet Street-Porter and Jane Hewland, who created *Network 7* (1987–8). Described by the *TV Times* as "TV's first electronic tabloid", this was a two-hour Sunday lunchtime package with a number of elements, only small parts of which were music related. The show boasted "fantastic fashion, sensational stories, sizzling style" but was an odd mix of celebrity gossip, the latest Gerry Anderson animation series* and

* A private detective spoof called *Dick Spanner PI*.

earnest discussions of issues of the day. But it was innovative, fast-moving and successful, and this ultimately led to the cancellation of *Whistle Test* when Street-Porter was poached by the BBC to revive the Corporation's own young-persons' output. Redistributing the *Whistle Test* budget, she set about creating a twice-weekly, early-evening strand called *DEF II* (1988–94). This was a collection of individual programmes covering everything from travel (*Rough Guide*), current affairs (*Reportage*) and football (*Standing Room Only*) to employment (*Job Bank*), cult adventure series (*Battlestar Galactica* and *Mission: Impossible*) and imported sitcoms (*The Fresh Prince Of Bel-Air* and *Wayne's World*), but music was far more prominent than in *Network* 7.

One of the first *DEF II* music shows was strangely called *FSd* (1988) and came from BBC Scotland. It aimed to showcase the indie music world, through performances and insights behind the scenes. Among those featuring were the Soup Dragons, Hue And Cry, Deacon Blue, Primal Scream and a number of lesser-known Scottish bands, but *FSd* only lasted one short run. Another early offering was *That Was Then, This Is Now* (1988–9), a series of films looking back over the careers of various artists, discovering through interviews and performance footage how fame had arrived and what they were up to at that moment in time. Among those feted were the Pet Shop Boys, Spandau Ballet, Depeche Mode, the Clash, Joe Jackson and Eddy Grant.

Frenchman Antoine de Caunes applied his Gallic charm, quirky wit and deliberately thick foreign accent to *Rapido* (1988–92), an English language version of a French music show, although the featured artists were international and included lots of big names. Initially broadcast late at night, this was incorporated into *DEF II* in 1989.

Snub TV (1989–91) was another interesting contribution, proving that you don't need big budgets to create stimulating music television. It started life as an export, put together to give Americans a taste of British indie music, and was then snapped up by the BBC. Initially hosted by Jeanette Lee, but known for mostly avoiding a "face" presenter, *Snub TV* was fortunate to be on air at the time when the Manchester music scene was beginning to take off and gave a television debut to the Stone Roses, but it wasn't entirely UK-focused – emerging acts from around the world were also included. Not all those featured were chart virgins but House of Love, Sonic Youth, the Pixies, Inspiral Carpets, James, Manic Street Preachers and Ocean Colour Scene, for instance, all appeared on the show before achieving chart success.

Producers Brenda Kelly and Pete Fowler, both formerly of Rough Trade records, developed the series on a shoestring but, turning a handicap into a virtue, were thus able to strip away the gloss of television, shooting their own low-budget videos and grabbing interviews in the odd hour that bands might be available while rehearsing, rather than running to the expense of hiring a studio.[25]

Black music in all its forms – soul, funk, rap, house, reggae – was showcased in *Behind The Beat* (1988–9), which combined performance with reportage. The programme was firmly centred on the big names – James Brown, the O'Jays, Barry White, Prince, Michael Jackson, Alexander O'Neal – but lesser-known acts did get a look-in, as did some soulful white performers. When it ended, it was replaced by *Dance Energy* (later renamed *Dance Energy House Party* and then *D Energy*, 1990–4) that was hosted by rapper Normski and focused more closely on house, hip hop and funk. There was a DJ of the week, dance news from around the world, a dance chart and comedy from Vas Blackwood. Anyone from Run DMC, the Dream Warriors and PM Dawn to the Shamen, EMF and Boyz II Men might feature. "*Come Dancing* it isn't," the *Radio Times* helpfully explained. Under the banner *Dance Energy Lift Off*, the show also offered a chance for unsigned artists to win a record deal.

Put together, *Behind The Beat* and *Dance Energy* can be seen as steps toward the wider embrace of multiculturalism on British television, while the overall output of *Network 7* and *DEF II* had its own cultural impact, significantly changing the way programmes for young people were made, introducing accessibility, informality and a degree of interactivity that predated the internet age.

Dance music was also the essence of another series, this time on ITV, screened late at night. *The Hit Man And Her* (1988–92) was a weekly exploration of club culture, or perhaps the dance equivalent of *Match Of The Day*, bringing highlights of the action from a different venue every week. The hosts indicated in the series' title were Pete Waterman and

Michaela Strachan. The first programme came from Mr Smith's club in Warrington and from there the show moved on to other clubs in the north of England and in Scotland – the Hacienda in Manchester, Roxy 2 in Sheffield, the Ritzy in Nottingham, etc. Waterman and Strachan rubbed shoulders with DJs, shouted barely audible questions to clubbers and admired the floorshows as programmes were recorded, quickly edited and broadcast the same night. Wrapped up in the package were videos of dance hits, some live music, fashion items, and games and competitions. On-screen graphics revealed the tracks being played, while selected stage dancers – including Clive, a black dancer in a blond wig – moved from venue to venue with the show.

★ ★ ★

Despite the cancellation of *The Tube* and the dispersal of its production team, Tyne Tees was keen to keep a hand on the musical rudder and so came up with a show for ITV that could be recorded in the vacant *Tube* studio. The result was *The Roxy* (1987–8), less a *Tube* substitute and more a potential rival for *Top Of The Pops*. This was produced by Alastair Pirrie, former presenter of *Razzmatazz*, which had also by now run its course. Once again, however, Tyne Tees ran into the same old problem when ITV did not guarantee the programme a networked slot. Although all the regions did screen it on the same day, they did so at different times, which meant it struggled to build a presence from the start.

Concept-wise, the show made out that it came from the Roxy Theatre, a faded thirties dance hall, complete with balcony and boxes, although there was no such place, everything being done in the confines of Tyne Tees' Studio 5. Still, there were five stages on which chart acts could perform, introduced by David Jensen and Irish presenter (later a successful artist) Kevin Sharkey. The chart used was the Network Chart, as prepared for Independent Local Radio stations, and later editions reflected that in being retitled *Roxy – the Network Chart Show*, by which time Pat Sharp had replaced Jensen and the show had been relegated to the graveyard, post-midnight slot in some regions. Breaking up the chart coverage, former Radio Luxembourg DJ Benny Brown reported on the international chart scene, a "video vote" encouraged viewers to ring in with a choice of film for the next edition, and pop gossip was disseminated in a feature called "Roxy Confidential".

Apart from scheduling, what also hindered *The Roxy* was its location. Being produced in Newcastle had been a bonus for *The Tube*, but it was the opposite for *The Roxy* as it could only tempt bands north with the promise of a three-minute slot for their current hit and not the longer, more flexible sets of *The Tube*. Reluctance to take up the offer meant a greater reliance on videos, which inevitably failed to mark the show out as original. In less than a year, *The Roxy* disappeared.

As a substitute, ITV picked up *The Chart Show* from Channel 4 and also introduced *Chart Attack*. With Capital Radio DJ Mick Brown as host, this looked at a number of different pop charts, including the album chart, the indie chart and the American chart. *Chart Attack* was shown on weekends after midnight in the *Night Network* (1987–9) strand that had been developed to help ITV regions extend their broadcasting through the night, although not all the regions took it. Other Mick Brown contributions were a music magazine called *MBTV* and the celebrity-based *Night Network Pop Quiz*. The *Night Network* package was otherwise made up of recorded concerts, comedy and re-runs of vintage series such as *The Monkees* and *Captain Scarlet And The Mysterons*, but it did also include highlights of the sixties German music show *Beat Club*.

Those ITV regions that didn't adopt *Night Network* did at least get a chance to see another contribution from *So It Goes*' Tony Wilson. *The Other Side Of Midnight* (1988–9) was an arts talk show from Granada, covering books, film, theatre and art, as well as music, which included performances from the Fall and the Stone Roses.

* * *

Among the ITV regions, it wasn't just Tyne Tees that was still hoping to make a musical mark. Border Television in Carlisle, fortified by the appointment of former *Tube* producer Paul Corley, had already created *Bliss* for Channel 4 and now tried again with *APB* (1988) for the same outlet, the letters standing for "All Points Bulletin". This was an hour-long Sunday lunchtime magazine presented by Gaz Top (Gareth Jones) and was less about performance than talk and features, with sport and film sharing the focus. As well as discussing musical matters, artists divulged their pastimes and other aspects of their private life. Michael Hutchence talked about Harley Davidson motorbikes, the Proclaimers discussed country & western and Annie Lennox played harmonium in a church. Only one series made it to air.

The same year, an independent Scottish production company developed a strongly accented late-night variety show for Channel 4. *Halfway To Paradise* (1988–90), mixing music with comedy and sport, aimed to prove that there was still life beyond London and was produced at Glasgow's Black Cat Studio. The hooks of the show were the host Mr Sinclair, a bingo caller with yearnings for the fifties (played by actor Iain McColl), and an emphasis on artists and features from Scotland, Ireland and the north of England – a typical show combined items on Scottish panto dames, the darts player Jocky Wilson and pigeon fancying – although some global stars did appear. Among those performing over the two series were Hue And Cry, Steve Earle, Wet Wet Wet, the Pogues, Deacon Blue, the Proclaimers, Texas and Jesus And Mary Chain.

While Channel 4 embraced such projects for domestic consumption, it also had its eye on the international market and commissioned Malcolm Gerrie, now working at the independent production company Initial, to deliver a series with export potential. This new series was called *Wired* (1988), for which Gerrie brought in former colleague Chris Cowey as associate producer and also gave early television experience to music journalist Mark Cooper, who would go on to create *Later With Jools Holland* and subsequently become the BBC's Head of Music Television.

Wired was a show split in two. Half the content came from London, hosted by Tim Graham; the other half came from New York with Lenore Pemberton. Pinewood Studios was used for live performances and there were no bigger names than those that *Wired* attracted, Robert Plant, Whitney Houston, Prince, Tina Turner, Michael Jackson, Elton John, Johnny Cash, Nina Simone and Bruce Springsteen among them.

Journalistic features covered issues such as pop and the press and pop and politics, but there was also room for fun. One item was a drinking tour of New York with the Pogues.

Much was hoped of *Wired* but, despite the considerable budget and the calibre of the production team, the programme stumbled and lasted only one series. Gerrie believes it all happened just a bit too quickly in response to the eager demands of Channel 4. "They were desperate for a replacement for *The Tube*," he says. "The ink hadn't dried on my contract with Initial before we got this massive deal. A lot of the people who I would normally have around me were scattered so it became a real challenge to pull it all together." Also, the format was not right. "I felt we had to do something new, try some different things out, but there was again a tension between what I wanted and what the channel wanted. The channel wanted more of *The Tube*, basically. So the show ended up a bit of a compromise. For me, it was neither fish nor fowl and I wasn't really satisfied with the outcome."[26]

Cowey, who ran the live music end, agrees, describing *Wired* as "a slightly odd hybrid" that "was trying too hard to reinvent *The Tube*". "It lacked the excitement and the vitality and the kind of risky, scary feeling that you got on *The Tube*," he says. "It was an attempt to make things more smooth and more slick and probably threw the baby out with the bathwater." The changing music landscape also didn't help, he says, and Gerrie agrees. "It was a funny time, actually, the end of the eighties, beginning of the nineties, pre-Brit pop, the fag-end of post punk and New Romantics."[27]

Looking back, Mark Cooper suggests two main reasons for the show's failure to click. "The series foundered partly because the presenters weren't a hit," he says. "Tim Graham, who was a lovely man, just didn't capture the public's imagination or indeed the critics' imagination." The other reason was because the show was set up as an international production with foreign investment. "That meant that they had to book big-name stars who sold lots of records. What I learned from *Wired* is that you couldn't book a show on the assumption, because it had big artists on it, that people would watch it." Cooper also learned that if he was ever in a position to sign artists for his own show, he would want to be driven by taste and integrity, rather than "they'll be pleased with this in Brazil". "There were lots of great bookings on *Wired* but I could just see the way you could be led into a situation where you weren't driven entirely by the music."[28]

Music also played a part in the disastrous arts series *Club X* (1989), a daughter of *Network 7* for late nights, which came from a nightclub so noisy that at times you couldn't hear the presenters. But that was just one of the programme's many deficiencies that have seen it labelled as one of television's most inept creations, a sometimes outrageous, shambolic mix of performance art, drama and dance. Of more interest to music lovers would have been *The Session* (1989), a programme shown on Channel 4 the same night. This was a short series produced by RTE in Ireland and brought together musicians from different genres. In the first show, Steve Cropper was partnered by John Parr and gospel singer Bobby Whitlock. In another, the Pogues and the Dubliners played together for the first time on television and the Pogues also helped Joe Strummer out with a few Clash songs. Others guests included Elvis Costello and Nanci Griffith.

★ ★ ★

In contrast to the froth of the pop charts, world music found itself increasingly under the spotlight during the eighties, hastened by the commercial success of Paul Simon's *Graceland* album in 1986. A year earlier, Channel 4 had shown Jeremy Marre's *Beats Of The Heart*, a collection of films that covered musical traditions from regions as diverse as the Texas–Mexico border, Thailand and the deserts of China. Romany music, Brazilian samba and Bollywood also featured. The films had been made over a period of seven years. The theme was then picked up in BBC2's *Rhythms Of The World* (1988–93), which drew attention to musical superstars unknown to most people. Six series of films were produced, delving into such genres as conjunto from Mexico, rhumba from Zaire and chouval bwa music from Martinique. There were programmes on places as varied as New Orleans, Soweto and Transylvania, and profiles of Cuba's "Queen of Salsa" Celia Cruz, Nusrat Fateh Ali Khan, the great star of Qawwali religious music, and Cui Jian, the rock star sometimes called "the Bob Dylan of China". More familiar names also featured. The Rolling Stones were seen visiting Morocco, John Lee Hooker was joined by Malian musician Ali Farka Touré, and Peter Gabriel welcomed 70 international musicians to his Wiltshire recording studio.

At the end of the decade, Channel 4 tried to build on the world music concept by launching *Big World Café* (1989), a Sunday afternoon show recorded at the Brixton Academy and presented by Mariella Frostrup, Eagle-Eye Cherry and Jo Shinner. The second series was broadcast late at night under the shortened title of *Big World*, with Andy Kershaw replacing Cherry and Shinner. Andrea Wonfor, now working at Zenith North, put together the team and this included fellow *Tube* refugees Chris Cowey as producer and her own husband, Geoff Wonfor, as director of filmed reports. Alongside western pop names such as Gloria Estefan, New Order and Wet Wet Wet, the programme introduced artists such as Guinean singer Mory Kante, Congolese musician Papa Wemba and Bulgarian folk singers Trio Bulgarka, who'd worked with Kate Bush, to British viewers.

★ ★ ★

As the eighties drew to a close, a new era opened up in British broadcasting with the start of the first satellite television services. The idea of beaming television signals down from space began to take hold with the launch of a company called Satellite TV in 1982. The business wasn't licensed to broadcast to the UK and so other European countries were its initial target, the first 70,000 homes located in Norway and Finland. One of the early offerings was a chart countdown show hosted by Mike Read in London.

Satellite TV then piqued the interest of Rupert Murdoch and was acquired by his News International group, which changed the name to Sky and began to find a way into the domestic television market. While most of the UK at the time received its television via rooftop aerials, some pockets of the country, where geography made it impossible to receive signals, did have a cable feed and Sky used this to build a presence prior to launching a service direct to homes equipped with their own satellite dishes in 1989. Part of the early Sky cable service was a music show called *Skytrax* that featured videos and interviews presented by Pat Sharp and Gary Davies.

Music video shows were eagerly embraced by Sky and other cable/ satellite broadcasters because they involved little production expertise and cost. This also inspired the creation of an MTV clone called Music Box in 1984. This was another cable-only service but viewers without cable in the north of England were able to get a good look at the channel two years later, when Yorkshire Television experimented with 24-hour broadcasting and for five months ran Music Box – which it partly owned – through the night, from around midnight to 6 a.m. It wasn't enough to save the loss-making channel, however, and Music Box was folded into a general entertainment service called Super Channel in 1987.

In 1989, direct broadcasting by satellite (DBS) services began in the UK. The official supplier – licensed and regulated by the IBA – was British Satellite Broadcasting (BSB), but its launch was delayed by technical problems and it was beaten to air by Sky's "unofficial" DBS service that used a satellite owned and operated in Luxembourg. The two systems being incompatible, viewers had to decide which one to opt for, leaving both operations soon in financial trouble. This meant a merger in 1991 to create British Sky Broadcasting (BSkyB), or Sky as it is still generally known. Among the five channels offered by BSB before the merger was a music channel called The Power Station, which featured Chris Evans as its breakfast presenter, but this became a victim of the merger and was replaced by MTV in Sky's subscriber package. BSB also had a general entertainment channel, Galaxy, for which Jools Holland hosted a music and comedy show called *The Happening* that briefly transferred to Channel 4 in 1991.

* * *

Meanwhile, *Top Of The Pops* was still rumbling on, although it was by now showing its age. By the end of the eighties, its viewing figures had dropped to around 10 million but in truth only the big soaps at this time were getting the huge numbers that *Top Of The Pops* had enjoyed in the seventies. The broadcasting landscape had changed. There was now a fourth channel, satellite television had begun and there were more viewing hours on the terrestrial networks. What's more, the arrival of affordable home video recorders meant that you didn't need to stay in any longer to watch your favourite show. That said, the programme's individual decline may perhaps be attributed to some degree to the innovation that had actually helped it at the start of the decade. The music video was now being dropped into any number of programmes from breakfast time to the middle of the night. You didn't need to watch *Top Of The Pops* any longer to catch the latest hits.

With Michael Hurll in charge, *Top Of The Pops* also remained rooted in the ethos of light entertainment. This family focus may have shielded it from the pressures that eventually killed off *Whistle Test* but it meant that, in the fast-moving decade in which *The Tube* had come and gone and youth TV had been grabbed by the collar and given a good shaking, *Top Of The Pops* had changed little and was becoming increasingly irrelevant to music fans.

In 1988, when the programme's 25th anniversary was marked with a special edition compiled and hosted by Paul Gambaccini and Mike Read, Hurll handed over control to Paul Ciani.* There was some immediate innovation. A simultaneous broadcast in stereo on Radio 1 was added, the time a music video could be played for was restricted to two minutes, and there were changes to the frontline personnel. The latest new hosts included Nicky Campbell, Mark Goodier, Adrian John, Liz Kershaw, Sybil Ruscoe, Susie Mathis and Jakki Brambles, but also – one guesses in a bid to keep the show youthful – Ciani added presenters from children's television: Caron Keating from *Blue Peter*, Jenny Powell and Anthea Turner from the Saturday morning magazine *UP2U* and Andy Crane and Simon Parkin from the continuity "broom cupboard". It was a strange decision. The hosting of cutting-edge music programmes on BBC2 and Channel 4 had been successfully entrusted

* Michael Hurll went on to develop *The British Comedy Awards*. He died, aged 75, in 2012.[29]

to informed young enthusiasts, but the longest-running music show on British television was handed to presenters with no musical background whose day jobs involved talking to puppet ducks and shaping pieces of sticky-backed plastic.

Top Of The Pops had an identity crisis that would need attention in the nineties.

THE NINETIES

Cool Britannia

Just like the eighties, the nineties was a decade of rapid evolution in the world of television. At its start, satellite broadcasting was just beginning to take a hold. When it finished, satellite had gone digital and there were so many channels available, free-to-air or via subscription, to dish owners or those connected by cable, that the arrival of a fifth UK terrestrial channel went almost unheeded. It was also a decade when television went fully 24/7.

The opportunities for broadcasting more music were obvious, but instead of making music increasingly available to the general viewing public, schedulers broke up its audience and began to push it into the margins. There were, indeed, lots of new programmes featuring music but viewers often had to sit through other material to get to it or, if they wanted just music on its own, seek it out in the fringes of the schedule.

This trend was already evident at the start of the nineties as music on TV became ever more closely entwined with whatever was grabbing the attention of young people. It often found itself confined to youth strands, tucked away for insomniacs in the dark hours or built into "daring" magazine shows where the language could be ripe and outrage seemed to be the key motivation. Leading this particular charge was *The Word* (1990–5).

★ ★ ★

Terry Christian was a lad from the stagnant streets of Old Trafford whose future looked bleak until he found salvation in the form of Tony Wilson's *So It Goes* in the seventies. He adored Wilson's boundless enthusiasm for the new wave music scene and his unwavering commitment to all things Manchester. Wilson became an idol and later a mentor as Christian found his own way into broadcasting, championing new music from the North on local radio. When Wilson gave up the weekly music column he wrote for the *Manchester Evening News*, Christian took it on. The column was called 'The Word', and that seemed like a pretty good title to take to television when Christian and the music of "Madchester" went national.[1]

The Word has become synonymous with "shock TV" and it certainly caused a stir during its time on air. Presented by Christian along with Amanda de Cadenet, Michelle Collins, Mark Lamarr, Katie Puckrik, Dani Behr and others, it was conceived as an early evening mix of music, film and showbusiness, broadcast by Channel 4 in the old *Tube* timeslot, but its controversial, provocative approach saw it shifted to 11 p.m. less than three months after it began, where it sat better with the post-pub audience. During the course of its time on air, *The Word* did offer some musical highlights. Christian's input was important and Jo Whiley was a band booker on the show. Among those appearing were Oasis (TV debut), Nirvana, the Charlatans, Norman Cook, the Farm, the Happy Mondays, the Inspiral Carpets and Mark Morrison, but they were often overshadowed by the antics of drunken celebrities, hidden-camera routines darker than anything seen on *Candid Camera* and other deliberately outrageous features. These included nauseating challenges undertaken by "The Hopefuls", assorted members of the public so keen to appear on television that they would snog a granny, bathe in pig shit or eat a plate of corns and verrucas. Creator Charlie Parsons, who had previously worked on *Network* 7 and *Club X*, was given a brief to make the show "talked about" and succeeded so brilliantly that Channel 4 eventually had to take it off air.[2]

The Word was succeeded by the almost as provocative *The Girlie Show* (1996–7), produced by the *Rapido* team. Presented by Sara Cox, Rachel Williams, Clare Gorham and later Sarah Cawood, the programme placed control in the hands of feisty young females, treating viewers to "Toilet Talk" gossip, boisterous coverage of girls' nights out and a decidedly frank view of the world from women behaving badly. In this form, girl power arrived on Channel 4 six months ahead of the Spice Girls, but again the music input was somewhat eclipsed. Not to be outdone, ITV chipped in with its own ladette-driven entertainment in the form of *Hotel Babylon* (1996), fronted by Dani Behr. This was a post-midnight music, entertainment and "style" show aimed at the under thirties. It featured big names from the movie world – Michelle Pfeiffer, Spike Lee, Quentin Tarantino – among performances from such artists as Coolio, Shaggy, Tori Amos, Green Day and Shakespears Sister.

★ ★ ★

While it courted controversy with such series, Channel 4 was also still looking for a genuine replacement for *The Tube*, albeit one that was likely to be confined to late evenings. A rare attempt to cater for the more mature viewer was *Rock Steady* (1990). Promising live music, news, informed comment and reviews, this hour-long show – a television equivalent of Q magazine, with echoes of the Bob Harris *Whistle Test* years – was hosted by DJs Dave Fanning and Nicky Horne and had a theme song provided by Sting. The first edition included film of a performance by Eric Clapton at the Royal Albert Hall and among the later artists caught in the act were Tanita Tikkaram, Michelle Shocked, Carlos Santana, Fleetwood Mac, Kim Wilde and John Mayall. The show presented its own album chart and there were 'Spotlight' features on individual performers, exploring their influences and their approach to their work. Some live performances – including sets from Dave Edmunds, Wet Wet Wet and Marillion – were later broadcast under the name *Rock Steady Special*.

Unfortunately, *Rock Steady* didn't work out and so Channel 4 tried again with *Friday At The Dome* (1991). Presented from London's Dome

Club (actually the domed Kilburn National Ballroom), this came from the same production team and included Dave Fanning again as host, but this time with comedian Craig Ferguson adding some humour. Interviews, features on anything from death metal clubs to Bob Marley, and big concert performances formed the central planks of the show, and artists who obliged included MC Hammer, Alexander O'Neal, Robert Palmer and Erasure. There were also some interesting collaborations, such as the pairing of Aaron Neville and Dr. John, Will Downing and Ruby Turner, and Joe Elliott of Def Leppard and Liam Ó Maonlaí of Hothouse Flowers. Once again, however, the show proved short-lived and, in the absence of home-grown success, Channel 4 then imported *Electric Ballroom* (1993) from Ireland. This post-midnight collection of interviews, profiles, concert footage and live music included artists such as the Cranberries and Carter USM, but only five programmes ever went out.

ITV was also frustrating territory for music fans at this time. There was some good stuff but it was hidden away in the schedules, like Central's hour-long late-night package of live performances appropriately called *Bedrock* (1990–1). This featured the likes of Uriah Heep, Wishbone Ash, Rick Wakeman and newly reformed outfits such as Gong, Camel and even the Buzzcocks, but these weren't the only blasts from the past on air. Mike Mansfield also returned to reprise the director-in-the-gallery role he played in *Supersonic* in the seventies. This time around, his show was not studio-based but a series of concert performances of varying vintage under the banner *Cue The Music* (1991–6), with Mansfield introducing the acts from his control-room chair. Those captured in action included ELO, Big Country, the Mission, Blancmange, Tears For Fears and Steeleye Span.

Far more vibrant was a new music magazine called *The Beat* (1993–5), hosted by Gary Crowley, that aimed to showcase up-and-coming young talent across the genres but also delved into film reviews and fashion. It was generously allocated an hour of ITV airtime for three years but, once again, this came after midnight and at different times depending on where you were watching around the country. Teenage Fan Club, Stereo MC's, Pulp, Saint Etienne and Radiohead were among the acts involved, along with more established performers like Deacon Blue, Aztec Camera and the Cure. Performances came from the London Astoria theatre and footage from the Reading Festival was also part of the mix.

The Beat was joined in the early hours by *The Album Show* (1994–5), a weekly round-up of the latest chart with Lynn Parsons, while, a few years later, another ITV middle-of-the-night offering was *Rockmania* (1997–8). Hosted by David Prever, this 26-part series majored on "the quirkier aspects of show business, the music industry and popular culture".

Regional television contributions on both ITV and BBC were fewer and farther between at this time than in earlier decades, but BBC Scotland did produce a short series called *No Stilettos* (1993), which came from the Cottier theatre, a former church in Glasgow. Eddi Reader welcomed guests such as Aztec Camera, the Lemonheads, Pulp, the Cranberries, Edwyn Collins and David Gray, six years before his first hit. The show was then repeated on BBC2.

★ ★ ★

At the other end of the spectrum, pop music was increasingly becoming the domain of the kids' TV presenter, as revealed in the innocent, but long-lasting, *The O Zone* (1989–2000). This was a short, sharp burst of music news broadcast at various times of the week, from weekday mornings to early Friday evenings. At first daily, it later went weekly, offering young viewers the first TV coverage of the new Top 40 as well as assorted features that ranged from a look behind the scenes of a video shoot with Halo James to a glimpse of Jason Donovan's hectic lifestyle. Andy Crane, Andi Peters, Philippa Forester, Toby Anstis, Jayne Middlemiss, Jamie Theakston and Zoë Ball hosted the 10- or 15-minute programmes. The series also generated an equally short spin-off called *The Pop Zone* (1998–9), which aired on Saturday mornings as part of the programmes *Saturday Aardvark* and *Planet Saturday*. Hosted by guest stars such as Aqua, Peter Andre and Louise, this married features with interviews and competitions, and included reviews of new releases in a segment called 'Pop Picks'.

Top Of The Pops' own experiment with children's TV stars fortunately didn't last long and in 1990 the line-up of presenters was firmly Radio 1-based once again, with only Anthea Turner from the kids' club keeping her place. A year later, producer Paul Ciani, suffering from ill health, stepped aside and an old face returned to the team. Stanley Appel had started as a cameraman on the show in 1966 and had been working on *Top Of The Pops* as producer off and on since 1975. He was now offered an extended run at the helm.

Faced with declining audience numbers, Appel gave the show a radical overhaul – what he describes as "the Year Zero Revamp" – moving it into a larger, purpose-built studio at Elstree with its own rock lighting rig and rejigging the format so that there was less focus on the Top 40, more live bands and fewer videos. More controversially, he also reinstituted a miming ban, so all vocals needed to be performed live. This was not only unpopular with some musicians and producers but backfired on occasions when what went out barely resembled what was on the original record. A new theme tune by Tony Gibber – 'Now Get Out Of That' – was introduced, album tracks were brought back and hits from the American Top 10 were also factored in. A new rule stipulated that only records still in the UK Top 10 could feature more than once.[3]

It was Appel who oversaw the introduction of direct stereo broadcasting when the greater availability of suitably equipped television sets made Radio 1 simulcasts no longer necessary. His time in charge also saw the end of Radio 1 presenters as hosts. A couple of years ahead of the radio station's own purge of ageing DJs, Appel dropped the familiar faces in favour of newcomers Mark Franklin, Tony Dortie, Adrian Rose, Claudia Simon and Femi Oke, plus a few guest hosts (including, rather cheekily, Harry Enfield and Paul Whitehouse in their Smashie & Nicey DJ guise). By 1993, the presentation team had been pared down again, leaving most of the duties to Dortie and Franklin.

The musical changes taking place in that era were arguably beneficial to the show. House and techno – hardly likely to make exciting television whatever thrill they provided in clubs – were on the wane and melodic bands were on the way back. Britpop was breaking through and the boy band phenomenon had started, both of which should have brought in viewers, but still the audience numbers declined. To try and keep things vibrant, the show experimented with 3-D in a performance from Take That and also added live satellite links to bring in bands from around the world. In January 1994, Smashie & Nicey returned to celebrate the show's 30th anniversary with a *Top Of The Pops Party* and a look back at "three poptastic decades".

Appel remained in charge until February that year, when it was decided to take a new look at the series with the appointment of Ric Blaxill as producer. Refreshingly, as well as being a much younger man (early thirties), Blaxill's background was not in light entertainment but in Radio 1, where he produced the breakfast show, and he soon ditched Appel's presenters. Radio 1 names such as Simon Mayo and Mark Goodier returned, but there were lots of guest hosts, too, including Jarvis Cocker, comedian Jack Dee and singer Luther Vandross. Blaxill also relaxed many of the rules of the programme, allowing miming again and more flexibility in the selection of records, and he looked to improve the quality of the music by opening the door to new artists wherever possible and taking the opportunity to book big stars who happened to be in town, whether or not they were climbing the charts. The number of videos was again cut back, as was the focus on the studio audience, and another new set, new logo and new theme tune – 'Red Hot Pop' by Vince Clarke – were introduced. Blaxill's aim was to rebuild the family audience and he did have some success, with viewing figures starting to rise.

In September that year, a sister programme, *TOTP 2* (1994–), was launched on BBC2. "A music magazine for lapsed record buyers," in Blaxill's own words, this offered highlights of that week's *Top Of The Pops* combined with archive material and a preview of the following week's chart. Johnnie Walker provided the voice-overs. The inspiration may have been a short BBC2 series called *DJ's Heaven* (1993), in which the *Top Of The Pops* archives were raided to compile "tributes" to some of the programme's hosts, showing clips of their work and some of the artists they introduced. It kicked off with Dave Lee Travis – who somewhat ironically had just caused a stir by resigning live on air from Radio 1 – and subsequent editions featured Jimmy Savile, Tony Blackburn, John Peel, Simon Bates and Mike Read.[4]

In 1995, the BBC launched the *Top Of The Pops* print magazine and the same year the programme became allied to the *Eurovision Song Contest*, when a special edition of *Top Of The Pops* showcased all the songs in contention to be the UK entry, in a bid to re-establish some credibility for the process. By 1996, celebrity presenters had taken over almost entirely and among those counting down the chart were Mark Owen, Mark Morrison, Peter Andre, Harry Hill, Nigel Kennedy and Julian Clary. The viewing figures began to fall again.

⋆ ⋆ ⋆

While its flagship pop show was battling against decline, there was better news for the BBC on the more mature music front, with a warm reception given to its latest live music showcase. As if to prove that television is a circular medium, the BBC launched this new programme by spinning it off from an end-of-evening arts magazine, just as had happened in the sixties and early seventies when *Late Night Line-Up* gave birth to *Colour Me Pop*, *Disco 2* and, ultimately, *The Old Grey Whistle Test*.

The Late Show (1988–95) had begun as a weekly post-*Newsnight* discussion programme on BBC2 hosted by Clive James but the format was soon overhauled under other presenters. The revamp turned it into a four-nights-a-week live event, covering all areas of the arts, whether performance, design, architecture, literature or indeed music, with bands or solo artists brought into the studio. The idea of hiving off a dedicated music show came out of a continuing conversation between two members of *The Late Show* team. Janet Fraser Crook was directing much of the programme's music output and she encouraged its music producer, Mark Cooper, to consider launching a spin-off.

"*The Late Show* at that time was a very open place," says Cooper. "They had a studio four nights a week but a lot of the people who worked on it were more interested in the opportunity to make films." This meant that there was plenty of free studio space and time for performers to come in and play music. In keeping with the ethos of *The*

Late Show, these musicians could come from anywhere on the spectrum – jazz, folk, country, rock, whatever. They might be emerging artists or established performers, and their contribution generally followed what Cooper describes as "that naturalistic band-in-a-studio, plays-to-camera tradition the BBC has always liked". This worked within the context of *The Late Show* but Cooper was wary of taking that extra step and creating an off-shoot dedicated wholly to music. In the post-*Tube*, post-*Whistle Test* era, the landscape, Cooper says, "was littered with the corpses of dead music shows that hadn't really worked, so I was quite reluctant."

Eventually, Cooper approached Michael Jackson, *The Late Show*'s editor, who suggested that he contact Jools Holland as a potential presenter. The two were not properly acquainted, but a shared love of a wide variety of music meant that they hit it off from the start. After building a TV presentation career in the UK, Holland had been working in New York, hosting an eclectic music show called *Sunday Night* (later renamed *Night Music*) and the experience, Cooper believes, had renewed his appetite for this sort of project.

"Jools had been the *enfant terrible*," he says. "The guy who said 'groovy fuckers' on television." Now he seemed to have a different attitude. He wanted to do a show that was all about the musicians, an inclusive show rather than an abrasive show that was out to shock. Things began to come together. They already had a studio. Now the question was how many bands could it hold? And also, how could these bands be shot?

It was Janet Fraser Crook who drove the idea of placing the cameras in the centre of the studio, with all the artists arranged around the outside. This meant, theoretically, that the show would be hard to edit but it would certainly be more authentic as a result. "It was going to happen in front of your eyes and you, the viewer, were going to have the best seat in the house because the cameras, even more than Jools, were leading the audience," says Cooper. It wasn't an easy trick to pull off, with several cameras in play and a studio filled with artists, leads and equipment. "For the first five years we kept expecting to fall off the air or for things to crash into each other and quite often they did."

In 1992, the first programme, billed in the *Radio Times* as *The Late Show: Later*, promised two guest bands plus an additional acoustic set – a modest offering compared with subsequent output but even this was challenging, given the fact that they were sharing studio space with *The Late Show* and needed to finish recording before that programme went on air. "We'd get all these people in, rush to film them, rush to get them out and then I would edit what we had together," says Mark Cooper. The package would then go out at around midnight after *The Late Show*'s live broadcast had finished. But slowly things fell into place. By the time of the third programme, the name *Later With Jools Holland* (1992–) was confirmed in the *Radio Times* – symptomatic of the way in which the programme slowly evolved as a production while on air rather than being planned in detail from day one.

"We were very lucky because we were getting the chance to grow and pilot a show on air," says Cooper. "Channel 4 in that period tended to launch all their shows with a big fanfare and a lot of hype and then find out that, because they'd made the show so visible, they were stuck with the things that were wrong with them. They were very hard to fix. Because we had a kind of soft launch and we were a spin-off, we were allowed to develop in the shadows, relatively."

One of the early ideas quickly discarded was the booking of same-genre acts for each edition. "Initially, for the first five or six programmes, I was very into the curatorial thing and I thought we'd do it thematically every week," Cooper explains. "I gradually realised that actually the show was more interesting if the artists were categorically as different from each other as possible, provided they were good. They were interested to meet each other; they were impressed by each other." Together with filming in the round, this cross-pollination of different music forms – and the blending of old and young performers – was to prove fundamental to the programme's character and longevity. "Legends like being on with brand-new young artists, because it makes them feel young, and young artists like being on with people they've followed all their lives because it makes them feel proud," says Cooper. "At first, quite a lot of the time, the acts were slightly wary of the idea of being in a studio with other artists, particularly some of the more competitive ones. Now *Later*'s an institution, they all feel very pleased to be on and they automatically give to the process and want to be part of it. In a way, it feels larger than the artists, because it's been on so long, whereas at the beginning, the artists felt larger than the show."

To help foster this mood of collaboration, it was decided to ask all the studio guests to jam along with the programme's opening theme music. "That was a joke really," says Cooper. "It's more of a statement of intent than musically valid. It's something that's put together very quickly but the implicit sense is that 'Yeah, we're in it together; we're sharing in something larger than ourselves'. It restates the ethos."

Also underpinning the show from the outset was the fact that bands don't just do their bit and then clear off. Instead, they stay and respond to whoever else is on the show, and that "communal but gladiatorial" atmosphere, as it has often been called, has been the catalyst for a number of new personal and professional relationships. Thrust together in the confines of a television studio, soul mates have found each other. Marianne Faithfull and Courtney Love apparently became close friends after meeting on *Later*, and there have been some memorable match-ups on the show itself, including Alison Moyet and Sinéad O'Connor singing backing vocals for Dusty Springfield's last ever TV appearance.

That first series, tentative as it was, saw appearances from the likes of Shakespears Sister, Mary Chapin Carpenter, Robert Palmer, Shane MacGowan, Nick Cave, John Cale, Television, Simply Red, Morrissey and Chris Rea. It was successful enough for a second series to be commissioned and, by the time this came to air, *Later* had bedded down and was beginning to acquire gravitas. Through the appearance of names such as Al Green and Leonard Cohen – making his first BBC studio appearance since the sixties – the team recognised they were now in a position to attract the world's most significant artists and also do them justice. Following in their wake were the likes of Elvis Costello, David Bowie, Luther Vandross, Jackson Browne, Elton John and Bryan Ferry as the decade unfolded. Yet breakthrough artists remained just as important to the programme's identity. The largely unknown Portishead performing 'Glory Box' in 1994 was one stand-out moment for Mark Cooper. "The idea that we could really put people on the map started to emerge with that," he says. Other artists who made their TV debuts on the show include Stereophonics and Macy Gray. At the same time, the show also helped to re-establish old names or introduce them to a new audience. There was a Johnny Cash special, Dr. John appeared and there were performances from Bo Diddley and B.B. King. The central musical pivot through all this remained Jools Holland, whose own band provided the backing for some of the guests, and who himself added a bit of boogie-woogie piano to certain performances. There were short interviews, too, but music, as was the original intention, always came first and foremost.[5]

* * *

In eschewing all the frippery and sensationalism of other music shows of that era, *Later* led the way for a revival of the simple studio performance show, a genre that seemed to have died when *Whistle Test* was cancelled. Shortly after the first series of *Later* ended, BBC2 began broadcasting selected editions of MTV's *Unplugged* (1992–5; 1997), kicking off with Eric Clapton, progressing with Rod Stewart, kd lang and Annie Lennox and going on to feature such acts as Crosby, Stills & Nash, Pearl Jam, Elton John, Nirvana, Bob Dylan, Plant & Page, and Oasis.

The MTV series had begun in 1990 with Squeeze as the first guests and its format was even simpler than *Later*'s. The performers just rocked up with acoustic equipment and regaled the audience with non-electric arrangements of some of their best-known songs. Sometimes it was all very low key; at other times it was quite a bash – the Eagles may have been unplugged but they still brought a 37-piece orchestra for their *Hell Freezes Over* reunion.

Channel 4 also reverted to unadorned studio performance with a show called *Butt Naked*. This was a sister programme to *Naked City* (1993–4), a late-night music-culture magazine produced by the *Rapido* team and broadcast from a "top-secret" warehouse somewhere in London. Described in the *Radio Times* as "a music show that caters for all tastes – ranging from ambient to indie, from funk to grunge, from rap to rave", the series was hosted by Caitlin Moran and Johnny Vaughan and combined studio sets with discussions, interviews and humorous comment. Among the bands to appear were Blur, Brand New Heavies, Pulp, the Charlatans and Oasis. One regular feature revolved around busking, with a star name attempting to attract a bigger crowd and raise more money on the streets than a regular busker. Jason Donovan took the challenge in the first edition. For the spin-off *Butt Naked* (1994), some of the artists who were booked for *Naked City* were milked for another half an hour's worth of material to be shown in the early hours of the following weekend, with comedian Smiley (Michael Smiley) as host.

The same channel then made an even greater commitment to studio performance by commissioning a series called *The White Room* (1994–6). This was another production from former *Tube* producer Malcolm Gerrie. "I'd had an idea to do a new show, given everything that was going on in the music scene," he explains. "I was quite excited by that. Music shows that have really worked best have been when there's something happening out on the street that you can plug into. That was a fantastic time to plug into – that whole upswell of not just music but fashion and politics. But I felt that we just needed to strip everything back. I just wanted to do it in an empty room – there was something about the purity of that I really loved – but still have an element of creative mischief about it, in terms of either showcasing bands and music that you wouldn't normally see on mainstream TV or just mixing people together, and visually having some fun with it."

Credit for bringing the show to air goes to Channel 4's arts commissioner, Waldemar Januszczak, now a noted art critic and broadcaster himself. "Waldemar was, and is, a huge fan of music, as well as being a leading authority on art," says Gerrie. "So when we got talking, this idea of just a white room, he loved it. We were flabbergasted to get a commission from the arts department." But this unorthodox route to air meant that a softly-softly approach was needed at the outset, so as not to scare the powers that be.

With Januszczak a little nervous of selling it to the channel from an arts perspective, it was decided to make the pilot programme a single-genre affair – a more "arty", niche project that might tick more boxes at Channel 4 than a wide-ranging music show. The chosen genre was reggae, and the show featured artists such as Sly & Robbie, Toots, Rico Rodriguez and Chaka Demus & Pliers. "I'd always been obsessed with reggae and loved it," says Gerrie. "Jimmy Cliff delivered the best version of 'Many Rivers To Cross' I've ever heard him sing and you could see the potential for what it was going to look like with a white studio."[6]

The pilot was so good that it was broadcast in June 1994 and the first series then followed eight months later, recorded initially at Westway Studios in Shepherd's Bush, and then at Ealing Studios. Production took place the day before the Saturday night broadcast, with at least four acts featured every week. Radio 1 DJ Mark Radcliffe was the host, but his links, as he describes them, were "mercifully short". There were no interviews or videos, except for occasional retro clips.[7]

Working with executive producer Gerrie were two former *Tube* colleagues, producer Chris Cowey and director Geoff Wonfor. Cowey had a very clear vision of how this new, stripped-back show should come together. He planned what he describes as "a real reaction against music television", meaning a revolt against the formats and production techniques that had come to dominate music programming in the early nineties, with its fast edits, special effects and "wacky" youth culture. "I hated all that and I wanted to really clean it all out," he says. "A lot of my influence was archive, looking at old shows, because I always thought that when you had a great big tight shot, a big close-up of Aretha Franklin, the Queen of Soul, doing what she does best, you don't remember the flashing lights, you don't remember the set, you don't remember any of that ephemeral bollocks. What you do remember is a great song, done well by a brilliant artist. That's really what I was trying to do with *The White Room.*"

Although the influence was retro, Cowey suggests that the programme also appeared fresh and cutting edge. "It was a plain white set, no flashing lights and very little in the way of coloured lights," he says. "The excitement and the movement and the colour were to come from the acts." Bands were allowed to set up their own backline equipment but this was then obscured by white hides to create a clean, fresh appearance and, to sharpen the image, audience members and performers alike were encouraged to dress in black and white. "It needed to look different," says Cowey. "Music television had this completely clichéd look, and to some extent still does. *The White Room* was an attempt to get rid of all those clichés."

The way the programme would be shot was also going to be unusual. "I wanted it to be almost balletic so you would have a camera move that would last a long time and develop. You wouldn't necessarily follow the action – you would look for the most interesting bit." This is perhaps best illustrated, Malcolm Gerrie thinks, during an appearance by Oasis. "There's a wonderful shot of Liam Gallagher," he says. "When the middle eight comes in and the guitars are all kicking out, he just goes back and just sits down and leans against the bass drum. Geoff Wonfor just went in on his face. Any other director would have been on another boring guitar solo. Geoff just stayed on Liam's face. It's one of the greatest shots, just watching this music wash over Liam living in the moment. If you put pictures and music together, and the chemistry's right, that's when you get electricity, and that was one of those moments. I was sitting in the back of the gallery and I just turned into a huge goosebump."

The show, unbeholden to the charts, immediately attracted big names. Stevie Wonder appeared in the first show, followed in later editions by the likes of Prince, Little Richard, David Bowie and Iggy Pop (in infamously see-through trousers), but there was always a strong Britpop element, this being its heyday. "Oasis were the house band. Even when they weren't on, they were at the show," says Gerrie. "They'd just rock up and sit on the floor or take over the bar. There was a real, fabulous vibe." Paul Weller was another regular as the show – just like *Ready, Steady, Go!* in the sixties and *The Tube* in the eighties – became a place to be seen among serious musicians. Mutual respect extended to on-stage collaborations, with Noel Gallagher and Paul Weller jamming a version of 'Talk Tonight', Lou Reed and Dave Stewart (who also wrote *The White Room*'s theme music) getting together on 'Walk On The Wild Side', and Damon Albarn and Ray Davies performing 'Waterloo Sunset'.

"The blurb that we wrote to go with the programme was 'the best music irrespective of genre, race or chart position', and that's really what *The White Room* was about," explains Chris Cowey. "It was a showcase for really good music. In terms of audience appreciation and numbers, it did better than *The Tube* and *Wired*, and really captured a lot of people's imagination."[8]

Sadly, *The White Room* proved short-lived. The team had hoped that the show would have a long future, but Channel 4 thought otherwise. Mark Radcliffe jokes that he did warn them against booking East 17 in what was the third and final series but it was actually another regime change at Channel 4 that, just as it had hastened the demise of *The Tube*, now saw off *The White Room*.[9]

"It was an arts commission and the question was asked: 'Should arts be spending money on a music show?'" explains Malcolm Gerrie. "*The White Room* could have been Channel 4's *Later*. It could still be on now but they let it go."[10]

★ ★ ★

With *Later* established in the BBC2 schedules, its production team began to branch out by adding a New Year special. *Jools's Annual Hootenanny* (1993–) was a modern take on the old Andy Stewart-type Hogmanay celebrations regularly shown on television in the sixties. The "hootenanny" of the title literally means an informal performance by folk singers, although that definition was stretched somewhat in the very first edition, which featured Sting, the Gipsy Kings and Sly & Robbie, and has been further loosened since.

"Jools was very keen to have a show that featured his growing Rhythm & Blues Orchestra," explains producer Mark Cooper, "and the show initially was a combination of artists singing with Jools. It didn't have much audience, we had no drink in the studio and it started at midnight, so there was no build up to midnight."

It was only in 1998 that the show was given the chance to actually lead viewers into the new year, when it kicked off at 11.55 p.m., and ever since – with even earlier start times – it has been counting down the old and ringing in the new with a line-up of star names. In the 1995 show, Blur performed 'Park Life' with Phil Daniels for the last time; in later years Elton John, Eric Clapton, Coldplay, Lionel Richie, Robert

Plant, Amy Winehouse, Paul McCartney, Eddie Floyd, Kylie, Emeli Sandé, Bobby Womack and Jeff Beck have been just some of the names to feature in a show that now parties for more than two hours. A pipe band brings a traditional flavour to the midnight hour and celebrity guests enjoy a festive drink in the small audience. Although the show is timed to meet the bongs of Big Ben, it is actually recorded a few weeks earlier.[11]

* * *

At the turn of the nineties, television schedulers discovered a new way of appeasing viewers who wanted more coverage of niche styles of music without scaring off mainstream audiences and, more importantly, advertisers. The vacant broadcasting hours during the night were ideal for showing programmes that had a restricted appeal – programmes built around heavy metal or dance, for instance.

With the exception of *ECT*, heavy metal had always been in short supply on British television, so it was with some surprise and no doubt huge pleasure that metal-heads welcomed a new performance-and-interview series, even though it probably meant setting the video recorder because of its late transmission. There were in fact three different shows in all, one stemming from another. It all began with *Power Hour* (1988–90), which was broadcast by a handful of ITV regions as part of their overnight service, and was hosted by Nikki Groocock and the artwork designer Krusher (Steve Joule). It then developed into *Raw Power* (1990–3), a collection of videos, news and competitions, which came from London's Marquee club and was fronted, at various times, by Phil Alexander, Nikki Groocock, Ann Kirk and again Krusher (with his Jack Russell terrier, Bullseye). The show had connections with *Raw* magazine but was later renamed and reformatted as *Noisy Mothers* (1994–5). This was seen in more parts of the country than the previous two offerings, but still only well past midnight.

In contrast, *BPM* (1992–5) was a sort of follow-up to *The Hit Man And Her*. Hosted by David Dorrell and Brenda Tuohy, the show came from a different UK nightclub each week. Among the pounding beats and flashing lights, there were DJ profiles, interviews and a look at the dance chart. A more exotic take on the club scene then came at the end of the decade with a Channel 4 show called *The Dog's Balearics* (1999–2000), which saw Dermot O'Leary, Jayne Middlemiss and DJ Brandon Block surveying hard-core dance at the Café Savannah in San Antonio.

For fans of black music, the offerings were similarly restricted. The days of *Soul Train* and *Behind The Beat* were over and it wasn't until the arrival of *Flava* (1996–2001) on Channel 4 that things began to look up. This midnight-hour series covered all areas of black music from ragga, jungle and garage to rap, swing and soul, initially only via videos. There were no presenters or live acts at the outset, but this soon changed to bring in guest hosts such as Colour Girl and Jamelia and performances from new artists. In 2001, Miss Dynamite took over as presenter. Among those featuring were Mark Morrison, 2 Pac, Little Kim, Debarge, Destiny's Child, Beverley Knight and Millie Jackson. One edition in 1999 was entitled Asian Flava and featured such names as Malkit Singh, Jas Mann and Asian Dub Foundation. The same year, an early-evening special offered a profile of Melanie G (as Spice Girl Melanie Brown/Mel B was known at the time).

⋆ ⋆ ⋆

While performance and music magazine shows remained trapped in twilight time during the nineties, music documentaries at least were tolerated in more sensible programming hours. Channel 4's *Mojo Working* (1992), for example, was a 13-part series looking into the roots of modern music, focusing on the likes of Muddy Waters, B.B. King, Chuck Berry, Little Richard, the Rolling Stones, the Doors, John Lennon and Jimi Hendrix. It explained how these greats had inspired future performers, using archive footage and feedback from those who had been influenced by their work. More comprehensive was *Dancing In The Street: A Rock And Roll History* (1996), which was a BBC co-production with WGBH Boston in the USA. The 10-part series took five years to make and cost around £5 million. Comprising archive footage and exploratory interviews with influential artists from each of pop music's eras, it had a much narrower remit than Tony Palmer's earlier *All You Need Is Love*, beginning in the fifties and progressing through to rap. Episodes along the way highlighted the work of Elvis, Phil Spector, the Beatles, Bob Dylan, the Rolling Stones, Jimi Hendrix, Marvin Gaye, David Bowie, Bob Marley, the Clash and others.

Once again during this decade, the BBC's *Arena* arts series also turned its spotlight onto popular music, most notably in four films collectively entitled *Tales Of Rock'n'Roll* (1993) that delved into the history of certain classic records, rediscovering the inspiration behind the songs. It opened with *Peggy Sue*, meeting Peggy Sue Gerron Rackham – the very same girl mentioned in two of Buddy Holly's hits, who was at the time running a drainage business in California. It continued with *Heartbreak Hotel* and its roots in a suicide note found in Miami, before looking at *Walk On The Wild Side* and meeting some of the colourful New York characters who had featured in Lou Reed's lyrics. The final film was devoted to *Highway 61 Revisited* and followed the road that led from the Canadian border to New Orleans, stopping at Bob Dylan's home town of Hibbing, Minnesota.[12]

Otherwise, *Arena* contributed numerous stand-alone documentaries, including *The Strange Story Of Joe Meek* (1991), *The Grateful And The Dead* (an intriguing tale of how the Grateful Dead secretly funded the work of undiscovered British orchestral composers, 1993), *Trouble Man – The Last Years Of Marvin Gaye* (1994), *Punk And The Pistols* (1995) and the two-part *The Brian Epstein Story* (1998).

Following the success of *Walking To New Orleans*, Jools Holland hit the road again for a Channel 4 travelogue called *Mister Roadrunner* (1992). This time the destination was the Tennessee/Mississippi area, which he roared through on a Vincent Rapide motorcycle in search of the region's musical roots, paying particular attention to the cities of Memphis and Nashville. Rufus Thomas, Charlie Rich, Betty Wright and Yvonne Fair were some of the people Holland encountered as he explored and enjoyed the South's bubbling mix of country, blues, soul, hillbilly and rock'n'roll. Robert Palmer, David Gilmour and Mica Paris also contributed tracks. Geoff Wonfor again directed the 90-minute film and Stephen Fry provided the narration.

Holland and Wonfor were also soon to collaborate on a project that was about as big as it gets for music documentaries when the three surviving Beatles agreed to sit down and tell their remarkable story, for the first time, in their own words. Archive material had been gathering for more than two decades at Apple, the Beatles' company, with a view to producing such a document but so many things had got in the way that no progress had been made towards completing the project. By the early nineties, however, the time was ripe to make this happen. What turned out to be a six-part series shown on ITV was financed totally by the band members themselves, which gave them full editorial control, and they asked Wonfor, who had directed a film of Paul McCartney's *Liverpool Oratorio* in 1991, to pull things together with producer Chips Chipperfield.

Wonfor brought in Holland to conduct many of the interviews as McCartney, Harrison and Starr reflected on the whole Beatles story, beginning with their childhood days and concluding with the break-up of the band. The trio were also filmed together for the first time in many years. Archive revelations from John Lennon filled out the story, as did retro footage of the band in action, re-runs of promotional videos they made in the sixties, out-takes from *Magical Mystery Tour*, personal snapshots and scraps of home-movies generated within the group itself. Adding to the buzz was the fact that two new songs – 'Free As A Bird' and 'Real Love' – were released to coincide with the series going on air in November 1995, both recordings built up from primitive home demo tapes of songs made by John Lennon in the seventies. These tracks featured on the accompanying CD and video collections that also included rare studio work, alternate takes and other previously unreleased material. Inevitably, *The Beatles Anthology* (1995), as it became known, was shown around the world and a book with the same title followed.[13]

Holland and Wonfor went back on the road towards the end of the decade when they were commissioned by BBC2 to supply a series called *Beat Route* (1998–9). In much the same vein as their two previous travelogues, this collection of six half-hour films took them to Budapest, Seville, Havana, Beirut, Chicago and Dublin, with Holland leading the viewer on city tours that were focused not on the obvious sights but on musical movers and shakers, be they flamenco dancers in Spain or Van Morrison in Ireland. He also lent a hand with a bit of boogie-woogie piano from time to time.

A documentary series set closer to home was *Routes Of Rock* (1999–2000). This was shown in a handful of ITV regions and looked at places in London that had shaped pop music history, taking in concert venues such as the Marquee and back-street pubs where bands cut their teeth, as well as more abstract places like the shop where David Bowie once worked or grungy flats where future superstars lived before fame beckoned. Through interviews and archive material, subjects ranging from the fashions of Carnaby Street to the punk explosion were referenced over two series. Ken Howard, co-writer of sixties hits for the likes of the Honeycombs, the Herd and Dave Dee, Dozy, Beaky, Mick & Tich, but by this time an experienced documentary maker, was the executive producer.

★ ★ ★

The nineties also saw the beginning of a different kind of documentary – "insight" shows that pieced together the history of a band or an album through interviews with the parties concerned. Leading the way was the BBC's ambitious adaptation of Pete Frame's even more ambitious *Rock Family Trees* (1995;1998). Frame began compiling these labour-of-love documents back in the early seventies, combining his loves of both technical drawing and music. The first tree, all about the band Blood, Sweat & Tears, appeared in *Zigzag* magazine in 1971 and, by the end of the decade, he was in a position to fill a book with similar efforts. This then led to a number of follow-up volumes.[14]

The BBC series used some of Frame's intricate artwork as illustration, alongside old stills, album covers, record labels, magazine cuttings and so on, but the lifeblood of the series was the contribution of the musicians themselves as they divulged little anecdotes about how bands came together and then, inevitably, went their own separate ways, so leading to the formation of new bands. John Peel added an explanatory voice-over, when necessary. Two series were produced, the first covering

'The Fleetwood Mac Story', 'The Birmingham Beat', 'Deep Purple People', 'New York Punk', 'The British R 'n' B Boom' and 'The New Merseybeat'; the second dealing with 'California Dreamin'', 'Sabbath, Bloody Sabbath', 'The Mersey Sound', 'Banshees And Other Creatures', 'The Prog Rock Years' and 'And God Created Manchester'.

In a similar vein was the independently produced *Classic Albums* (1997; 1999–2000; 2003–6; 2008–12), shown at various times by both the BBC and ITV. Producers Nick de Grunwald and Bous de Jong came up with the idea after working on a documentary called *The Making Of Sergeant Pepper* (screened as an edition of *The South Bank Show* in June 1992) and started looking for other albums that, they considered, were "not just a collection of great songs, but which also tell a story about the time and the people who made them". Among the albums examined were Jimi Hendrix's *Electric Ladyland*, Paul Simon's *Graceland*, Stevie Wonder's *Songs In The Key Of Life*, Fleetwood Mac's *Rumours*, Meatloaf's *Bat Out Of Hell*, U2's *The Joshua Tree*, Bob Marley & the Wailers' *Catch A Fire*, Pink Floyd's *Dark Side Of The Moo*n, Nirvana's *Nevermind*, Jay-Z's *Reasonable Doubt* and Peter Gabriel's *So*. Archive material, rare fan footage and interviews with those involved with the making of each album helped explain all.[15]

* * *

As well as beating its own path to the nation's television receivers, music continued to be part of the general entertainment mix across all channels, although the days of the Black & White Minstrels and *Seaside Special* had long gone and what was once termed "light entertainment" was becoming more daring and edgy. *Don't Forget Your Toothbrush* (1994–5) was a Channel 4 show that mixed games with entertainment, giving members of the studio audience a chance to win an exotic holiday that had to be taken straight away – hence the need to bring a toothbrush, not to mention a passport, to the live Saturday-night broadcast. Chris Evans hosted the manic show, supported musically by Jools Holland and his band. Guests from the music world belted out the odd tune but also found themselves on the spot in a weekly quiz, struggling to prove that they knew more about themselves than a clued-up super fan. Despite huge popularity, the programme only ran for two series, Evans giving it up to create the even more successful *TFI Friday* (1996–2000; 2015).

With the initials in the name apparently standing for "Thank Four It's", *TFI Friday* was broadcast live from Riverside Studios. An hour-long, early-evening show (repeated later the same night), it was the closest Channel 4 came to finding a replacement for *The Tube*. Evans, at the top of his game, developed the concept for his own Ginger Productions company. Jonathan Ross was his first choice of presenter but this was knocked back by the channel and so he himself took on the role, hosting proceedings from a bar above a performance area.[16]

Evans recognised the fact that music alone on television doesn't get the viewing figures of general entertainment so, while live performance formed the core of each edition, it was buttressed by lots of other features – chats to star guests, big-prize competitions (the first TV show to give away £1 million) and assorted stunts and challenges, with on-screen assistance from the show's producer, Will Macdonald. Scripts were provided by Danny Baker.[17]

At its peak, *TFI Friday* was unmissably spontaneous and unpredictable. Shaun Ryder was dared not to swear but failed miserably, Geri Halliwell and Kylie Minogue snogged on screen, and Paul McCartney was seen racing away from the show in a speedboat up the Thames. Down on the stage, Britpop bounded free and artists like the Manic Street Preachers, Lightning Seeds, the Beautiful South, Kula Shaker, David Bowie, U2 and Supergrass entertained the partying crowd.

If any programme summed up the good times, Cool Britannia mood of the late-nineties, *TFI Friday* was it, but it came to an end after just four years, falling victim to the confused world in which Chris Evans was living at the time. Evans had quit his job as Radio 1's breakfast presenter when boss Matthew Bannister refused to give him Fridays off in order to prepare for the show. He had bought and sold Virgin Radio for millions, was partying heavily and, generally, in his own words, going "off the rails". For the last few editions of *TFI Friday*, he wasn't even the host, with guest presenters having to fill in, including Elton

John on the final show. Happily, Evans' career was to bounce back, as was *TFI Friday*, when it was revived as a one-off to celebrate its 20th anniversary in 2015, which led to a new series later in the year. This time, the show was presented from the Cochrane Theatre in Holborn, the Riverside Studios having been demolished to make way for a new arts/television/residential complex.[18]

★ ★ ★

The *Eurovision Song Contest* in the nineties belonged to Ireland, which notched up four victories. But there was some success for the UK, when Katrina & the Waves stormed the 1997 event with 'Love Shine A Light', and there were also runner-up spots for Michael Ball, Sonia and Imaani. More encouragingly, some of the entries in this decade actually did sound as if they came from the same era: Frances Ruffelle's funky ballad 'We Will be Free (Lonely Symphony)' in 1994, rappers Love City Groove with 'Love City Groove' in 1995 and the breezy pop of Gina G's 'Ooh Aah … Just a Little Bit' in 1996. By the end of the decade, however, the quality of the song seemed more irrelevant than ever, with political voting – which had always been a problem – increasingly warping the results.

Pop trivia also made a comeback in this decade. Chris Tarrant presented a revival of *Pop Quiz* on BBC1 while, in the dark hours, some ITV regions broadcast *Pop Down The Pub* (1998), which saw celebrities competing in a fake boozer for the chance to win an engraved tankard. Phil Alexander supervised the drinking and larking about. Alexander also hosted the follow up, *Popped In, Crashed Out* (1999–2000), in which he invited a couple of musical guests to "his flat" for a few beers, talked to them about music past and present, showed them some videos and encouraged them to take part in an informal quiz with rubbish prizes.

Far more successful, not least because of its somewhat larger budget, was BBC2's *Never Mind The Buzzcocks* (1996–2015). Once the topical comedy quiz *Have I Got News For You* had been established, and a sports equivalent called *They Think It's All Over* had followed it onto the air, it seemed an obvious next step to give pop music the same treatment. Unlike *Pop Quiz*, this new show was only played for laughs and was totally flexible with rules, allowing celebrity guests to run riot as they tackled offbeat questions and challenges – guessing hummed record intros, picking out stars of the past from identity parades, adding the next line of a lyric, etc. Not really trying to keep order was host Mark Lamarr who was succeeded by Simon Amstell in 2006 and then by a run of guest presenters until Rhod Gilbert was installed as a fixture in 2014. The first team captains were Sean Hughes and Phill Jupitus, with later captains including Bill Bailey and Noel Fielding. These were each joined by a couple of guests from the worlds of comedy and music.

★ ★ ★

Having established themselves as ratings successes in the eighties, music awards ceremonies continued to provide annual highspots for both viewers and broadcasters. *The Smash Hits Poll Winners' Party* ran throughout the decade, Phillip Schofield giving way to other hosts, including Simon Mayo, Andi Peters and Ant & Dec. The BBC finally relinquished the event in 2001, after launching its own *Top Of The Pops Awards*, and Channel 4 then took it over. There was no show in 2003 because US artists, it was reported, declined to appear, and then it all came to an end when *Smash Hits* magazine folded in 2006.

The BBC also launched coverage of the new Mercury Prize. This contest began in 1992 as a musical equivalent of literature's Booker Prize. Its role is to select the finest 12 albums of the year, with the spotlight finally falling on the overall best album, as judged by an independent panel of musicians and experts under the chairmanship of the rock journalist and academic Simon Frith. Television didn't catch up with the event until 1994, when the announcements were covered as part of *The Late Show* on BBC2. Since 1996, however, the ceremony has been broadcast annually (usually live but sometimes in a highlights package), either by the BBC or Channel 4.

Television has also been covering the MOBO Awards – the first black music awards in Europe – since 1996, the year of its inception.

ITV handled the first two years, but didn't network the show, then Channel 4 took over with highlights packages. From 2005, the BBC or ITV has offered live coverage, but only on BBC3 or ITV2, with just highlights on their main channels.

⋆ ⋆ ⋆

After its rather formal introduction to television, *The British Record Industry Awards* was in need of a make-over as the eighties drew to a close, but what the British Phonographic Industry (BPI) who ran the event didn't foresee was the show turning into a farce. Making the name more snappy by shortening it to *The Brit Awards* in 1989 had some logic; booking Mick Fleetwood and Samantha Fox as the hosts did not. Faced with the challenge of finding two presenters who might be able to handle a complicated live television production in which anything could go wrong, not many producers would have opted for a veteran rock drummer and a page-three model. It could have been an inspired move but was never likely to be. The show looked odd from the start when the little-and-large combination took their places on the stage but things rapidly took a turn for the worse as they battled their way through the ceremony, introducing the wrong acts, apologising for technical cock-ups and going 10 arduous rounds with the autocue. It was entertaining viewing, certainly, but for all the wrong reasons.

The following year the organisers played it safe. The event was downscaled from the Royal Albert Hall to London's Dominion Theatre and in came Jonathan King as producer for the BPI. To try to re-establish credibility, former *Ready, Steady, Go!* presenter Cathy McGowan was hired as host. Considering what had gone before, it couldn't help but be a better event, but it still didn't set the world alight. King remained in charge for the next two years, with Hammersmith Odeon as the new venue in 1992, but all confidence in on-stage hosts had by now dissipated and it was left to an unseen Simon Bates to announce the winners. The show – temporarily renamed *The Brits* – was dying on its feet, viewing figures were sinking and the BBC was losing interest.

Rob Dickens, chairman of Warner Music in the UK, was in charge of The Brits for the BPI. He knew drastic change was needed and he hoped Malcolm Gerrie, former producer of *The Tube*, would ride to the rescue. Gerrie had first been approached after the Fleetwood/Fox fiasco but was wary of getting involved in something over which he didn't have complete control.

"The music industry and the television industry have always been very strange, awkward, uncomfortable bedfellows," he says, and the disaster at the Royal Albert Hall hadn't made the relationship any more friendly. Despite the parlous position the event was now in, the BPI still wouldn't give Gerrie the guarantees he needed to go ahead and rebuild the show at that time and so he walked away. Two years later, a desperate Dickens was back. "Do whatever you want," he said.

"Rob was fantastic, so supportive of me," Gerrie reveals, "but even then, the first few BPI Brit meetings I went to were pretty bloody, despite what he'd said. It was basically a back-slapping party and there was a shadow of Jonathan King over the whole fiasco. I think the logo was a British bulldog and a union jack. Naff, naff, naff. So I got rid of all of that and started to bring it into the modern world."

With big stars now avoiding the event, the first thing Gerrie set out to do was find a performer of repute who would agree to take part in the show. He chose Peter Gabriel and persuaded him to perform. "I thought we needed somebody big, really credible, really nice, that everybody loves." Bridges had to be rebuilt with such names, he said. They needed to know that they weren't going to be mucked around. "That was the beginning."

With the safety net of transmission a day after the event, a new broadcaster was found in ITV. The venue was switched to the grander scale of Alexandra Palace and Richard O'Brien of *The Crystal Maze* was installed as host. The show developed from there, becoming bigger and more powerful every year. Elton John and Ru Paul co-hosted the 1994 event, which saw the BPI voting system overhauled to broaden the range of acts and provide a more accurate reflection of the musical environment.* Also at this point, Gerrie came up with the novel idea of collaboration performances for the show and had in mind an initial pairing of Björk and PJ Harvey. "When I mentioned this at the Brits committee, they thought I was mad," he says. "Everybody would switch off. ITV thought it was a suicide mission. But they were just amazing and that pointed a way for a unique collaboration every time – so we had Robbie and Tom Jones, Jay Kay and Diana Ross."

Chris Evans was anchor for the 1995 show, which Madonna opened with a live performance. A year later, the restored ambition of the event was crystallised in a move to Earls Court and a guest performance by David Bowie. "Long gone are the days when the Brit Awards were a bit of joke," declared the *Radio Times*. Ben Elton, Johnny Vaughan and Davina McCall, in turn, then hosted the revitalised show through to the end of the decade.

"We just built it up and built it up and built it up, allowing a bit of freedom for things to happen, which they did," Malcolm Gerrie says with a laugh, recalling how Danbert Nobacon of Chumbawamba poured a bucket of water over Deputy Prime Minister John Prescott in 1998 and drunk DJ Brandon Block wandered onto the stage, thinking he'd won an award in 2000. But the big story concerned Jarvis Cocker's invasion of Michael Jackson's set in 1996, wiggling his bum to ridicule the pomposity of the performance. "It got 11 and a half million viewers and was on the front page of every newspaper in the world," says Gerrie. "Thank you, Jarvis!"[19]

Going into the new millennium, the BPI had a show to be proud of, one that was being watched around the world and was even beginning to outshine the prestigious Grammy Awards ceremony in America.

---

* This change to the rules was long overdue, with established stars from the big record labels perennially collecting the major awards, even though there was much more of interest going on. To lampoon the Brits and draw attention to the need to revamp the voting procedure so that it could recognise and encourage new talent, the *NME* reincarnated its own annual awards as *The Brats*. Highlights of the 1998 Brats, presented by Eddie Izzard, were broadcast by Channel 4. Reverting to their old name, the NME Awards were then covered by Channel 4 on a number of occasions during the 2000s.

Little Ladies in the *Rock Follies* sequel.
MANTLEMEDIA LTD/REX/SHUTTERSTOCK

Paula Yates and Jools Holland 'in the tube'.
ITV/REX/SHUTTERSTOCK

Malcolm Gerrie with Bono.
ERICA ECHENBERG/REDFERNS

eding the World at Live Aid.
E CAMERON/REDFERNS

een rule over Live Aid.
PERFOTO/GETTY IMAGES

Antoine de Caunes, *Rapido's* French host.
PHILIPPE LE TELLIER/GETTY IMAGES

DEF II's Rapido.
PHILIPPE LE TELLIER/GETTY IMAGES

Samantha Fox and Mick Fleetwood's worst nightmare: The Brit Awards 1989.
DAVE HOGAN/HULTON ARCHIVE/GETTY IMAGES

ter With Jools Holland and guests Mick Hucknall, PJ Harvey, Tricky, Siouxsie Sioux and Budgie, and Leon Russell.
ORE CSILLAG/REX/SHUTTERSTOCK

lp rehearsing for *Later With Jools Holland.*
ORE CSILLAG/REX/SHUTTERSTOCK

Oasis within *The White Room.*
DES WILLIE/REDFERNS/GETTY IMAGES

Mark Radcliffe fronts *The White Room.*
RICK COLLS/REX/SHUTTERSTOCK

Simon Amstell with the 411's Suzie Furlonger in a Christmas edition of *Popworld.*
CLAIRE GREENWAY/GETTY IMAGES

Club 7 members hit the beach.
C FORD/JASON KIRK/ONLINE USA

arne Cotton and BBC children's presenter Adrian Dickson at
› Of The Pops.*
RETH DAVIES/GETTY IMAGES

Andi Peters, the kids' TV host who became executive producer of *Top Of The Pops.*
MARK ROBERT MILAN/FILMMAGIC

The late John Peel in his element at Glastonbury.
MARTYN GOODACRE/GETTY IMAGES

★ ★ ★

In June 1996, *Top Of The Pops* lost the Thursday night slot it had inhabited for most of its 32-year existence. For scheduling convenience, it was switched to Fridays to try to raise the BBC1 audience share against ITV's *Coronation Street.* It certainly did that but at the expense of the show's own figures, which were halved – perhaps not surprisingly, given that much of its regular audience was probably heading to the pub at that time of the week. To compensate, a Saturday night repeat was added but it didn't help restore the show's fortunes and producer Ric Blaxill bowed out early in 1997.

What followed was another major shake-up. *Whistle Test* producer Trevor Dann had returned to radio after the demise of that show but, through internal BBC reorganisation, now found himself Head of Music Entertainment and in overall charge of *Top Of The Pops.* He knew things needed to change.

"There was a producer called Mark Wells who had been put in temporarily," he says. "He was a kind of glitz-and-glamour entertainment producer and I thought that what we needed was somebody who was a bit more earthy and down with the music." Wells went on to bigger and better things, eventually becoming Controller of Entertainment at ITV, and instead Dann reached out to Chris Cowey, who had just enjoyed success with *The White Room.* Cowey didn't need asking twice. It was a show he had grown up with and he understood its importance. He also felt it could be made so much better.[20]

"*Top Of The Pops* was a real appointment to view. Everybody had to see it," he says, thinking back to his teenage years. "You were afraid to miss it because then you couldn't be down with the cool kids and you just didn't know what was going on. It was like the equivalent of not being on Facebook now. It was that important. It took me about five seconds to say 'Yeah', because I'd always perceived *Top Of The Pops* as a bit of a 'close but no cigar'. It didn't seem to be really curated. It seemed to be put together almost like painting by numbers, where they had all these rules. If you knew enough about the business, you could write the running order for *Top Of The Pops* before the BBC did. You wouldn't play anything two weeks in a row, you wouldn't play anything that was going down, etc. I thought, and presumably one or two people at the BBC thought, that, if you can apply *The White Room* criteria to *Top Of The Pops*, then we'd have something. So I took the job."

Cowey knew he had his work cut out to restore the programme's fortunes but he had a plan to do just that. "The week before I started, *Top Of The Pops* had dropped below two million viewers for the first time ever. There was too much chat, too many graphics, too many silly things going on, so I worked out that I could cram eight live performances and a chart rundown into it, and that was it."[21]

It was a difficult time to come into the show, which was struggling with a rapidly evolving music industry. The way the charts were collated and presented had changed at the end of the eighties. Instead of coming out on a Tuesday, they were now released on a Sunday, which meant that a Friday *Top Of The Pops* – following five days later – lost all topicality. Additionally, the way in which records were now marketed destroyed the look and the dynamic of the charts.

"The record industry had decided that the only way you could make a hit record was to put it out to radio weeks before it was actually released, thereby ensuring that advance orders made it go in at number one," says Trevor Dann. "The old dynamic of the chart, where records entered low and rose, peaked and then fell, changed completely. Every number one was a new record and that meant that *Top Of The Pops* was not playing big hits, it was playing new releases, in effect. So it was playing an old chart that wasn't very interesting because we all knew it from Sunday and it was playing unfamiliar music."[22]

Chris Cowey confirms the analysis. "The charts at that time were subject to very clever and sharp marketing practices by the record companies, which meant that they would discount things in the first week so they were never going to achieve a higher position than they did in their debut week. What I had to try and do was to see through that and try and create a good show despite the chart rather than because of it, and to have some diversity. Typically there'd be some faceless dance act with a drum machine at number nine and a new single from the Pretenders at 15. I would put the Pretenders on, because they're bigger box office, they'd be better live and it just makes a better programme."

It was all about having a wide-ranging and thought-through musical strategy, he says. "I always say that if people watch a whole edition of *Top Of The Pops* and they like everything on it, then they need therapy, because you really shouldn't. I thought that some of the stuff I put on was absolutely bollocks, but that's the way it should be, as long as it's got an audience. It's not just about loving music: it's about understanding the audience as well. I remember as a kid watching *Top Of The Pops* and we used to argue about it at home. My brother would like one thing; my sister would like another thing; my mum and dad would hate most of the things but occasionally they'd like the odd bit. I wanted to bring that argument, that debate, back into people's living rooms."

One of the first things that Chris discussed with Trevor was introducing more live performances as a means of revitalising the show, and this became a hallmark of his period in charge. "If you want to watch videos, watch MTV," he says. "That's how videos got such traction. There were far too many people trying to make music television who didn't know the first thing about it and it's an easy option. *Top Of The Pops* should be about bands performing on a level playing field – all in the same place at the same time, as far as possible."

He succeeded in getting most people to play live. "I persuaded a lot of bands who were *Top Of The Pops* refuseniks in the past to do it. I got the Spice Girls to sing live. I think I even got Steps to sing live once. Somebody bothered to work out that 92 per cent of the bands during my period of *Top Of The Pops* at least sang live.

"Occasionally, there were acts who clearly wouldn't be able to reproduce anything even vaguely approximating the record," he says, citing Norman Cook in his Fatboy Slim guise. "You just can't do that live and also it doesn't make a great deal of sense, so he was one of the few exceptions where I would allow a video, but we always customised the video in some way so it didn't look like the video you would see on MTV. We'd have him holding up a *Top Of The Pops* logo in it somewhere, or whatever."

Cowey also changed the branding of the show and the theme music. "I didn't want it to be called 'TOTP'," he says. "I banned people using 'TOTP' because you'd never hear a kid upstairs on a bus saying: "Did you see TOTP?" I insisted on it being written and said in full. The logo I created was a combination of the old Atlantic Records label and the *Billboard* masthead. I crunched those things together because I wanted it to be evocative. I knew the audience was that broad. I wanted it to be new enough for punters now, but really evocative for their parents." For the theme music, Cowey worked with DJ re-mixer Ben Chapman to bring back a version of 'Whole Lotta Love', the track that had characterised the show in its seventies heyday.[23]

On the presentation front, out went the celebrities and a small team of regular hosts took over. Jayne Middlemiss, Zoë Ball, Jamie Theakston, Kate Thornton, Gail Porter, Richard Blackwood, Dermot O'Leary, Lisa Snowdon, Liz Bonnin and Sarah Cawood were the predominant faces of the six-year Cowey era, with a sprinkling of guests towards the end.

The programme had also continued to expand beyond its weekly slot. In 1997, a Sunday afternoon show began on Radio 1, immediately prior to the new chart rundown. Hosted by Jayne Middlemiss, this was an idea of Ric Blaxill's to capitalise on the down time that artists endured during the production of the TV show. He thought it would be good to grab some interviews while everyone was hanging around between rehearsals and recording, and he also set up an acoustic area in which they could perform additional material for the radio show. This continued on Cowey's watch, as did the Saturday BBC2 repeat, although Cowey now recut this for an adult audience, showing rock bands at full length, complete with guitar solos, and allowing the odd profanity. *TOTP 2* was similarly enhanced, Cowey taking the opportunity to insert extra tracks recorded when artists appeared on *Top Of The Pops*, although this was later abandoned when *TOTP 2* became a pure archive show with Steve Wright adding wry commentaries.[24]

In 1999, *Top Of The Pops* went on a six-week tour and was recorded in cities around the UK. This drummed up a lot of regional publicity and helped bolster viewing figures that had now bounced back to around five million, assisted to some degree by positive developments in the world of pop, although in the BBC above Cowey there was a feeling that this halting of decline was probably only temporary.

"Just in that era we'd hit Britpop and it was that kind of era where live music was back," says Trevor Dann. "Also we were helped for that brief period by the fact that pop music was now on the front pages so there was an appetite to see Robbie Williams or Steps. I think we slightly rode that wave for a while but we just couldn't keep it going."

Recognising the battle *Top Of The Pops* still faced to be viable, Dann continued to look for more multi-platform options, even being tempted by the thought of a dedicated *Top Of The Pops* channel. "I thought we could maybe expand our way out of the problem, but the problem was that the mother ship, which was the main weekly show, was dying and all these other things just didn't feel cool and modern because everybody associated the brand with the failure of the main show."[25]

As the millennium ticked over, the digital age kicked in. This presented new opportunities for *Top Of The Pops* but also new challenges – challenges it would find impossible to overcome.

★ ★ ★

The growing reputation of the Glastonbury music festival in the eighties inevitably attracted the attention of television producers. Beginning in 1970 – inauspiciously the day after Jimi Hendrix was found dead – when 1,500 hippies gathering to watch Marc Bolan at Michael Eavis's Worthy Farm, near Pilton, Somerset, were charged £1 for entry and offered all the milk they could drink, the festival ran for a couple of years then disappeared. It was kicked back into life in 1978 and stuttered along for a while before finally beginning to find its stride.

The first television coverage came in 1982 in the form of recordings shown later that year, after midnight, to some ITV viewers. This material – including music from Judie Tzuke, Roy Harper, Randy California, Richie Havens, Osibisa and Aswad – was then re-used in other ITV night-time programmes through the eighties, with some performances also repackaged as editions of *Cue The Music* in the nineties. In 1990, BBC1 paid a visit as part of a short Sunday evening series called *Festival*, with host Bill Oddie nosing around the site, but it wasn't until 1994 that TV vans rolled up in numbers to bring the event to a national audience.

It was the Tyne Tees crowd, alumni of *The Tube*, that drove this initiative, picking up on an idea that had occurred to them while that show was still on air. "Sometime around about 1984–5, we decided we'd go and check it out," recalls producer Chris Cowey. "We got a train from Newcastle down to Bristol Temple Meads, got into a hire car, drove to Glastonbury, straight to Worthy Farm, parked at the side of the stage – literally at the side of the stage – and walked out to watch the Style Council." Chris and his colleagues liked what they saw and figured it might be interesting to broadcast the event at some point. That point arrived about 10 years later, when the team talked the Eavis family into allowing Channel 4 access.

Plans for that first broadcast were disrupted when the main Pyramid Stage burned down just over a week beforehand, and Channel 4 also had a scheduling issue, trying to work out how to slot in the coverage among its regular shows. In the end, seven programmes – under the title *4 Goes To Glastonbury* (1994–5) – were shown over the course of the festival weekend, with most of the action coming late at night or on Sunday afternoon. It worked well enough for the channel to repeat the exercise the following year. In the hands of presenters Mark Lamarr, Mark Radcliffe, Mark Kermode, Marc Riley, Katie Puckrik and Johnnie Walker, the channel had shown that Glastonbury could be televised.

"We did it very successfully for two years: 13 hours of live broadcasting over the weekend," says Chris Cowey. "I think it was the Channel 4 coverage that made it really leap up from being a hippie-dippy, historical festival. Everybody could see the potential of having great live music, this amazing backdrop and all these amazing people". The fact that these people were clearly really committed music fans and that there was so much counter-culture stuff going on made for a really thrilling package, he says. "It wasn't just about the performance. It was about going up to the healing fields and about the old, crusty farmers." But the wind was changing at Channel 4, pennies were being counted and, just as it cancelled *The White Room*, Cowey's other major project of the time, the broadcaster decided to drop the event.[26]

Glastonbury took a year off in 1996 and when it returned in 1997 the BBC swooped on the rights. The coverage kicked off on BBC2 in the early hours of Saturday morning, with John Peel and Jo Whiley hosting highlights of the event so far, as the mud welled up around spectators' ankles and the secondary Other Stage began to sink. If the festival had experienced trouble with the weather before, it was nothing compared to the deluge that turned that year's gathering into a swamp, but highlights, previews and reports continued over the weekend, with Jools Holland linking the final offering on Sunday night. By later standards, it was a rather cautious toe in the knee-deep Glastonbury water but nonetheless a "terrifying" undertaking, in the words of its producer, Mark Cooper.[27]

There was more adventure in the 1998 production, with performances from a third location – the Jazz-World stage – added to sets on the Pyramid and Other Stages, and the presentation trio of Peel, Whiley and Holland trekking across the fields to visit other tents. More significantly, programming wasn't just confined to lunchtime and late-night highlights packages: a little prime-time exposure was also built in, but this was small beer compared to the technical advances that really opened up the Glastonbury coverage the following year.

In September 1998, the BBC's first new digital channel, BBC Choice, went on air. With its younger audience profile, it was an ideal outlet for additional Glastonbury programmes and, starting in 1999, it was able to accommodate lots of live material to complement the highlights packages on BBC2. In the hands of Radio 1 presenters Kevin Greening and Mary Anne Hobbs, an extra 23 hours of coverage were transmitted over the three days, providing a glimpse into how the broadcasting of Glastonbury was likely to improve and develop in the digital era.

* * *

Apart from allowing additional coverage of Glastonbury, the BBC's new digital output had other benefits for the music follower. One of BBC Choice's first programmes was *Inside Tracks* (1998–2000). Described as a "music programme for the serious music fan", this was a weekly late-night show featuring live artists, music news and interviews that came from the BBC's Maida Vale studios. The bands included XTC, the Cranberries, Feeder, New Flesh For Old and the Bluetones, and there were reports from festivals and features on such topics as the history of women in music. It was hosted by Kevin Greening at first, but then comedian Sean Hughes – team captain on *Never Mind The Buzzcocks* – took over, at which point the show was renamed *Sean Hughes' Inside Tracks*.

Inside Tracks could, perhaps, be seen as the BBC's answer to a programme that Channel 4 had introduced earlier that year. *Jo Whiley* (1998–2000) was another late-night mix of live performance and talk hosted by the Radio 1 DJ, whose guests included Shirley Manson, Cerys Matthews, Babybird and Tony Wilson. This evolved into *The Cut With Jo Whiley* (2001) that was recorded just before broadcast. The White Stripes, Ryan Adams and Basement Jaxx were some of the performers, while Macy Gray, Jay Kay and Brett Anderson, among others, answered Wiley's questions.

* * *

In 1997, the UK gained a fifth terrestrial television channel and with it a little more airtime for pop and rock music. In March that year, Channel 5 was launched, with the Spice Girls guests of honour on opening night, and less than a year later it introduced its own weekly chart programme in a daring attempt to rival *Top Of The Pops*.

The Pepsi Chart (1998–2002) was a groundbreaking programme that became hugely successful on the international stage. "*The Pepsi Chart* made broadcasting history," says its producer, Malcolm Gerrie, explaining its significance and how it came about. "The wonderful Dawn Airey, who ran Channel 5, wanted a chart show but couldn't really afford the level of production I thought it should be." Sponsorship was an obvious answer but this was against the rules of the ITC, as the commercial television regulator was by now known: unless a programme was covering an established sponsored event, sponsorship was not permitted.

To figure out a way forward, Gerrie got together with the late Nick Milligan, who was head of advertising and sales at Channel 5, and advertising guru Robert Dodds. They already had a potential sponsor in mind. "Robert had the Pepsi account and they were beating a path to his door," he says. Pepsi wanted to get more involved in music and it had money to spend, so between them, Nick and Robert came up with an ingenious solution.

The plan was to launch a Pepsi Chart "event" that would run as a genuine club night at a London venue. They could then go to the ITC and say: "We have the Pepsi Chart event, sponsored by Pepsi. We think it would be a good idea to stick a few cameras in and shoot it."

"It was the most extraordinary meeting," adds Gerrie. "You know when somebody knows they've lost, before they've even started to fight? They were like: 'Very clever. We'll get back to you.' I think it was a combination of admiration and abject hatred."

The club event had only been running a matter of a few weeks so the lawyers swarmed all over the proposal, but by the letter of the law, it was legitimate, and the regulator gave way. "It was the first programme ever on British television that wasn't a sports show or an event to be sponsored 100 per cent," Gerrie says.[28]

The Pepsi Chart was initially broadcast from London's Hanover Grand theatre, later moving to the Sound Republic nightclub. The first hosts were actress Rhona Mitri – known for being the promotional face of video game heroine Lara Croft – and DJ Eddy Temple-Morris, but after a few months Neil Fox – who already hosted the Pepsi Chart show on commercial radio – took over. Abbie Eastwood and Matt Brown were later hosts.

Producing the show at a real venue, rather than in a TV studio, was a bonus for Gerrie. He felt it enhanced the atmosphere. To create more spontaneity, performers were deliberately under-rehearsed and, to maintain as much of the live buzz as possible, the 30-minute show then went out with minimal editing a day after it was recorded. When a five-minute chart update on Monday nights was factored in, the show performed reasonably well, attracting 1.5 million viewers at its height, but its real value came in overseas sales, with more than 100 territories taking the format.[29]

★ ★ ★

By 1998, the programme simply known as *The Chart Show* had been running for 12 years. It was time for something different, the brains at ITV concluded. At the same time, the channel was also looking for a product that could seriously challenge the BBC's domination of Saturday morning television, and so the two projects came together. The result was a new live show called *SM:TV*, to be hosted by up-and-coming presenters Ant & Dec, along with MTV VJ Cat Deeley. This would be followed immediately by a live music show called *CD:UK*, fronted by the same team.

SM:TV's bundle of comedy, competitions and music, wrapped around teenage dramas and cartoons, was – just like *Tiswas* against *Multi-Coloured Swap Shop* in the seventies – a much more anarchic and spirited affair than its BBC rival, *Live And Kicking*, and easily won the Saturday morning ratings battle. *CD:UK* (1998–2006) – the abbreviation initially standing for "Countdown: UK" although this became less obvious – was a blend of live performance, video footage, news, interviews, vox pops and, at the outset, some music trivia from Dr Pop (radio producer Phil Swern). The fact that the show was commissioned for a whole year shows just how much ITV wanted it to succeed.

CD:UK was a bubbly package, produced by former *Top Of The Pops* supremo Ric Blaxill and driven by its three popular presenters. Starting with small viewing numbers, it grew its audience to the point where big international stars were more than happy to appear. To attract names such as Beyoncé, Christina Aguilera, Britney Spears, Paul McCartney and U2 to a children's TV studio on a Saturday morning was quite a feat. Unfortunately, when Ant & Dec moved on to bigger and better things in 2001, both shows took a hit. *SM:TV* was terminated two years later but *CD:UK* continued for a while longer. Deeley hung around until 2005, joined by a succession of other presenters, including *Hollyoaks* star James Redmond, *Big Brother* winner Brian Dowling and Tess Daly. On Deeley's departure, Holly Willoughby, Dave Berry, Myleene Klass, Lauren Laverne and Johnny Pitts saw the show to its inevitable cancellation as viewing numbers fell away. It might not have ended there, however. The show was then picked up by Channel 5, who clearly sensed an opportunity with *Top Of The Pops* on its way out, but the show never did make it back to air.

More pop on weekends at this time came from Channel 4 with a show that started out as a summer holiday filler. *Planet Pop* (1998–2000) was launched as part of *The Bigger Breakfast* – a morning package of American dramas and comedies that built on the audience generated by *The Big Breakfast*. As part of the mix, *Planet Pop* – hosted by, among others, Marc Crumpton, June Sarpong, Lauren Laverne and Scott Mills – delivered a half-hour collection of videos, location reports, gossip and star profiles. It then moved to Sunday mornings as part of the *T4* youth strand and also picked up five-minute update slots on weeknights.

* * *

The circular nature of television was exposed again at the end of the nineties when the BBC presented a musical comedy series called *No Sweat* (1997–8). This was a slapstick affair for children's hour about two teenagers at a Brighton school who decide to form a band in order to find overnight success and so get away from local bullies. Jimmy Osman (played by James Hurst) has just arrived in town having lived all over the country – north and south – and that, to his new buddy Greg Fuggle (Lee Otter), sounds like a good name for a band, if only they can find a couple more members. Eventually, Miles Smith-Jones (Tom Lowe) and Giles Beamish (Sam Chapman) are recruited from a posher school in the neighbourhood. The series tells of their attempts to get the band off the ground, with fantasy sequences that suggested how it might all turn out providing plenty of opportunity for musical interludes. In the second series, the band were seen on tour with their manager Mickey (David Cardy).

No Sweat was produced for the BBC by Initial and masterminded again by Malcolm Gerrie, who had felt that the idea of a "new *Monkees*" was overdue. He pitched the concept simultaneously to the record industry and the BBC. One of the people he approached was Simon Cowell, then working at BMG Entertainment, who referred it up the line to his chairman, John Preston. Preston leapt on the idea and told Gerrie: "I'm really interested in this. We've got a band, managed by Tom Watkins [former manager of the Pet Shop Boys, Bros and East 17], called North And South. Have a listen and see if you think they would be appropriate." Gerrie was also talking to Anna Home, head of children's programmes at the BBC. "She wanted something for that *Grange Hill* slot, ten past five on a Thursday – older audience, bit more edgy," he says. When he mentioned his idea of a *Monkees* for the nineties, she expressed an interest and told him to come up with the right format.

BMG's band fitted the bill and Anna Home commissioned the show, which proceeded to do very well. "It was a little series, really, not massive budget, and it got huge ratings," says Gerrie. It also did good business for the record company, with North And South notching up four UK chart successes, including the Top 10 hit 'I'm a Man Not a Boy'. Plans for a third series, however, were scuppered when the band split, suddenly leaving Gerrie and the BBC with a massive hole to fill. The show had been inked into the schedule for a further 26 weeks so a replacement band was needed, and fast.

Gerrie hastily contacted some of the country's biggest managers and the first to get back to him was Simon Fuller, former manager of the Spice Girls, who said he desperately wanted to be involved and promised to find a band within two weeks. "By then I'll have some tapes and pictures for you to look at and we'll put the band together," he said. "I've got some really great kids." Gerrie admits to having his doubts but also thinking "If anybody can pull it off, it's him."

He returned to the BBC and told them that all was going to be fine, even though the still embryonic band did not have a record deal or even a name. Securing that couple of weeks' grace, he met again with Fuller. "He'd done a short list of who he wanted so I listened to them," says Gerrie. They could sing and they looked great but the key question was whether they could act. "We didn't have any audition tapes or anything." It turned out they could so the next thing to sort out was a recording contract, which brought on board Polydor, whose young MD Lucian Grainge – despite the vagueness of the proposal – was not surprisingly seduced by the guarantee of a 26-week television contract and the impressive track-records of both Simon Fuller and Malcolm Gerrie.

"I thought that was it," says Gerrie. "Then we started doing the budget. We decided we didn't want to shoot in England. We wanted to shoot in Miami, because it was sunny and sexy – just more exotic; like *The Monkees*, upbeat, feel-good. The budget went through the roof. Then we felt that we should shoot it on Super 16 [film] so it would be really glossy, not just videotape. The budget went through the roof again, so we had this massive deficit."

To fill the financial hole, Gerrie approached executives at BBC Worldwide, the Corporation's international marketing arm, and persuaded them to write out a big cheque. Simon Fuller chipped in, as did Endemol, which by now owned Gerrie's company, Initial. But there was still a half-million pound shortfall and the BBC was yelling for production to begin. The last place Gerrie could turn to was Polydor again, where Lucian Grainge somehow found the required cash, even though he had no money to put into television projects. It saved the day and set the ball rolling, starting with a publicity trip to the Mipcom television trade show in Cannes, where programmes are bought and sold internationally.

"BBC Worldwide organised the beach in front of the Carlton Hotel," says Gerrie. "We had the band arrive by motorboat. They sang three songs. I think it was live vocals to track. We had no script, no running orders, just a really sexy sizzle tape we'd put together. An hour later, I'd sold it to an American network, Fox Family. I had the best phone call I've ever made in my career, ringing Lucian up at home that weekend and saying: 'You've got your money back already and, very shortly, you're going to be in profit. Tell that to your board'. The show went to number one in the children's ratings and stayed there for every episode. And it sold everywhere around the world."[30]

The show in question was *Miami 7* (1999) and it introduced S Club 7 to the world. The group of talented youngsters that Simon Fuller had pulled together – Jon Lee, Tina Barrett, Bradley McIntosh, Rachel Stevens, Hannah Spearritt, Paul Cattermole and Jo O'Meara – played the part of a British band who take up an engagement at the inappropriately named Paradise Hotel in Miami, where not only are they expected to turn out covers of seventies hits, instead of their own music, but do other chores as well. Cue 13 episodes of fun and games in the Florida sunshine, with plenty of tunes to lubricate an impending record launch. And the hits just came rolling on in, starting with 'Bring It All Back', number one only a couple of months after the series' debut.

This being too good a concept to lose after just one outing, the group returned later in 1999 with the two-part *S Club Special – Boyfriends And Birthdays*, in which they head for Los Angeles. The next time they surfaced, they had reached their destination. *LA* 7 (2000) carries on their fame-and-fortune-seeking adventures in the American sun, with *Hollywood* 7 (2001) the third and final instalment of the story, unless you count also the feature film spin-off *Seeing Double*. If you factor in CD sales, revenue from a dedicated print magazine and merchandising spin-offs such as S Club dolls, it was really not a bad return on a project that very nearly collapsed before it went into pre-production.

In the sense that it was inspired by *The Monkees*, the S Club project was a sixties thing but it also reflected wider changes in the media, where television music programmes no longer stood alone but were increasingly required to form part of a multi-platform offer. As the 2000s arrived, this mixed-media approach to delivering music to the public, aided by the arrival of digital technology and the explosion of the internet, was to provide both opportunities and challenges for those working in music television.

THE NEW MILLENNIUM

Over On The Red Button

Simon Fuller had a vision for the future of the pop music market. Having witnessed how his S Club 7 project had straddled the worlds of television, recording and print, as well as good old-fashioned merchandising, the entrepreneur could now foresee other opportunities in the digital age.

Fuller's next step was the creation of an online pop music portal that looked to provide in one place pretty much everything a teenage music fan could want, its interlocking strands covering all bases from print media to music sales. The *Popworld* website opened in 2000 and eventually expanded its offer into live shows, online retail, radio, mobile phone interaction and even the production of Westlife chocolate bars, although at the heart of the business was its own television series.[1]

Popworld (2001–7) aired initially on Fridays on the brand-new digital channel E4, with a quick repeat on Sunday mornings in the Channel 4 *T4* strand, where it replaced *Planet Pop*. While there was plenty that was familiar – videos, live performances and interviews – the series adopted a refreshingly different approach from existing pop shows, based primarily around the personality and wicked sense of humour of its two presenters, 21-year-old comedian Simon Amstell and Miquita Oliver, a headstrong, 16-year-old girl who had been known to skip school to watch MTV. The show didn't hit its stride immediately but once Amstell and Oliver were given more freedom and control, it rapidly developed a cult following for its gloriously irreverent attitude to the pop scene and the stars of the day. To the subversive presenters, the music industry needed grounding. Not everything in the pop world was fantastic. Rather than fawning over guests, they preferred to wind them up, pitching oddball questions to throw them off guard and smirking sarcastically to the camera at any vacuous response. The pompous and the boring were easy targets and students, in particular, loved it.

There was more than a touch of the absurd, too. Some questions were posed by Richard and Trudy, two talking horses voiced by the hosts, while Lemar was interviewed by megaphone across a car park ("Lemar from Afar"). Amstell also acted as a counsellor ("the Si-chiatrist") to some bemused musicians, handed out cheese to celebrities at The Brit Awards and, declaring himself not good-looking enough to be on screen with Natalie Imbruglia, proceeded to conduct the interview with a paper bag over his head. Startled artists had to think on their feet and glib responses were cruelly exposed. Guests that gamely played along – Gary Barlow drawn into discussing his pubic hair – went up in viewers' estimation; those who failed to see the joke – a moody Kelly Osbourne – did not.[2]

Popworld was a big hit. Alongside its main Channel 4 outing – later switched to Saturday mornings – programmes were repeated on E4 and there were also editions on MTV. It was time for Fuller and his associates to expand the offer. A *Popworld* magazine began as a supplement in the *Mail On Sunday* newspaper in 2001, with former *Smash Hits* editor Gavin Reeve at the helm. It developed into a stand-alone monthly in 2003 but it couldn't buck the trend of declining print media sales and folded in 2004. For some reason, a second attempt, under the name *Popworld Pulp*, followed in 2007 but this was even more disastrous, surviving only two issues.[3]

Online coverage was expanded, too. In 2006, aspiring musicians were encouraged to upload material to the *Popworld Promotes* website, from where viewers could then, by downloading tracks, vote for performers to be given a spot in the TV show. Unfortunately, this initiative arrived too late as the presentation partnership that drove the programme quit shortly after and the show began a steady decline. Amstell – on his way to *Never Mind The Buzzcocks* – and Oliver – going into other TV presentation – were replaced by comedian Alex Zane and model Alexa Chung, but *Popworld* only lasted one more year. By that time, however, it had made its mark, both in twisting the way music on television was presented and in underlining how television was no longer a medium that stood alone in a multi-platform digital age.

★ ★ ★

The new millennium's promise of a digital broadcasting revolution was also quickly tapped into at *Top Of The Pops*, when BBC Choice began broadcasting an update show called *Top Of The Pops: The New Chart* in 2000. As for the main programme, in 2001, after a 10-year exile at Elstree and, latterly, Riverside Studios, it returned to BBC Television Centre with a special, one-hour edition entitled *Top Of The Pops Goes Large*, hosted by Jamie Theakston, Zoë Ball and Dermot O'Leary. Its new home offered five stages and a "Star Bar", allowing guests to be interviewed over a cocktail or two. The *Top Of The Pops Awards* (2001–2) was another innovation designed to make the show more relevant as it climbed towards its 2,000th edition, as was *Top Of The Pops Saturday*, reformatted as a morning programme for kids, featuring more performances and interviews.

Success in reviving the show domestically now encouraged producer Chris Cowey to look to the international market as a way of both making the *Top Of The Pops* brand more profitable and safeguarding the supply of overseas artists, who had become less inclined to jet across to London for a show that commanded only a fraction of the audience it had once attracted.

"What I wanted to do was to export not just the British programme but the logo, the opening title sequence, the methodology, the studio set, etc. and have people make their own versions in their own territories," he explains. The best Anglo-American material recorded in London could then be supplied to programme-makers in other countries, who would complete their package with local acts. Cowey flew around the world to sell the concept and came home with some remarkable deals. "I think within six or nine months it was in over 100 territories," he says. "That really buttressed the programme and gave it a lot of strength. That meant that we were getting all the best acts again on *Top Of The Pops*, which hadn't been the case for a few years." He coined a slogan to pull in these artists: "Do a worldwide promotional tour: come to London for the afternoon."

Regrettably, one territory where the efforts came to nothing was America, despite plenty of interest. "We got close enough to the US sale that I was actually thinking of where to live out there, because I was going to go set the whole thing up, but in the end that floundered on the fact that the BBC wouldn't let the Americans have any of the ancillaries [merchandising spin-offs]. They only would allow them to do it on the money that they made from commercial breaks. The Americans wanted a juicier deal than that so, although we got extraordinarily close, in the end it didn't happen."

This disappointment deepened Cowey's disillusion with the BBC, having already been knocked back on another adventurous idea, which was to open a *Top Of The Pops* nightclub. "What I wanted to do was to have a permanent *Top Of The Pops* venue," he says. "I wanted to move it into the Hammersmith Palais, have a big neon sign outside with my *Top Of The Pops* logo on it and open it six nights a week as a nightclub but one night a week we'd record *Top Of The Pops* there. The whole thing would have been rebuilt as a permanently branded *Top Of The Pops* set." He saw the venture as symbiotic. If big stars were not available on the nights the show was being recorded then they could be slotted in on other nights and recorded then. "What better way to buttress the attendance at a nightclub than to have Madonna appear in the middle of the night?" he asks. "People would be coming there to make sure they didn't miss anything every night of the week. We did a massive business plan and it meant that, effectively, *Top Of The Pops* would have cost the BBC nothing." Frustratingly, the project was rejected in favour of that move back to Television Centre.

But Cowey had one last idea to pitch before heading for the door, which was to switch the show to Sunday teatime and broadcast it live – a move he described as throwing a hand-grenade into BBC1's "blue-rinse brigade" programming that was built around programmes like *Antiques Roadshow* and *Songs Of Praise*. He reasoned that there was a huge available audience at that time, with nobody heading to the pub and most families at home, getting ready for school and work on Monday morning. His bosses listened and then revealed their own plan. They were thinking of moving *Top Of The Pops* to BBC2. Cowey told them that not only would that sound the death-knell for the programme, but they'd also need to find a new producer. "So that was the end of me and *Top Of The Pops*," he says. "I saw that the BBC's ambitions for the show were nowhere near as high as mine."[4]

Nothing happened on the BBC2 front immediately but there was talk of the show moving to BBC3, although this was rebuffed by its controller, Stuart Murphy, who said he wouldn't have it. It did not fit in with the channel's ethos of bringing forward emerging talent. So on BBC1 it remained and in 2003, with audience numbers back down to around three million, it was time for another throw of the dice. The new man charged with saving the series was a surprise choice – former children's TV presenter and one-time *Top Of The Pops* host Andi Peters.[5]

⋆ ⋆ ⋆

By this time, *Top Of The Pops* had acquired plenty of competition as a chart-based television show. *The Pepsi Chart* ran on Channel 5 until 2002 and was replaced by a series called simply *Pop* (2002) that was a little different in setting out to draw attention to breaking acts as well as established names. It was recorded at the newly reconstructed Marquee Club in Islington and hosted by Lauren Laverne and Matt Brown, although just one series was produced, leading to another, more chart-focused show taking its place. *The Smash Hits Chart* (2003–4) was made by Emap, publisher of the magazine of the same name, and saw hosts Sam

Delaney and Anita Rani introduce acts from a chart compiled not just from music sales but also airplay and viewer requests. Its initial popularity led to Channel 4 poaching the show after six months. Undeterred, Channel 5 fought back by immediately launching the *Flaunt Chart Show* (2003). This was produced by BSkyB's Flaunt music channel before that was re-orientated as a gay music outlet. The show didn't just focus on music but also included style tips and features on celebrity lifestyles, with the chart this time ignoring sales data completely and taking its stats simply from viewers' text votes. It ran for only six months and was superseded by another reworking of the idea called *The Chart* (2004–5), which featured albums as well as singles.

Having stolen the *Smash Hits* show, Channel 4 came a cropper when the *Smash Hits* magazine went under, so to fill the void it developed yet another chart show called *hit40uk* (2004–5). This melange of videos and gossip was based on a commercial radio series and built around a chart that was compiled from sales, airplay and votes from listeners. Hosted by DJ Simon (now Stephanie) Hirst, it was shown in the *T4* strand on Saturday mornings and also after midnight.

While none of these shows had any longevity, it appears that commercial broadcasters could sense that the market for chart-related music programmes was by no means sewn up by the BBC and that, maybe, there was a big opportunity just lurking around the corner. It's hard not to picture them as vultures waiting for the carcass of *Top Of The Pops* to drop.

One of Channel 4's longer-lasting chart-centred innovations was *The Album Chart Show* (2006–12), in which bands performed live in front of a large audience – generally at the Koko Club in Camden – introduced by Joe Mace and later Sara Cox and Nick Grimshaw. The programme later evolved into a show called *London Live*, mostly screened on the music channel 4Music, but with some editions shared on Channel 4. The Koko Club was also home to *Koko Pop* (2010–2), a Saturday morning show for Channel 4, hosted by Jameela Jamil with the Popsicles Crew dancers.

* * *

Under the auspices of Malcolm Gerrie, *The Brit Awards* had been totally transformed in the nineties. What had once been a laughing stock had developed into, arguably, the world's premier music awards show. By the time Gerrie stepped down in 2000, some 140 international broadcasters were taking the coverage. It had become a global spectacular, meticulously planned but always with a little danger, that slight possibility of something spontaneous happening to give it an edge. "Miss *The Brits* and you miss a bit of musical history," Gerrie said at the time.[6]

Following Gerrie's departure, the show worked its way through a catalogue of new and returning presenters, starting with Ant & Dec, Frank Skinner, Zoë Ball, Davina McCall, Cat Deeley and Chris Evans. In 2007, for the first time since the 1989 debacle, the show was broadcast live, with Russell Brand given the job of ensuring it all went to plan. A year later, the Osbourne family were the unlikely choice to front the show and in 2009 the duties were shared by Kylie Minogue, James Corden and Mathew Horne. While not quite catastrophes on the Fox and Fleetwood scale, neither of these last two events went particularly smoothly. Sharon Osbourne swore at Vic Reeves as he was announcing an award and Corden and Horne were perhaps not quite as funny as they thought themselves to be. Peter Kay took over in 2010 and then James Corden returned to begin a four-year run as host with the show now setting up home in the O2 Arena. Ant & Dec were brought back as presenters from 2015.

The event's eye-catching collaborations continued – Justin Timberlake and Kylie Minogue in 2003, the Pet Shop Boys, Lady Gaga and Brandon Flowers in 2009, Dizzee Rascal and Florence Welch in 2010 – and there were other notable moments, not least in 2011 when Adele's spine-tingling performance of 'Someone Like You' quickened her inevitable rise to global fame. The following year, Adele's appearance was memorable for another reason: she flipped the finger at the organisers after her acceptance speech was abruptly terminated.

One thorny issue was the Outstanding Lifetime Contribution Award, traditionally the climax to proceedings when the winner – always a big established act with a long career behind them – would perform a medley of their greatest hits. One problem was that attrition would sooner or later result in the winners becoming less noteworthy, thus diminishing the status of the award. Another was that the winner had to agree to perform live which is why neither the Rolling Stones nor Led Zeppelin ever won it but, ludicrously, the Spice Girls did in 2000 when even their most vociferous supporters would find it difficult to claim their career had lasted a lifetime. (It was subsequently revealed that Paul McCartney had been offered the award that year but was unwilling to accept.)* In the event the Outstanding Contribution Award – the 'Lifetime' was dropped somewhere along the way – was abandoned after Robbie Williams won it in 2010.

Malcolm Gerrie, while recognising the scale and the demands of the project, is disappointed by the general tameness of the show today and the way in which the event has developed since his departure. "It's a big show to do properly, but I'm just really saddened by what's happened to it now," he says. "It's just become dull and bland. I'm not saying that you've got to get into trouble every year – you haven't – but take some risks editorially. Now it's produced, effectively, by the British record industry, by the BPI, so it's this huge commercial thing."[7]

That said, more than 30 years after it made its television debut, *The Brit Awards* remains one of television's big musical events of the year and, as long as the star names still want to appear, it seems likely to remain that way for some time.

★ ★ ★

An unexpected development in the early 2000s was the return of the television talent show. The idea of auditioning singers, presenting them on screen and allowing the public to decide which of them might become stars dates back to the fifties, with programmes such as *Carroll Levis And His Discoveries/The Carroll Levis Show* (1956–9) and the long-running *Opportunity Knocks* (1956; 1964–78; 1987–90), hosted initially by Hughie Green. Such shows were not dedicated to musicians: the

---

★ It is thought McCartney objected to the term 'Lifetime', though it's possible his band wasn't ready at the time to commit to the required live performance.

winners might just as easily have been muscle men flexing their pecs to music or doggerel poets churning out their latest rhymes but it was a route to chart success for a number of bands and singers over the years. While the Beatles (in proto form as Johnny & the Moondogs) failed to impress Levis and secure a place on his show, *Opportunity Knocks* could claim to have discovered Mary Hopkin, the Real Thing and Paper Lace, while its later rival *New Faces* (1973–8; 1986–8) brought us Sweet Sensation, Sheer Elegance and Showaddywaddy. In the new millennium, however, a new generation of talent shows emerged that were entirely focused on the lucrative pop music market. They were also more brutal and voyeuristic, exploiting all the emotion that goes with the territory. From modest beginnings, such shows became a powerful force, using their enormous audiences to create instant celebrities and even dictate which records would next top the charts.[8]

It all began with *Popstars* (2001), not a talent show in the conventional sense but a 13-week, fly-on-the-wall documentary series based on a format imported from Australia. It followed the creation of a new pop group, from the placing of an advertisement for members, through numerous auditions to the launch of the first single. Potential recruits received lessons in style, choreography and media relations before five of them were selected to become, hopefully, a viable group. Making the tough decisions was a panel of judges made up of executive producer and former dancer "Nasty" Nigel Lythgoe, publicist/manager Nicki Chapman and Polydor A&R (new talent) director Paul Adam. The selected candidates emerged under the collective name of Hear'Say and their first release, 'Pure And Simple', went straight to number one. There was consolation for the five runners-up when they were fashioned into Liberty (later Liberty X) and signed their own recording deal.

The same team next came up with *Popstars: The Rivals* (2002), which tweaked the format to show the creation of competitive boy and girl groups. Hosted by Davina McCall, with Pete Waterman, Geri Halliwell and Boyzone manager Louis Walsh as judges, this series led to the formation of One True Voice and, far more significantly, Girls Aloud.

Popstars: The Rivals was not a documentary like *Popstars* but a full-on talent contest that reflected the success of another show that had arrived in the interim. This was *Pop Idol* (2001–3), which took the original *Popstars* concept and pared it down to its essentials. This time, the viewing audience voted for their favourites, whittling down the number week by week after considering comments made by the judging panel of Nicki Chapman, Pete Waterman, DJ Neil Fox and Simon Cowell, who was head of A&R at RCA records at the time. There was just one prize up for grabs, a solo recording contract for the successful candidate, and it went to Will Young who defeated Gareth Gates in the final. The instant success of both finalists – both scoring number one hits – screamed loud and clear that this was a sure-fire way to build new stars and dominate the pop charts. In a second series, Michelle McManus came out on top and, while her chart career proved short-lived, she also reached number one. Everyone was a winner – the contestants, the record labels and, not least, the TV producers.

For *Pop Idol*, *Popstars* judge Nigel Lythgoe had retreated behind the scenes, where he was joined by pop mogul Simon Fuller. Together they developed the concept and sold it on to the rest of the world, most notably to the USA where, as *American Idol* – featuring Simon Cowell again as a judge – it unearthed Kelly Clarkson as its first winner. But the days of *Popstars* and *Pop Idol* were numbered once Simon Cowell concluded he could take the basic idea and make it even better. The result was *The X Factor* (2004–), which would become a central plank of ITV's weekend viewing for many years and discover such names as Leona Lewis, Alexandra Burke, Jedward, Olly Murs, JLS, Little Mix and One Direction (not all of them actually winners of the series).

Unlike *Pop Idol*, *The X Factor* was open to all ages above 16, but otherwise there were a number of similarities – so much so that Simon Fuller sued for copyright violation and the matter was settled out of court. The on-screen process this time began with auditions, progressed through "boot camp" for those with promise, followed by personal mentoring from the judges, and concluded with live Saturday night performances that once more saw the survivors slowly culled by viewer votes. Cowell again appeared as a judge, sharing the duties over the years with Sharon Osbourne, Louis Walsh, Dannii Minogue, Cheryl Cole, Kelly Rowland, Tulisa Contostavlos, Gary

Barlow, Nicole Scherzinger, Mel B, Rita Ora and Nick Grimshaw. Kate Thornton was the original host, succeeded by Dermot O'Leary and then, for one year, Olly Murs and Caroline Flack. Hundreds of thousands of hopefuls applied for the show and the power of the series at its height was remarkable, guaranteeing that the winner's first single release would top the UK chart in Christmas week. Not surprisingly, the format was again sold around the world.[9]

The BBC, noting ITV's huge success, commissioned its own reality-talent show in the form of *Fame Academy* (2002–5; 2007). Based on a European format, this took the *Pop Idol* concept and built in elements of the eighties American drama series *Fame*, where students paid their dues in sweat to earn the right to fame and fortune in the performing arts. So, as well as the now-familiar scenes of ropey auditions, hissy-fits and tears that characterised the candidates' "journeys", *Fame Academy* showed the hopefuls going back to school. Billeting them in a north London mansion, with its own music suites and dance studio, it roused contestants at 6.30 each morning for a gruelling regime of vocal training and choreography, rounding off the week with a sing-for-survival ordeal live on television. Cat Deeley, Patrick Kielty and Claudia Winkelman hosted and the two series' winners were David Sneddon and Alex Parks. Celebrity versions for *Comic Relief* were also produced.

The BBC returned to the idea when it adapted a Dutch format into *The Voice UK* (2012–16), which pretty much followed the same patterns as all the other shows, except for an initial twist in which contestants were chosen on their voice alone by celebrity coaches/judges, whose seats were turned away from the stage, and a later round of one-on-one sing-offs. Tom Jones, will.i.am, Jessie J and Danny O'Donoghue from the Script were the initial mentors, with Kylie Minogue, Ricky Wilson of the Kaiser Chiefs, Rita Ora, Paloma Faith and Boy George added at various times later. Holly Willoughby and Reggie Yates were the original hosts, replaced from the second series by Emma Willis and Marvin Humes. The format has now been acquired by ITV.

* * *

The decision to bring in Andi Peters as Chris Cowey's replacement at *Top Of The Pops* was made by Wayne Garvey, the BBC's Head of Entertainment, and Mark Cooper, Head of Music Entertainment. The unexpected appointment brought echoes of the "yoof" TV shake-up of the eighties when Janet Street-Porter was poached from Channel 4 to take charge of the BBC's young people's output. Now Peters was lured over from the same broadcaster after successfully producing the youth programming strand *T4*. "Andi has a proven track record in developing new programming for the teenage market," explained Garvey as he broke the news, thus offering a clue as to the future direction of *Top Of The Pops*. What was once a family show was being refocused.[10]

Mark Cooper sums up the situation. "*Top Of The Pops*, certainly in the seventies and eighties, was a show for all the family and for all audiences. There was something for mum and something for dad and something to unite the family and something to get them arguing or divide them," he says. "The family audience had evaporated to some degree, not because of Chris but because of the whole way the BBC and media had gone. When Radio 1 relaunched in the early nineties, it stopped being the 'Nation's Favourite' and became a show for young people and that sort of mirrored the way music was going to become more and more niche for different demographics." The glue wasn't there to hold the family audience together, he says, and it showed in the audience figures. "Suddenly you had a show that used to deliver, in its heyday in a three-channel world, 17, 18, 20 million, delivering three-and-a-half, three million on BBC1 on a Friday night, not necessarily attached to a new chart story. In pure television-ratings terms, it wasn't functioning."[11]

The music industry was also in turmoil in 2003. Singles sales had collapsed that year, down around 40 per cent – abetted by the arrival of Napster and other downloading websites – and this suggested a lack of interest in the charts (the Radio 1 chart show figures also took a dip). But it was in the BBC's interests to keep *Top Of The Pops* alive. Those international deals were still valuable and it would have been a shame to lose the programme just as it was approaching its 40th anniversary.[12]

The brief for Peters was to give *Top Of The Pops* more impact by introducing "big moments" that would encourage viewers to switch on – moments such as U2 playing in the horseshoe in front of Television Centre or Eminem on *HMS Belfast* on the Thames. Within weeks of Peters' appointment, the show had been totally revamped and relaunched, at great expense, as *All New Top Of The Pops*. A new studio, a new logo and a new theme tune – a reworking of Tony Gibber's nineties theme 'Now Get Out Of That' – were all acquired. Twenty-two-year-old Tim Kash was chosen to be the programme's regular host, in the belief that his weekly presence would foster viewer loyalty, and also that his background as a presenter on MTV would bring across some of that audience. Stages were made higher to introduce more of a "concert" atmosphere and the show went out live again but greater emphasis was now placed on interviews and music news at the expense of performances. The number of acts was cut from around eleven a week to just seven and the focus on hits was diluted as Peters decided to play the industry's game and include singles that were being marketed ahead of going on sale. Interactive votes were introduced so that the audience could tweak some of the content of the show as it went along. Unfortunately, the experiment with Tim Kash didn't work out and Fearne Cotton and Reggie Yates were soon brought in to liven things up but, sadly, it was all to no avail.[13]

Top Of The Pops was a sinking ship that took on more water when it finally lost its Friday night BBC1 slot and was switched to Sunday evenings on BBC2. The audience figures could no longer justify the prime spot in the schedule but there was also a recognition that, in the new millennium, immediacy was everything. A chart show that was broadcast five days after the chart was first announced no longer made sense, when information and entertainment were available on demand via the internet. Running the show directly after the new chart was released was a better option. There was certainly some logic to the move but the fact that the programme was relegated to BBC2 was an admission of weakness. The audiences tumbled again, collapsing to just over a million, less than half the number the Friday night shows were getting. The writing was on the wall and, reluctantly, it was time to put *Top Of The Pops* out of its misery.

"Andi's relaunch didn't really work, in terms of reigniting and finding a new audience," concedes Mark Cooper. "That induced a loss of faith in it from the channels and from the Director of Television so they moved it onto BBC2 for a year and then they killed it. For them, it was a show that no longer spoke to the present. For somebody who was making it, it was enormously disappointing, but it's hard to argue with their logic."

The sinking ship finally went under when the last weekly show was broadcast on July 30, 2006. It was a bittersweet affair, with former presenters of various vintages providing the links. The Rolling Stones had kicked off the show back in 1964 and they did so again, with an archive performance of, somewhat appropriately, 'The Last Time'. It wasn't quite the end for *Top Of The Pops* as the show has survived in retro form as *TOTP 2* – with Mark Radcliffe, since 2009, the latest DJ to provide the witty comments – and in re-runs of whole programmes on BBC4. *Top Of The Pops* also remains firmly part of the traditional British Christmas, with seasonal specials still rolled out every year.

"The beauty of doing it at Christmas is you have a built-in sense of occasion and it has a known and effective place in the schedule," says Mark Cooper. "So the Christmas show and the New Year show work and we love doing them. It's very nostalgic for us and a great review of the year in pop but that doesn't suggest that the conditions exist to return to a weekly show. That feels like it belongs in another world. It belongs, a bit like the music press or record shops, to a specific era, a golden era for people of a certain age, but the game's changed."[14]

Former producer Trevor Dann agrees and, in hindsight, knows that the programme was on its way out in the mid-nineties when he took over. "Once a brand is on the way down, you've just got to let it die," he says. "As it turned out, we tried wrongly to rescue a brand that had no validity any longer. It is a shame in some ways but my learning from these 'brands' is that they mostly go on too long. I think *Whistle Test* ran out of steam and should have been canned before it was and definitely the same with *Top Of The Pops*."[15]

Chris Cowey, however, takes a different slant. "What the BBC have done with *Top Of The Pops* is cultural vandalism," he says. "The BBC shouldn't care about the ratings. *Later* is brilliant but it hasn't got a programme that does music in a comprehensive way that *Top Of The Pops* does. That is because of executives chasing ratings and chasing their own careers, instead of realising that what you had in *Top Of The Pops* was a national treasure, which could have been one of Britain's biggest exports – and indeed was for a long period of time. Somebody let that slip through their fingers." There could still be a future for the show, he says, but it would mean working in the modern world.

"I think television has lost a lot of confidence and, to some extent, thrown the baby out with the bathwater by being afraid," he says. "When *Top Of The Pops* finally died, somebody said: 'It's because of MTV and the internet'. Bollocks. MTV has been going since 1981. The internet had been going for a long time. It's because we'd been making it really, really badly and, if the BBC didn't give it any love, how did they expect the punters to give it any love? It's a cracking format. It's a cracking programme and it could still do incredibly well. To do it right requires a big business plan that includes radio, print, TV, online – that right-across-the-board thinking. There's no kind of halfway, fudgy way of doing it. You've got to go for it." He reckons, produced in the right way, *Top Of The Pops* would both deliver the viewing figures and be a commercial success, although the latter might be something that could trouble the BBC. "There's the rub," he says. "The BBC have to be really, really cautious about how commercial they are. Pop music is rapaciously commercial and the marriage of those two things has always been uneasy. Maybe it could be done through ITV or BT or Sky but it would require people to buy into not just a concept for a television programme but a concept for a whole business. In that way, it would be self-sustaining, cost the network nothing and do a great job for them."[16]

* * *

While *Top Of The Pops* coughed, spluttered and finally gave up the ghost, other music shows continued to come and go. The most refreshing were live performance programmes, such as *Re:Covered*

(2002–3), which was shown on BBC Choice and then BBC3. Dermot O'Leary was the host and associate producer, welcoming artists to the Riverside Studios in Hammersmith to answer a few questions and do their thing before a live audience. Three bands or singers in each show played their own songs plus some covers (hence the title), with the first show featuring the Pet Shop Boys, Stereophonics and Natalie Imbruglia. Over time, Craig David covered the Beatles' 'Come Together', Busted played Simon & Garfunkel's 'Mrs Robinson', the Thrills had a go at Michael Jackson's 'Billie Jean' and Jamiroquai tackled Roxy Music's 'Love Is The Drug'.

BBC Choice also offered *The Beat Room* (2000), a BBC Scotland production first seen as an opt-out from the channel in Scotland. As well as presenting live local bands, this introduced 'Top Of The Poppets', a slice of satirical comedy featuring puppets of stars such as Robbie Williams, Madonna and Destiny's Child.

Once BBC Choice had morphed into BBC3, among its other contributions was *Trevor Nelson's Lowdown* (2003–4), in which the Radio 1 presenter jetted around the world to celebrate urban music with big names from the field. It was later repeated on BBC2.

From The Basement (2007–9; 2013), on the other hand, had no host. Inspired by the most memorable performances from *The Old Grey Whistle Test* (Bill Withers has been cited), it aimed to bring television music back to basics, to allow musicians to play directly to the camera and not a studio audience. "TV world is a pretty hostile environment for your average musician to have to walk into and bare his soul on cue," declared the programme's creator Nigel Godrich, the internationally renowned producer of Radiohead and other acts. Forget the fast cuts, the zany hosts, the down-with-the-kids speak: this show just let the artists play in a film studio (the Chaplin Stage at the Charlie Chaplin Studios in LA), when they were ready, and filmed them in high definition (and later 3D). Godrich was himself in charge of the sound that was recorded on analogue tape. The plan was to allow the musicians to be themselves, unencumbered by the usual constraints of making a television programme. The show began life as a download but was soon snapped up by the subscription channel Sky Arts, as well as other international broadcasters. Among those participating were the White Stripes, Damien Rice, Jarvis Cocker, PJ Harvey, Fleet Foxes, Gnarls Barkley, Eels and Radiohead.[17]

At the same time as Nigel Godrich was recording the first bands for *From The Basement*, a similar series – another reaction to the over-production of music shows that had begun in the eighties – was coming together at London's hallowed Abbey Road studios. *Live From Abbey Road* (2007–9; 2011) was based around the same premise of just letting the performers perform without the hindrance of an expectant audience or a demanding director. Shrewdly using the famous studio name as a draw for both artists and viewers, this was a project devised for international sales. Featured artists included Paul Simon, Corinne Bailey Rae, the Red Hot Chili Peppers, Kasabian, Damien Rice, the Killers, Muse, Iron Maiden, the Script, Brian Wilson, Florence + the Machine and Ed Sheeran. The series was shown first on the More4 channel before airing on Channel 4 and led to two spin-off series, the first being *Abbey Road Debuts* (2010–11), a 15-minute showcase for rated new bands such as Everything Everything, Mount Kimble and Trophy Wife, which was hosted by John Peel's son, Tom Ravenscroft. The second was *Abbey Road Studios: In Session* (2012–13), whose guests included Paul Weller, the Maccabees, the Vaccines and Alt-J.

Of the other new music shows in the 2000s, *Orange Playlist* (2004–7) stands out. After prevailing with *The Pepsi Chart*, and fortified by his success in getting sponsors to fund music shows for television, producer Malcolm Gerrie developed this late-night, celebrity-based music-and-chat show for ITV. Guests – Minnie Driver, Michael Stipe, Lennox Lewis, Pete Doherty, John Simm and others – shared their musical preferences with host Lauren Laverne (later Jayne Middlemiss) and explained the role music had played in their lives. They also had to make past, present and future choices of music, select a dedication track and plump for their all-time favourite piece. "We just said to them: 'Carte blanche. You just choose any tracks you want'," says Gerrie. "It was like a *Desert Island Discs* format really, paid for by Orange. Once we'd done *The Pepsi Chart*, the floodgates were open." Early episodes were filmed in studio; later programmes were shot on location.[18]

Music also came into the Channel 4 weekday breakfast schedule with the launch of *Freshly Squeezed* (2006–12), a 25-minute, cheaply-assembled, studio-based ramble through the latest videos, combined with specially recorded performances, interviews and album reviews. There was also a gig guide, movie news and dates from 'This Day In Pop'. Presenters worked in pairs and included Rick Edwards, George Lamb, Sarah Hendy, Phil Clifton, Jameela Jamil, Nick Grimshaw and Alexa Chung, over the show's six-year run.

⋆ ⋆ ⋆

The political bias that had always, to a degree, skewed the voting in the *Eurovision Song Contest* progressed to a new level during the early years of the new millennium. With the number of countries expanded to take in former Soviet territories and the introduction of public telephone and online voting, the quality of the song became even less important than before, although it would be hard to argue that this was the sole reason for the failure of some of the UK entries. The highest position achieved since 2000 has been Jessica Garlick's joint third with 'Come Back' in 2002 but this is a blip on the graph, as most of the British contributions have finished way down the list, and there have even been some embarrassing last positions. Arguably, Andy Abraham's 'Even If' and Josh Dubovie's 'That Sounds Good To Me' didn't deserve this ignominy, but the same couldn't be said for Jemini's tuneless rendition of 'Cry Baby' in 2003 that scored zero points.

Garlick and Abraham were just two of a number of TV talent show contestants to represent the country at this time and their international obscurity possibly didn't help the cause but even bringing in successful names such as Blue didn't do the trick, nor did resurrecting Engelbert Humperdinck or Bonnie Tyler. As it meanders on beyond its 60th anniversary, Eurovision remains as it has nearly always been, a glitzy entertainment show with little connection to the real music world.

⋆ ⋆ ⋆

One area of music programming that really blossomed in the 2000s was the documentary. The BBC's *Arena* continued to include popular music among its arts essays, offering a mix of original output and some previously made films. These included Martin Scorsese's *No Direction Home – Bob Dylan* (2005), *Pete Doherty* (2006) and *Today Carshalton Beeches – Tomorrow Croydon* (a look at DJ John Peel's role in encouraging unsigned bands, 2007). There was also *Caroline 199 – A Pirate's Tale* (2007), *Produced By George Martin* (2011), Martin Scorsese's *George Harrison: Living In The Material World* (2011) and *Magical Mystery Tour Revisited* (2012).

Other BBC documentaries included *Walk On By: The Story Of Popular Song* (2001). Narrated by Clive Owen, this eight-part series by Alan Lewens explored the greatest hits of the 20th century, from Scott Joplin's 'Maple Leaf Rag' to Britney Spears' 'Baby One More Time'. Through archive footage and interviews with leading players, the story traced the development of popular songwriting from its earliest days in the ghettos of New York City, where immigrants from all over the world congregated and shared their musical heritages. Greats like Gershwin and Berlin were justly prominent as were partnerships such as Bacharach & David, Goffin & King, and Lennon & McCartney.

In complete contrast, Channel 4 imported *The Osbournes* (2002–5) from MTV. On the face of it, a fly-on-the-wall documentary about the Black Sabbath singer and his family, this was really a laugh-a-minute glimpse into a dysfunctional universe, with Ozzy, Sharon and kids Jack and Kelly rubbing along in a Beverly Hills mansion. The joy of the series came from the fact that this was no sycophantic, stage-managed tribute programme: the Osbournes were seen warts and all. The head of the family may have been a global rock star but here he cut a shambling, though comically likable, figure. "He's Homer Simpson come to life," executive producer Greg Johnston told the *Radio Times*. "He can't pretend for the camera – he just is." Some of the constant expletives were inevitably bleeped out but if you wanted the whole unexpurgated extravaganza you only had to wait a few days for an unedited repeat.[19]

⋆ ⋆ ⋆

The most significant development of the new decade for those with an interest in the history and culture of popular music was the additional airtime provided by the new digital channels – and particularly BBC4. This allowed producers to make good use of archive material that otherwise would never have seen the light of day. BBC4 thus began re-running whole *Top Of The Pops* shows and devoting most Friday evenings to wallows in rock nostalgia, pulling together excerpts from *The Old Grey Whistle Test* and other live performance shows. There was also room for externally made documentaries on certain genres of music or individual artists such as Neil Sedaka or Alice Cooper. One recurring idea was the *Britannica* series, in which one particular strand of music was analysed in its British context, be it *Folk Britannica*, *Psychedelic Britannica*, *Heavy Metal Britannica* or even *Synth Britannica* – looking at the worlds those styles of music emerged from, how they were interpreted in Britain and how they then reflected British culture.

"It's a huge privilege to grow the Friday night on BBC4," says BBC Head of Music Television, Mark Cooper. "I love curating the archive, even in the compilations that we do, whether it's *One-Hit Wonders At The BBC* or *Goth At The BBC* or *Hip Hop At The BBC*. It's very rich pickings. With the exception of some programmes in *Arena*, there really wasn't that historical music documentary tradition in TV until the 2000s and now it's part of the landscape."[20]

One interesting concept was *Pop On Trial* (2008), a series of hour-long, archive-fuelled debates about the merits of each of pop's decades, from the fifties to the nineties. Stuart Maconie took on the role of chairman and contributors included Neil Innes, Gaz Coombs, Martin Fry and Paolo Hewitt. In a grand finale, a jury comprising Paul Morley, Noddy Holder, Lauren Laverne and David McAlmont, having heard evidence delivered by advocates Pete Wylie, DJ Eddie Piller, David Quantick, Miranda Sawyer and Caitlin Moran, decided which era was the best. For the record, the seventies won.

Complementing the work done on BBC4 has been the subscription-based Sky Arts channel. This began life as Artsworld, launched by former Channel 4 boss Jeremy Isaacs in 2003, but it ran into financial difficulties leading to a takeover by BSkyB, at which point the name was changed. Alongside a diet of opera, classical music and fine art, the channel delivers popular music in the form of concert footage, the *Classic Albums* series and other documentaries. There was also a chat show, *Talks Music* (2013–14), a musical equivalent of the US series *Inside The Actors Studio*. This was hosted by its executive producer Malcolm Gerrie who found himself in front of the cameras because the channel didn't like any of the proposed presenters. "It was really just a simple idea of digging deep into the body of work of a range of artists who had, I felt, turned the page of contemporary music," he says. Among those featured were Jeff Beck, Nile Rogers and Giorgio Moroder.[21]

* * *

With the demise of *Top Of The Pops*, the granddaddy of British music programmes is now *Later With Jools Holland*, which is still delivering the goods after a quarter of a century on air. It has reached this milestone by changing very little. A small audience was added quite early on, then some tables and chairs for additional guests, and the number of bands in each edition has expanded since the very first days, but essentially *Later* has remained gimmick-free. It's just musicians playing in an intimate setting. There's no attempt to recreate the atmosphere of a grand-scale event like a live concert. Instead it allows television to deliver music in the way it often does best, which is close up and without fuss, as *Whistle Test* found out over many years. The draw for the artists is not the money, but the musical integrity of the programme and the chance to perform two or three numbers from their most recent album rather than just whipping in and out with the latest hit. They also appreciate the care taken to deliver the best audio, trusting Mike Felton, who has been the sound man on the show from the start, as they trust the rest of the team, starting with fellow musician Jools, director Janet Fraser Crook, Mark Cooper and Alison Howe, who joined as producer in 1998. Over the years big names have always been keen to appear – Robbie Williams, Coldplay, David Gilmour, Paul Simon, Morrissey, Red Hot Chili Peppers, Scissor Sisters, Tony Bennett, Lou Reed and more in the new millennium – and breakthrough artists have their chance. Adele made her television debut in 2007, sharing the studio with Paul McCartney and Björk.

The biggest change that has occurred has come behind the scenes, following the closure of the BBC's Television Centre in 2012. Always eager for more space, *Later* had expanded out of the modest studio it first shared with *The Late Show*, and had gradually acquired more and more room at the BBC. Now it needed to relocate completely. A new home was found in Maidstone at the studios built for the ITV company TVS in 1982 but now an independent production facility.

"The nature of *Later* is that we've always just pushed the envelope, wanting to get more artists in, make it bigger, have more variety," says Mark Cooper. Maidstone provided the facilities for that but it has added to the show in other ways, too, he says. "It's got a great sound desk, which is crucial, because groups don't like doing music shows if they don't sound good, and the audience are very enthusiastic. It's not in the heart of the West End where people are blasé about the many artistic things on offer." Cooper also feels being away from the towering presence of Television Centre is a bonus. "In a way, it's slightly more ours because at Television Centre the artists were entering the hallowed portals, alongside Ronnie Corbett or Morecambe & Wise or Jeremy Paxman, and there was always a slight sense of alien territory, whereas in Maidstone it feels more like something shared with the artists. They can tell the show's about them."

A more obvious development was the addition of a second weekly show. While the main programme has remained comfortably ensconced on a Friday night, a shorter outing was introduced earlier in the week in 2008, primarily as a pragmatic response when the BBC changed its funding models and concluded it couldn't continue to spend so much money on a show that wasn't broadcast in peak hours. By introducing an extra half-hour edition that went out at 10 p.m., the programme could continue to wash its face. What gave the whole thing a lift, however, was the decision to broadcast this show live. "We've loved doing that," says Cooper. "I think the artists like it: it raises their game. Jools loves it as a musician: it raises his game. It adds a kind of spontaneity and commitment to the performances. It feels like the show goes up 15–20 per cent in terms of excitement. If you're pre-recording, to some degree, you've always got that slight ability to second-guess yourself. When there is no safety net, you're going to try and do your best work. So it's been great. It's put *Later* in front of a broader audience and it makes it more accessible to more viewers."

The main hour-long version of the programme is actually recorded on the same night, immediately before the live edition. "I think the first show relaxes people, makes them comfortable in the room," adds Cooper. "It tends to be the first two songs of the pre-recorded show that people screw up, because they're nervous, however big they are. Being in a room, confronted by your peers, seems to make a lot of people nervous. By 10 o'clock they tend to have conquered those nerves and feel more in the zone. But some of the performances in the Friday night show we now move over from the live show because they're the better performances."[22]

A quarter of a century on, *Later* is still doing the business. It's a remarkable achievement for a show with such a relatively small audience. It could only be possible at the BBC. When discussions continue about how the Corporation should be funded, and how it uses its resources, it is perhaps worth remembering that if *Later* had been conceived for a commercial network it wouldn't have survived one series.

* * *

While there is more music on television today than there has ever been, very little can be seen during peak hours on mainstream – what used to be known as terrestrial – channels. With the exception of *Later With Jools Holland*, archive material on BBC4 and some festival coverage, music has been mostly siphoned off into dedicated channels or the fringes of the schedules. There's no *Top Of The Pops*, so promotional appearances by artists are now often confined to chat shows hosted by Jonathan Ross, Alan Carr and Graham Norton. The marginalisation of music that began in the nineties has continued.

As further evidence of this, you only have to consider the new music shows offered by Channel 4 since the turn of the millennium. It's an extensive list, from a broadcaster that traditionally has been a fine partner for pop and rock music, but nearly all of these programmes have been broadcast in the post-midnight *4Music* strand, which was launched in 1999.

The *4Music* programming, seen on one or two nights of the week, was a mixed bag, ranging from individual concerts to cheap video shows. *4Play* (1999–12), a long-running series of interviews and performances, was the most durable but the strand also encompassed series already discussed such as *Jo Whiley*, *Flava*, *The Osbournes*, *The Album Chart Show*, *Live From Abbey Road* and *hit40uk*. Other elements of Channel 4's overnight service included *All Back To Mine* (1999–2000), in which Sean Rowley paid visits to the homes of music stars – people like Norman Cook, James Dean Bradfield and Moby – to inspect their record collections, and *The Barfly Sessions* (2000), featuring indie bands introduced by Dermot O'Leary at the Barfly Club in Camden and other venues.

House Of Rock (2000–2) was a collection of short satirical cartoons featuring dead musicians who share a house – Freddie Mercury, Marc Bolan, John Denver, Notorious B.I.G. and Kurt Cobain, with John Lennon later replacing Bolan – while *Ear Candy* (2003–4) was a window for new music talent presented by Colin Murray. In *Rock 'n' Roll Myths* (2004) Sean Rowley tried to discover the truth behind such hoary tales as Robert Johnson selling his soul to the devil, Keith Moon driving his car into a swimming pool and Mick Jagger and Marianne Faithfull's alleged innovative use of confectionery.

Ibiza Rocks (2006–12) provided coverage from the Balearic island's annual music festival, with Zane Lowe and later Annie Mac, while *Transmission* (2006–7) was a performance show, hosted by Steve Jones and Lauren Laverne, that travelled around the UK. "Up-and-coming" Lily Allen featured in the first edition, alongside Dirty Pretty Things, the Klaxons and the Kooks; later contributions came from the Zutons, Primal Scream, Kasabian, Babyshambles and Funeral For A Friend.

Spectacle: Elvis Costello With … (2008–9) was an international production, with Elvis and Elton John acting as executive producers. Costello talked to an eclectic array of guests – the Police, James Taylor,

Bill Clinton, soprano Renée Fleming, Herbie Hancock and others – about their music, and joined them in some renditions.

Mercury Prize Sessions (2009–14) offered coverage of gigs at The Hospital Club, London, featuring a mixture of established and rising artists, from Florence + the Machine, the Coral and Graham Coxon to Tom Odell, Bastille and George Ezra, while *360 Sessions* (2010–12) was another travelling music series, this time giving artists such as David Gray, Mark Ronson, David Guetta and Nelly Furtado a chance to reveal the places they like best when making music or just chilling, taking in destinations such as LA, New York, London and Tokyo.

On Track (2010–11) was an adventurous series created by Universal Music and hosted by Tom Ravenscroft that saw performers take a step back in time by cutting recordings directly to vinyl at London's Metropolis Studios. Each guest performed three of their own tracks, plus a cover version of a number that had helped shape their career. This cover was then available for streaming and download. Among those taking part were Foals, Ellie Goulding, Bombay Bicycle Club, the Kaiser Chiefs and James Morrison.

Another recording studio show was *Launched At Red Bull Studios* (2012–15), introduced by Dan O'Connell and later Annie Mac. This featured conversations with, and songs from, artists hotly tipped for success. Two acts were given a chance to shine in each 30-minute show. Early exposure was given here to Sam Smith, Bastille, Royal Blood, James Bay and Years And Years, recommended as artists to watch by the likes of Gary Barlow, Ed Sheeran and Rita Ora. *Four To The Floor* (2014), meanwhile, was another short but innovative series that focused on modern non-mainstream music, combining live performances with animations and videos.

The title *4Music* was gradually phased out on Channel 4 after it was adopted for a separate digital channel, formerly called The Hits, in 2008. 4Music is now just one of a huge number of satellite/cable channels devoted to music. Most are subscription based and each has its own agenda, be it urban, funk or metal. Some trade on the back of radio stations – Kiss, Magic, Heart, Capital; others have been tied into magazines – *Kerrang!*, *Smash Hits!*, *Heat*. Effectively, you can have wall-to-wall rap, rock or dance from dawn to dusk and through the night, if that's what you need.

* * *

By the early 2000s, the Glastonbury festival had inked itself into Britain's summer calendar as an event not to be missed, rubbing shoulders with Wimbledon, Royal Ascot and the Henley Regatta. Undoubtedly, the BBC's involvement helped. From tentative beginnings in 1997, the Corporation's coverage had developed into a broadcasting highlight of the year, aided by the arrival of digital television. Using BBC Choice, the BBC was able to deliver more coverage and present more facets of the festival, such as when, in 2000, the channel began paying visits to the Dance Tent. In that same year also, coverage on BBC2 began to infiltrate more peak hours, rather than being confined to the extremes of the television day.

By 2003, BBC Choice had been replaced by BBC3 and the new channel fully embraced the Glastonbury weekend, dedicating almost all its output to the event, Edith Bowman and Colin Murray at the helm. Another platform was opened in 2005, when BBC4 began offering selected sessions for its own, more mature audience. This was a particularly trying year for all concerned with heavy downpours hindering the start and the BBC having to abandon one of its presentation areas because of flooding.

Back in 1998, the BBC had pioneered its "red button" service, which gave viewers access to news, weather and other information and also the chance to enjoy feeds from sporting and other outside broadcast events that could not be accommodated in the normal schedules. The service could have been made for Glastonbury. With so much happening at any one time, the opportunity to show more was a godsend. By 2013, the BBC was providing five feeds from the festival through the remote control red button, allowing viewers to choose which stage to follow. In the same year, the BBC's online service was streaming live music from six stages to home computers, tablets, smart phones and smart TVs. Glastonbury, suddenly, was everywhere. "As the BBC has grown into the digital offer and the online interactive offer, Glastonbury has grown with it," says executive producer Mark Cooper. "You could argue that it's at the very heart of the way the BBC itself has grown in the 20 years since we first went there."

All these new services, of course, mean greater commitment both financially and in human resources on the part of the BBC. It is not hyperbole to suggest that the Corporation sends a small army to cover the event. Around 300 people decamp to Somerset to bring the show to air and they are all needed. "We film something like 160 artists," says Mark Cooper. "It's not like the Olympics, where the BBC is adding presentation to someone else filming. Everything that you see on the BBC we're responsible for, so we are the infrastructure." It's a massive undertaking, with countless challenges. "You're on a working farm, in a valley with huge communications issues," says Cooper. "You're working in a wonderful, extraordinary landscape, full of people, so there are all the technical challenges of that and we live in a very different world now. When we started at Glastonbury, everything was on tape. We were just on BBC2 and we had a limited number of hours. There was no ability to time-shift things and put them on to suit you. Now we're streaming five or six stages live and we're trying to offer a distinct Glastonbury for each channel, demographically and artistically".

There's also a commitment to conveying the atmosphere and spirit of the festival and giving viewers a sense of the forces that shape Glastonbury, through specially made features and reports. And, as well as covering scheduled acts live, the BBC now also has its own acoustic stage where acts can play directly to the television audience. "You can have very different Glastonburys," says Cooper. "You can be down the front, being a teenager enjoying James Bay or Ellie Goulding, or you can be watching Lionel Richie or you can be at West Holts watching an eclectic funk band from Japan. It's a broad offer. We try and lead the audience to different stages but you can go on your phone and stream any artist that's on live and curate your own Glastonbury."

Yet Cooper knows that what he calls "the event side of it", those big, live moments when the headliners hit the stage, is still what drags people away from their personal devices and back to the television. "We've very deliberately built Glastonbury in the schedule to be something that's quite rare," he says. Rather than just playing highlights from a festival that's already packed up for the night, it's become a thrilling, anything-can-happen live event. "I can't think of many other festivals that are covered with that breadth but also that sense of 'liveness'," he adds. "This is Kanye West and there is no mediation. We love that."

Getting agreement to show live material does require trust on the part of the performers, he says, and careful negotiation that sometimes spills out into the public domain, as it did with the Rolling Stones in 2013. "For them, a lot's at risk, in terms of how they sound and how they look. Some of the artists, particularly the legendary, more old-school artists, feel at risk. But that's also what produces great work and excitement and the public's desire to engage with it."

There are issues, of course, with live coverage, particularly if it's going out before the 9 p.m. family-viewing watershed, so care has to be taken over which acts to feature at this time. The Sunday teatime slot on BBC2 is one of those live occasions but the sort of performers booked for this – Neil Diamond, Tom Jones, Paul Simon, Kenny Rogers – are unlikely to scare the horses. "You're not going to have issues with Lionel Richie or Dolly Parton, in terms of language, and with the headliners we feel free to go to them live," says Cooper. "But the acts between 7 and 9 have been a problem because they can use a bit of cheeky language."[23]

The success of the BBC's work at Glastonbury has led to the coverage of other festivals such as T in the Park, Reading and Leeds. It has also made the staging of a massive international event such as *Live 8* (2005) much more straightforward than was the case with its forebear, *Live Aid*, 20 years earlier.

Live 8 took place on July 2, 2005 in London's Hyde Park. Bob Geldof was again the driving force behind the concert although the primary purpose this time was not to raise money but to draw attention to Third World debt, putting pressure on leaders of the G8 countries, who were shortly to meet in Edinburgh, to address this issue. By cancelling debt, increasing financial aid and reforming trading arrangements, the lives of millions of the world's poorest citizens would, in theory, be improved. "Make Poverty History" was the mantra.

Tickets for the event were not sold but given away in a texting lottery. The rest of the world was able to watch the event at home courtesy of the BBC. The show was notable in that Geldof had managed to persuade the four members of the classic seventies line-up of Pink Floyd to bury the hatchet and reform for what turned out to be the very last time. Also among those featured in extended coverage on BBCs1 and 2 were Paul McCartney, Elton John, Sting, Coldplay, U2, the Who, Madonna, Robbie Williams, R.E.M., Scissor Sisters, the Killers, Mariah Carey and Stereophonics, while the hosts were Jonathan Ross, Jo Whiley and Fearne Cotton, helped by a number of comedians and even David Beckham. A satellite event at Philadelphia's Museum of Art was introduced later by Graham Norton and bits of other related concerts around the world were dropped in between the London performances.[24]

* * *

Glastonbury today epitomises how far coverage of rock and pop music on British television has come in 60 years and also sums up the challenges facing today's television producer looking to deal with how people consume media in the 21st century.

Television is no longer just about a handful of channels and people do not sit placidly in front of the set for a whole evening. Choice now extends to hundreds of possibilities supplied digitally, by cable and satellite, and if you miss something you can catch up via the +1 service or the likes of the BBC's iPlayer and the ITV Hub. The arrival of the home video recorder in the late seventies and its successor the DVD recorder in the 2000s, along with systems like TiVo and Sky+, revolutionised how people used television and shaped their viewing experience but even these methods of self-programming now seem old hat given that on-demand services from cable and internet providers have made it possible to watch thousands of programmes at the push of a button or a click of a mouse.

The red button facility and streaming have changed the way broadcasting output is distributed, meaning that, while television will continue to provide music fans with musical entertainment, the days when it was the primary medium for seeing musicians perform are behind us. In 1957, *Six-Five Special* was important in the evolution of music in Britain because it gave young people across the country access to new developments and new faces. It showed them what otherwise they might only have been able to read about or hear on the radio. Sixty years on, music performance, news and information are available instantly. Obscure Korean musicians can become global stars within seconds, Gangnam style. Television, as powerful a medium as it remains, just can't compete with that and now has to be seen as just part of a multi-platform mix of entertainment and news providers.

Within television, even if you count talent contests and performances in chat shows, the mainstream channels now offer less music than for many years. It has even disappeared from late nights and weekend mornings in favour of interactive gaming and cookery shows. The thinking seems to be that, as music is so easily available elsewhere, television doesn't need to bother with it, although paradoxically the same argument is never applied to news coverage.

In truth, the audience for music programmes has never been enormous, *Top Of The Pops* in the seventies being an anomaly, and the way in which the music market is now segmented into niches means that – with the exception of the *Live 8*s or some of the headline acts live from Glastonbury – the days when families or even groups of friends would sit down together to watch music on television have gone.

Today, you take your music when you want and how you want. The era of waiting for *The Old Grey Whistle Test* on a Tuesday, *Top Of The Pops* on a Thursday and *The Tube* on a Friday is over, but I wonder how many of us who remember those eagerly awaited weekly thrills would trade them for the instant access of today.

Source Notes

Many sources have been consulted during the research for this book, beginning with the invaluable weekly listings magazines the *Radio Times* and the *TV Times* that provided the road map for the whole adventure. The work done by Kaleidoscope, the non-profit making organisation devoted to the appreciation of classic television, has also been extremely useful and its series of research guides are highly recommended to anyone engaged in a project like this. For background overviews on the music front two books stand out: Pete Frame's *The Restless Generation*, which covers the British rock'n'roll years with infectious enthusiasm, and Bob Stanley's *Yeah Yeah Yeah*, which merely takes in the whole history of pop music and does so with style. Research for my previous work, *The Penguin TV Companion*, has provided the television essentials, while the Official Charts Company supplies the chart statistics quoted in this book. Numerous other points of reference have been eagerly consulted along the way, as outlined in the notes below, which draw particular attention to quotations used and articles of particular relevance to certain passages in the text. References to BBC WAC relate to the BBC Written Archives Centre at Caversham, Berkshire, and the files consulted therein.

The Fifties

1. *Never Had It So Good*, Dominic Sandbrook (Abacus, 2005), p. 435; *The Restless Generation*, Pete Frame (Rogan House, 2007), p. ix
2. Correspondence from Bill Ward, 20 September 1951, and R.G. Walford, Copyright Department, 2 October 1951, BBC WAC T12/153/1; 'Presenting the Month's Hit Tunes', *Radio Times*, 11 January 1952
3. 'Diana Coupland' (obituary), *Guardian*, 24 November 2006; Narration: Hit Parade, undated, BBC WAC T12/153/2; correspondence from Tom Sloan, Assistant Head of Light Entertainment, Television, 26 October 1955, BBC WAC T12/153/3
4. BBC Audience Research Report VR/52/24; correspondence from Cecil McGivern, Controller, Television Programmes, 15 January 1952, and Bill Ward, 23 January 1952, BBC WAC T12/153/2
5. Correspondence from Francis Essex, 22 December 1955, BBC WAC T12/153/3
6. Trailer script, BBC WAC T12/272/2; 'Off the Record', *Radio Times* 6 May 1955
7. Correspondence from Bill Cotton Jnr, undated, BBC WAC T12/272/5, and Joanna Spicer, Head of Programme Planning, Television, 18 May 1955, BBC WAC T12/272/1
8. Correspondence from Ronald Waldman, Head of Light Entertainment, Television, 9 March 1955, BBC WAC T12/272/1
9. Assorted correspondence, BBC WAC T12/272/1 to BBC WAC T12/272/5
10. 'Jack Jackson' (obituary), *Times*, 17 January 1978
11. Picture caption, *TV Times*, 12 October 1958; 'Silence is Golden for Paddy and Pam', *TV Times*, 22 March 1959
12. 'How It Became "Cool For Kent"', *TV Times*, 30 March 1958; 'Kent Walton' (obituary), *Daily Telegraph*, 28 August 2003, and *Guardian*, 8 September 2003 (accessed online March 2016)
13. Author interview with Dougie Squires, 27 November 2014; *Coming to You Live!*, Dennis Norden (Methuen, 1985), p. 27
14. Author interview with Dougie Squires, 27 November 2014
15. *TV Times*, 3 November 1957 & 24 November 1957
16. 'The Cool Cats Are "On The Tiles"', *TV Times*, 27 April 1958; 'Tipster', *TV Times*, 11 October 1957
17. *Hansard*, 6 October 1960
18. 'Joan Kemp-Welch' (obituary), *Guardian*, 29 July 1999 (accessed online March 2016)
19. Author interviews with Trevor Peacock, 27 November 2014, and Jack Good, 22 April 2015

20. Correspondence from Jo Douglas, 2 January 1957, BBC WAC T12/360/3
21. 'Bridging the Gap', *Radio Times*, 8 February 1957
22. Correspondence from Jo Douglas, 2 January 1957, BBC WAC T12/360/3
23. 'Josephine Douglas' (obituary), *Times*, 13 July 1988; programme notes for *The "Six-Five" Stage Show*, 1958
24. Correspondence from Tom Sloan, Assistant Head of Light Entertainment, Television, 16 January 1957, BBC WAC T12/360/5, & 22 March 1957, BBC WAC T12/360/3; author interview with Pete Murray, 27 November 2014
25. Author interview with Jack Good, 22 April 2015; correspondence from Cecil McGivern, Deputy Director of Television Broadcasting, 18 February 1957, BBC WAC T12/360/5; correspondence from Kenneth Adam, Controller of Programmes, Television, 7 February 1958, BBC WAC T12/360/4
26. Author interview with Jack Good, 22 April 2015
27. Correspondence from Jo Douglas, 25 April 1957; Jo Douglas and Jack Good, 28 January 1957; Jo Douglas, 29 January 1957; and Jo Douglas, 6 February 1957, BBC WAC T12/360/3
28. Sleeve notes written by Ken Sykora for the album *Ain't It A Shame* by the Bob Cort Skiffle (Decca 1957); 'Noise for "Young in Spirit" Fills Silent Hour', *Manchester Guardian*, 18 February 1957
29. BBC WAC Light Ent Scripts, Reel 65/66, *Six-Five Special*, 16/02/57
30. 'Noise for "Young in Spirit" Fills Silent Hour', *Manchester Guardian*, 18 February 1957
31. BBC Audience Research Report VR/57/95
32. Correspondence from Duncan Wood and Dennis Main Wilson, 31 January 1958, BBC WAC T12/360/4
33. Author interview with Trevor Peacock, 27 November 2014; correspondence from Ronald Waldman, Head of Light Entertainment, Television, 18 March 1957, BBC WAC T12/360/6; correspondence from Cecil McGivern, Deputy Director of Television Broadcasting, 1 April 1957, Jo Douglas, 3 April 1957, and Jack Good, 5 April 1957, BBC WAC T12/360/7
34. Correspondence from Tom Sloan, Assistant Head of Light Entertainment, Television, 18 March 1957, BBC WAC T12/360/3; 'Lowdown on the Big Shake-Up', *6.5 Special* (*Daily Mirror*, 1958), p. 3
35. BBC memo stipulating text for audience tickets, 28 January 1957, BBC WAC T12/360/3; *Hand-Jive at 6.5*, Jack Good (Southern Music, 1957); correspondence from Jack Good, 20 December 1957, BBC WAC T12/360/3; *6.5 Special* (Daily Mirror, 1958)
36. *6.5 Special* (Network DVD)
37. Correspondence from Jack Good, 5 July 1957, Tom Sloan, Assistant Head of Light Entertainment, Television, 15 July 1957, W.L.S. Streeton, Head of

Programme Contracts, 29 November 1957, Ronald Waldman, Head of Light Entertainment, Television, 18 December 1957, Jack Good, 20 December 1957, and M. Kinchin Smith, Acting Establishment Officer, Television, 3 January 1958, BBC WAC T12/360/2; author interview with Jack Good, 22 April 2015

38. Correspondence from Kenneth Adam, Controller of Programmes, Television, 13 January 1958, BBC WAC T12/360/4
39. Correspondence from Tom Sloan, Assistant Head of Light Entertainment, Television, 23 January 1958, and Duncan Wood and Dennis Main Wilson, 31 January 1958, BBC WAC T12/360/4; 'Lowdown on the Big Shake-Up', *6.5 Special* (*Daily Mirror*, 1958), p. 3
40. 'Lowdown on the Big Shake-Up', *6.5 Special* (*Daily Mirror*, 1958), p. 3; 'Three Leaving Cast of "Six-Five Special"', *Times*, 26 March 1958; 'Josephine Douglas' (obituary), *Times*, 13 July 1988; 'Freddie Mills Found Shot Dead in Car' and 'Mr Freddie Mills' (obituary), *Times*, 26 July 1965
41. 'A Typist Made His Name… ', *6.5 Special* (*Daily Mirror*, 1958), p. 7; correspondence from Dennis Main Wilson, 20 May 1958, BBC WAC T12/360/4
42. Author interview with Jack Good, 22 April 2015
43. 'Oh Boy! – It's a Musical Powerhouse', *TV Times*, 15 June 1958
44. Author interview with Jack Good, 22 April 2015; 'Oh Boy! – It's a Musical Powerhouse', *TV Times*, 15 June 1958
45. Correspondence from Tom Sloan, Assistant Head of Light Entertainment, Television, 4 July 1958, and Kenneth Adam, Controller of Programmes, Television, 4 November 1958, BBC WAC T12/360/4
46. 'Oh Boy!', *TV Times*, 30 November 1958; 'Silent Spectacle', *TV Times*, 2 November 1958
47. Author interview with Jack Good, 22 April 2015; 'About Cherry', *TV Times*, 14 December 1958
48. 'Peerless', *TV Times*, 7 December 1958; 'The Stately Hoax of England?', *TV Times*, 18 January 1959
49. http://www.kittybrewster.com/members/k_1.htm (accessed March 2016)
50. 'Blonde in "specs"', *TV Times*, 22 February 1959
51. Author interview with Marty Wilde, 13 May 2015
52. Author interview with Jack Good, 22 April 2015
53. Ibid.; *My Life, My Way*, Cliff Richard (Headline, 2008), pp. 61–2
54. Author interview with Jack Good, 22 April 2015
55. 'Oh Boy! – It's a Musical Powerhouse', *TV Times*, 15 June 1958
56. Author interview with Marty Wilde, 13 May 2015
57. Author interviews with Jack Good, 22 April 2015, and Vince Eager, 12 October 2015
58. 'New nickname', *TV Times*, 30 November 1958

59. Author interview with Jack Good, 22 April 2015
60. Author interviews with Marty Wilde, 13 May 2015, and Jack Good, 22 April 2015
61. 'The New Beat Show Wham!!', *TV Times*, 17 April 1960; author interview with Jack Good, 22 April 2015
62. Author interview with Jack Good, 22 April 2015
63. 'Oh Boy! What A Great Hit', *TV Times*, 30 June 1979; 'If It's Good It's Rock 'n Roll', *TV Times*, 7 July 1979; author interview with Jack Good, 22 April 2015
64. Author interview with Jack Good, 22 April 2015
65. Author interview with Marty Wilde, 13 May 2015
66. Correspondence from Eric Maschwitz, Head of Light Entertainment, Television, 9 October 1958, BBC WAC T12/360/4
67. Correspondence from Kenneth Adam, Controller of Programmes, Television, 4 November 1958, BBC WAC T12/360/4
68. *The Cliff Richard Show* tour programme notes, 1964
69. 'Dig This New Year!', *Radio Times*, 26 December 1958; BBC Audience Research Report VR/59/13
70. 'New Beat', *Radio Times*, 27 March 1959
71. Author interview with Vince Eager, 12 October 2015; BBC Audience Research Report VR/59/267
72. 'Stewart Morris' (obituary), *Independent*, 9 February 2009 (accessed online March 2016)

The Sixties

1. http://www.findagrave.com/cgi-bin/fg.cgi?page=gr&GRid=54475252 (accessed March 2016)
2. Correspondence from Tom Sloan, Assistant Head of Light Entertainment Group, 16 January 1959, and Memorandum of Agreement Re 'Juke Box Jury', 18 March 1959, BBC WAC R73/281/1
3. *Jacobs' Ladder*, David Jacobs (Peter Davies, 1963), pp. 148–9
4. Author interview with Susan Stranks, 17 September 2015; BBC Audience Research Report VR/65/14; author interview with Pete Murray, 27 November 2014
5. Author interview with Susan Stranks, 17 September 2015
6. 'Juke Box Jury', *Radio Times*, 26 September 1964
7. Juke Box Jury Running Order, 7 December 1963, BBC WAC N31/5/1; *Life*, Keith Richards (Weidenfeld & Nicolson, 2010), pp. 183–4
8. BBC Duty Office Log, 21 January 1967

9. Correspondence from Paul Fox, Controller BBC1, 13 October 1967, and David Jacobs, 29 December 1967, BBC WAC T12/1,102/1
10. Author correspondence with David Gell, 14 October 2014
11. Sleeve notes for the EP *Discs-A-Gogo* (Decca, 1963)
12. Author interviews with Bernie Price and Terry Woolcock, 3 February 2015
13. 'Kent Walton' (obituary), *Daily Telegraph*, 28 August 2003, and *Guardian*, 8 September 2003 (accessed online March 2016)
14. Author interview with Tony Prince, 5 February 2015
15. 'Vintage Year for Pop', *TV Times*, 23 December 1962
16. Author interview with Janice Nicholls, 8 October 2013
17. *This Is Where I Came In*, Brian Matthew (Constable, 1991), pp. 143–8
18. *Shout!, The True Story of the Beatles*, Philip Norman (Pan, 2004), pp. 166–7
19. Correspondence from Head of North Regional Programmes, 6 September 1963, BBC WAC N25/344/1
20. *The Beatles Tune In*, Mark Lewisohn (Little Brown, 2013), pp. 737, 777
21. Author interview with Johnnie Hamp, 16 February 2015
22. *The Jack Good Story*, Alex Kerr, Banbury Live radio (accessed 21 November 2014)
23. Correspondence from Alan W. Swales *et al*, 9 December 1963, and Barney Colehan, 16 December 1963, BBC WAC N31/5/1
24. 'Ready Steady Go!', *Melody Maker*, 3 October 1964; *Ready Steady Go! – the Weekend Starts Here*, Radio 2, 14 February 2006
25. Author interview with Vicki Wickham, 20 November 2015
26. Author correspondence with David Gell, 7 December 2013
27. Author interview with Vicki Wickham, 20 November 2015
28. *Oh, What a Circus*, Tim Rice (Hodder, 1999), pp. 88–9; http://www.dailymail.co.uk/femail/article-567024/Shes-leaving-home---The-woman-inspired-Beatles-classic-quit-Spanish-house-built-illegally.html (accessed March 2016)
29. *Ready Steady Go! – the Weekend Starts Here,* Radio 2, 14 February 2006; 'The With-It World of Rockers and Mods', *TV Times*, 1 December 1963; 'How We Made Ready, Steady, Go!', *Guardian*, 19 August 2013
30. Author interview with Vicki Wickham, 20 November 2015; *Revolt Into Style*, George Melly (Penguin, 1972), p.171
31. 'Having a ball', *TV Times*, 5 April 1964
32. 'Shooting Stars!', *TV Times*, 19 April 1964
33. Programme listing, *TV Times*, 2 August 1964
34. Author interview with Vicki Wickham, 20 November 2015
35. 'Ready Steady Goes Live!', *TV Times*, 27 March 1965
36. 'How We Made Ready, Steady, Go!', *Guardian*, 19 August 2013
37. Author interview with Vicki Wickham, 20 November 2015

38. Ibid.
39. *Rod, The Autobiography*, Rod Stewart (Century, 2012), pp. 65–6
40. *The Story Of Top Of The Pops*, Steve Blacknell (PSL, 1985), pp. 9–22; *Top Of The Pops, Mishaps, Miming And Music*, Ian Gittins (BBC Books, 2007), pp. 6–11; *Top Of The Pops 50th Anniversary*, Patrick Humphries and Steve Blacknell (McNidder & Grace, 2014), p. 185
41. BBC Audience Research Report VR/64/11
42. Correspondence from Tom Sloan, Head of Light Entertainment Group, 17 August 1965, BBC WAC T12/1,324/1, & 29 March 1966, BBC WAC T32/1,957/1
43. 'Samantha Juste' (obituary), *Independent*, 19 February 2014 (accessed online March 2016)
44. Correspondence from Tom Sloan, Head of Light Entertainment Group, 2 July 1965, BBC WAC T12/1,324/1
45. Correspondence from Johnnie Stewart, 30 April 1965, and Joanna Spicer, Assistant Controller Television, 9 December 1965, BBC WAC T12/1,324/1
46. Correspondence from Johnnie Stewart, 2 August 1967, BBC WAC T12/1,324/1; *The Complete Beatles Chronicle*, Mark Lewisohn (Chancellor Press, 1996), p. 225
47. 'End of miming on television', *Times*, 23 July 1966, p. 9
48. Author correspondence with John Williamson, 12 June 2015
49. Interview with Don Smith by John Williamson, 24 April 2013; agreement signed by Dave Dee, 15 September 1966, BBC WAC T12/1,323/1
50. Interview with Don Smith by John Williamson, 24 April 2013
51. *Wicked Speed*, Annie Nightingale (Kindle edition: CB Creative Books, 2014)
52. Correspondence from Elizabeth Cowley (undated), BBC WAC T32/1,957/1
53. BBC Audience Research Report VR/66/10; correspondence from Tom Sloan, Head of Light Entertainment Group, (undated), BBC WAC T32/1,957/1
54. Correspondence from Michael Peacock, Controller BBC1, 8 June 1966, BBC WAC T32/1,957/1
55. Various documents, BBC WAC T12/808/1
56. Correspondence from William Cave, Chief Assistant Science and Features, 30 September 1965; programme proposal, 29 April 1966; Round the World Project State of Progress, Febuary 1967, BBC WAC T14/2,723/2
57. Andrew Wiseman Translation of Soviet Telex, 21 June 1967, BBC WAC T14/2,723/2; Opening Sequence – Studio Introduction BBC WAC T14/2,723/4
58. Correspondence from Derek Burrell-Davis, 17 May 1967, BBC WAC T14/2,727/1
59. Final Estimate of Television Outside Broadcast, BBC WAC T14/2,727/1

60. *Arena: Magical Mystery Tour Revisited*, BBC2, 6 October 2012
61. BBC Audience Research Report VR/67/823; 'Christmas Television', *Guardian*, 27 December 1967
62. *The Complete Beatles Chronicle*, Mark Lewisohn (Chancellor Press, 1996), pp. 262–7
63. 'Beatle puts controversy before boredom', *Guardian*, 28 December 1967; *Arena: Magical Mystery Tour Revisited*, BBC2, 6 October 2012
64. *Luck And Circumstance*, Michael Lindsay-Hogg (Knopf, 2011), pp. 119–135
65. Author interview with Tony Palmer, 5 August 2015; The Greatest Ravers of Them All (proposal), BBC WAC T53/113/1
66. Author interview with Tony Palmer, 5 August 2015
67. 'All My Loving', *Radio Times*, 2 November 1968; 'Violence on television', *Guardian*, 5 November 1968; 'A personal pop credo', *Observer*, 10 November 1968
68. Author interview with Tony Palmer, 5 August 2015
69. Correspondence from Tony Palmer, 11 November 1968, BBC WAC T53/113/1
70. Author interview with Tony Palmer, 5 August 2015
71. Promotional Material, BBC WAC T53/76/1
72. Correspondence from Rex Moorfoot, Head of Presentation, Television, 6 June 1968, BBC WAC T53/76/1; author interview with Tony Palmer, 5 August 2015
73. Correspondence from Tony Palmer, 10 June 1968, BBC WAC T53/76/1, and Paul Fox, Controller BBC1, 4 December 1967 & 4 March 1968, BBC WAC T47/178/1; author interview with Tony Palmer, 5 August 2015
74. Author interview with Tony Palmer, 5 August 2015
75. Ibid.
76. 'Pop music, Socrates and Sandie Shaw… that's Jonathan's world', *TV World*, 30 September 1967
77. 'When the Stones staged a free for all', *TV Times*, 1 September 1969

The Seventies

1. Author interview with Bob Harris, 12 May 2015
2. 'Pop's changing face: LPs sell like singles', *Radio Times*, 15 January 1970
3. Author interview with Mike Appleton, 9 September 2015
4. Ibid.
5. Author interview with Bob Harris, 12 May 2015
6. Author interview with Mike Appleton, 9 September 2015
7. Author interview with Bob Harris, 12 May 2015
8. Author interview with Ayshea, 7 August 2015
9. Author interview with David Jensen, 26 February 2016

10. http://www.mirror.co.uk/3am/celebrity-news/how-queens-bohemian-rhapsody-pop-6742180 (accessed March 2016)
11. 'In the world of Pop everybody's a teenager', *TV Times*, 22 November 1975; 'Pop Power: It's in the hands of ITV's big three', *TV Times*, 6 November 1976
12. 'James Paul McCartney', *Times*, 11 May 1973
13. *The South Bank Show Final Cut*, Melvyn Bragg (Sceptre, 2010), pp. 1, 7
14. 'Pop Power: It's in the hands of ITV's big three', *TV Times*, 6 November 1976
15. Author interview with Johnnie Hamp, 16 February 2015
16. http://www.nme.com/news/nme/4068 (accessed March 2016); 'O'er col and cwm', *Observer*, 15 April 1979
17. 'Johnnie Stewart' (obituary), *Guardian*, 6 May 2005 (accessed online March 2016)
18. Author interview with Tony Palmer, 5 August 2015
19. Ibid.
20. Author interview with Mike Appleton, 9 September 2015
21. Author interview with Bob Harris, 12 May 2015
22. Author interviews with Mike Appleton, 9 September 2015, and Bob Harris, 12 May 2015
23. Author interview with Mike Appleton, 9 September 2015
24. *Punk Rock: An Oral History*, John Robb (Ebury, 2006), pp. 259–263
25. 'Something rotten… ', *Guardian*, 5 August 1986
26. 'Revolver', *TV Times*, 22 July 1978
27. Author interview with Bob Harris, 12 May 2015
28. Author interview with Mike Appleton, 9 September 2015
29. Ibid.
30. Author interview with Bob Harris, 12 May 2015

The Eighties

1. Author interviews with Malcolm Gerrie, 16 & 23 September 2015
2. Author interview with David Jensen, 26 February 2016
3. *Top Of The Pops, Mishaps, Miming And Music*, Ian Gittins (BBC Books, 2007), p. 145
4. Author interview with David Jensen, 26 February 2016
5. *Black By Design*, Pauline Black (Serpent's Tail, 2012), pp. 252–3
6. 'Rock by the river', *Radio Times*, 2 January 1982
7. 'A new wave', *Radio Times*, 10 September 1983
8. *Rod, The Autobiography*, Rod Stewart (Century, 2012), p. 295; *I Want My MTV*, Rob Tannebaum and Craig Marks (Plume, 2012), pp. 143–58
9. Author interview with Trevor Dann, 15 September 2015

10. Author interviews with Malcolm Gerrie, 16 & 23 September 2015
11. Author interview with Chris Cowey, 15 July 2015
12. *The Tube Anthology, The Best Of Series 1* (Network DVD)
13. Author interview with Chris Cowey, 15 July 2015
14. Author interviews with Malcolm Gerrie, 16 & 23 September 2015
15. Author interview with Chris Cowey, 15 July 2015
16. Author interview with Mike Appleton, 9 September 2015
17. Author interview with Trevor Dann, 15 September 2015
18. Author interview with Mike Appleton, 9 September 2015
19. Author interview with Trevor Dann, 15 September 2015
20. Ibid.
21. Author interview with Mike Appleton, 9 September 2015
22. Author interview with Trevor Dann, 15 September 2015
23. Author interviews with Malcolm Gerrie, 16 & 23 September 2015
24. 'Andrea Wonfor' (obituary), *Independent*, 22 September 2004 (accessed online March 2016)
25. 'More pop and less champagne', *Guardian*, 23 March 1989, p. 31
26. Author interviews with Malcolm Gerrie, 16 & 23 September 2015
27. Author interviews with Chris Cowey, 15 July 2015, and Malcolm Gerrie, 16 & 23 September 2015
28. Author interview with Mark Cooper, 19 January 2016
29. 'Michael Hurll' (obituary), *Guardian*, 20 September 2012 (accessed online March 2016)

The Nineties

1. www.terrychristian.tv (accessed March 2016)
2. 'How The Word changed television for ever', *Guardian*, 10 August 2010 (accessed online March 2016)
3. 'How we made Top of the Pops', *Guardian*, 4 February 2014 (accessed online March 2016)
4. 'Back in the groove', *Radio Times*, 4 February 1995
5. Author interview with Mark Cooper, 19 January 2016
6. Author interviews with Malcolm Gerrie, 16 & 23 September 2015
7. *Thank You For The Days*, Mark Radcliffe (Simon & Schuster, 2010), p. 266
8. Author interviews with Chris Cowey, 15 July 2015, and Malcolm Gerrie, 16 & 23 September 2015
9. *Thank You For The Days*, Mark Radcliffe (Simon & Schuster, 2010), p. 267
10. Author interviews with Malcolm Gerrie, 16 & 23 September 2015
11. Author interview with Mark Cooper, 19 January 2016

12. 'Whatever happened to Peggy Sue?', *Radio Times*, 17 April 1993
13. 'The Beatles: A magical history tour', *Radio Times*, 25 November 1995
14. *Pete Frame's Rock Family Trees* (Omnibus Press, 1980), Introduction
15. 'Classic cuts', *Radio Times*, 26 July 1997
16. *Memoirs Of A Fruitcake*, Chris Evans (HarperCollins, 2010), pp. 10–11
17. *It's Not What You Think*, Chris Evans (HarperCollins, 2009), pp. 243–4
18. *Memoirs Of A Fruitcake*, Chris Evans (HarperCollins, 2010), p. 72
19. Author interviews with Malcolm Gerrie, 16 & 23 September 2015
20. Author interview with Trevor Dann, 15 September 2015
21. Author interview with Chris Cowey, 15 July 2015
22. Author interview with Trevor Dann, 15 September 2015
23. Author interview with Chris Cowey, 15 July 2015
24. 'Look what they've done to Top of the Pops', *Radio Times*, 21 June 1997; author interview with Chris Cowey, 15 July 2015
25. Author interview with Trevor Dann, 15 September 2015
26. Author interview with Chris Cowey, 15 July 2015
27. Author interview with Mark Cooper, 19 January 2016
28. Author interviews with Malcolm Gerrie, 16 & 23 September 2015
29. 'No change at the top?', *Guardian*, 1 May 1998; author interviews with Malcolm Gerrie, 16 & 23 September 2015
30. Author interviews with Malcolm Gerrie, 16 & 23 September 2015

The New Millennium

1. 'Cadbury and Popworld launch Westlife bars', *Marketing Week*, 19 July 2001 (accessed online March 2016)
2. 'Bands on the run', *Guardian*, 9 April 2006 (accessed online March 2016)
3. 'Popworld moves into publishing', *Media Week*, 4 October 2001 (accessed online March 2016); 'Popworld Pulp folds after two issues', *Media Week*, 18 April 2007 (accessed online March 2016)
4. Author interview with Chris Cowey, 15 July 2015
5. 'The final countdown', *Guardian*, 24 November 2003 (accessed online March 2016)
6. 'Just reward', *Radio Times*, 4 March 2000
7. Author interviews with Malcolm Gerrie, 16 & 23 September 2015
8. *The Beatles Tune In*, Mark Lewisohn (Little, Brown, 2013), pp. 197–9
9. http://news.bbc.co.uk/1/hi/entertainment/4482216.stm (accessed March 2016)
10. http://news.bbc.co.uk/1/hi/entertainment/3100933.stm (accessed March 2016)

11. Author interview with Mark Cooper, 19 January 2016
12. 'It's all new. It's different. It's, um, Top of the Pops', *Times*, 15 November 2003; 'Ratings for "nation's favourite" Radio 1 hit new low', *Independent*, 31 July 2003 (accessed online March 2016)
13. 'It's all new. It's different. It's, um, Top of the Pops', *Times*, 15 November 2003; 'Chart attack', *Radio Times*, 15 November 2003; 'Putting the fizz back into pop', *Radio Times*, 22 November 2003
14. Author interview with Mark Cooper, 19 January 2016
15. Author interview with Trevor Dann, 15 September 2015
16. Author interview with Chris Cowey, 15 July 2015
17. http://www.fromthebasement.co.uk/ (accessed March 2016)
18. Author interviews with Malcolm Gerrie, 16 & 23 September 2015
19. 'Off their rocker', *Radio Times*, 28 May 2002
20. Author interview with Mark Cooper, 19 January 2016
21. Author interviews with Malcolm Gerrie, 16 & 23 September 2015
22. Author interview with Mark Cooper, 19 January 2016
23. Ibid.
24. *The Penguin TV Companion*, 4th edition, Jeff Evans (Penguin, 2011), p. 573

Index